1982

EDWARD POLS

The Acts of Our Being

A Reflection on Agency and Responsibility

The University of Massachusetts Press   Amherst, 1982

Contents

Preface

The issue this book deals with is far too important to be left to professional academic philosophers. By saying that, I intend no discourtesy to them, for part of me belongs to their company. If the issue were one for which they could indeed obtain "results," as certain professions can obtain results in their fields and impart them to the rest of us, we should all have to abide by their pronouncements, no matter how unpalatable we might find them. But the issue is whether we are authentically what most of the time we take ourselves to be—responsible rational agents, and that issue not only is the concern of all thinking persons but also falls within their competence in the sense, by no means obvious or easy to express, that this book is designed to establish. If that should be so, and at this point I ask the reader only to entertain that possibility, anyone who should venture to settle it by dismissing as a mere appearance, or as a prescientific and archaic delusion, the very perspective within which the issue arises would have missed the point of it. By no means all professionals take this line. Some, however, do; and if we suppose them to speak with authority, we may fail to give due weight to the nonprofessional authority each thinking person has in the matter.

The common thinking view, although much disturbed of late by what are perceived as the implications of science, is still that we are indeed responsible rational agents. But all who have gone into the matter, encountered all the familiar difficulties, and, like Milton's reasoning angels (fallen angels, as it happens), "found no end, in wand'ring mazes lost," must occasionally be tempted to think otherwise. If, after having been through something of that kind, I still rejoice to concur with the common thinker, I am nevertheless well aware that one must go very deep to show that the common thinker has been on the right track after all. I have gone as deep as I can; and because professional philosophers have shaped the issue for today in a running dialogue with science and with scientists speaking as philosophers, I have not hesitated to work with one or another of their idioms when that seemed called for. But since I am trying to express the sense—a sense so far unnoticed, or at least not clearly expressed—in which the common thinker is the final arbiter of this question, I have done my best to make the book intelligible to those who are not academic philosophers as well as to those who are. Certain material I take to be of importance only to the latter group I have put into the notes at the end; some of them are therefore rather long.

Certain parts of the book have already appeared in the *Review of Metaphysics*. Chapter 6 is a later version of "Action and Its Physiological Basis" (31, no. 3 [1978]: 365–86). Section 4 of chapter 1 and sections 2–6 of chapter 7 descend, considerably expanded, from "The Ontology of the Rational Agent" (33, no. 4 [1980]: 689–710). A shorter version of sections 1–6 of chapter 2 appears as "The Conditions of Ontic Responsibility" (35, no. 2 [1981]: 297–319). The *Review of Metaphysics* has played an essential role in the lively debate about metaphysical issues now taking place in this country. I note that many of the writers I am most in disagreement with have also appeared in it, together, of course, with many whose views are closer to mine. I am grateful for the hospitality of its pages.

25 January 1982
Bowdoin College

I

The Question of the Authenticity
of Responsibility

1

The Prima Facie Explanatory Value
of Rational Action

When we act, something comes into being: in the first place, our act itself; in the second, ourselves, for in some measure we come into being by virtue of our acts. So at least it seems, as we experience ourselves as agents-in-act, as we complete and possess this experience in a rational web of words; and there is nothing so important to our ontological self-respect as the conviction that goes with it, not perhaps of creating being, but at least of participating as coadjutors in a coming-into-being. Caught in that conviction, we see the very shape of time flowing out of us as our minds and bodies move in the order of the act.

The conviction, which includes the assumption that our rationality guides many of our acts directly and expresses itself indirectly in others, governs our respect for other persons no less than our respect for ourselves. We are all of us rational agents, if not always in fact, then at least in aspiration; and those who belong to the biological species and yet never reach the status of rational agent seem to us somehow deficient in humanity. There is in the first place—or so we assume without being quite clear what it means to assume it—something self-explanatory about being a rational agent. There are of course important explanations that bear upon agency and illuminate it in various ways—neurophysiological ones, for instance—but when everything that can be explained has been explained, there remains something that in a *prima facie* sense is both indispensable and needs no further explanation; and because of this, rational agency has itself a powerful *prima facie* explanatory value. In most circumstances this feature of agency manifests itself as a *prima facie* causal power, and it would appear inappropriate to separate the two features: it is because rational agents are *prima facie* causal powers that they can be used in *prima facie* explanation of other things.

No *prima facie* rational agents have more prestige in our times than scientists, and so we shall often turn to their work for examples in the course of this book. Their acts have causal consequences in a number of senses. Certain physical acts of the great Max Planck, for instance, produced the words and symbols that make up the manuscript of his 1879 doctoral dissertation. This causal power then helps explain the physical state of affairs of which the manuscript was a part. The real nature of his work can not be adequately described as the production of a physical object, so that the notion of causal power must be qualified in important ways if we are to do justice to his achievement. But even if we confine ourselves to the physical level, it is Planck we must invoke to explain the existence of the marks on those pages. Other explanations may be relevant and may illuminate features of the physical state of affairs that are not illuminated by appeal to his rational agency; nonetheless, that appeal *is* illuminating, and furthermore precisely that kind of illumination is necessary if we are really to understand why a certain state of affairs is as it is. The notion of responsibility depends upon this—indeed, it would be more accurate to say that it is part of what we mean when we say that someone is responsible for something, and when we insist, as we often do, that praise or blame, or even reward or punishment, is not just customary in such cases, but somehow ontologically appropriate.

The conviction that the rational agent is a causal power is in conflict with the view, common but by no means universal in philosophical discussion of action, that the causal relation is best understood as holding between events or between events and states.[1] We shall come to that question soon enough. If, however, rational agents should indeed be causal powers, certain of their rational acts have features that are difficult to accommodate under any rubric of causal power suited either to common sense or to science. I am thinking of acts much more momentous than the making of marks on paper as one writes, and much more momentous than the well-worn examples (flicking on a light switch, signaling for a turn while driving a car, clenching one's fist, and so on) that abound in action theory. Consider again the long train of rational acts Max Planck started in the late 1870s and brought to a culmination by stating the quantum principle in his famous 1900 paper.[2] When we say that he discovered the quantum principle by pressing to its conclusion a line of reasoning he began with his doctoral dissertation, we mean just that. Although it is an incomplete account, and one that could easily be amplified (for instance, by bringing in something from neurophysiology and something about the situation in research in physics at the University of Munich when he was young), we take it for granted that it is also essential to a complete explanation to say that he, Planck, made the discovery. As in the simpler example of writing, where we were concerned not with the sense of words and symbols but only with the ink marks on the page, so here: whatever conditions may enter into the internal constitution of an act, whatever influences may bear upon it from the outside, they do not wholly explain something that when all is said and done is still a *rational* act. Something in the act escapes in principle any analysis we can make of its conditions and the influences that bear upon it; and the explanatory value of the act depends upon this resistance to complete explanation.

But suppose, on the analogy of the ink marks on the paper, we try to think of Planck as a causal power whose effects are visible in the way science is carried on today—visible, that is, in certain states of affairs. Perhaps it does not strain the word "cause" out of all recognition to say so, but surely his influence was more indirect than the word suggests. In the first place, his acts culminated in the articulation of a principle that has itself an important explanatory value, and it is surely in the impact of this profound explanatory principle that his own influence chiefly consists. The influence can not then easily be assimilated to any of the usual contemporary cause-effect models, even if agents can be causal powers; for his acts of discovery are not the causes of the explanations discovered in the sense in which he is the cause of the ink marks (setting aside their meaning) on the paper. The quantum principle has an explanatory value, and rational acts of the kind we are attributing to Planck would be, if authentic, the ontological ground for the existence of an explanation of that kind and of other kinds as well. I do not mean that they would be the ontological ground of the principle but rather of the articulation of it in a way that can be used in an explanation. Whatever one ought to mean by "ontological ground," evidently one does not capture it precisely by saying that the rational acts were causes of which the explanations were effects, or that the explanations are effects of the causal power of the agent. We might wish in the long run to retain the notion of causal power, but we should have to modify in various subtle ways the sense we might have in mind if we were thinking only of such matters as making ink marks on a page or turning on a light switch. One reason for this is that a felt obligation to standards (norms, ideals) plays a role in such discoveries, and that the standards accordingly exercise an odd kind of power within the very dynamism of the acts. Planck's acts developed under an obligation, not just an obligation to the abstract notion of scientific truth but an obligation to see precisely as it is that feature of the nature of things that concerned him. The power of what the agent feels obliged by—as distinct from the feeling of being obliged, considered as a psychological fact—is considerable, and its role in the act can not be assessed simply or briefly. But its nature is not compulsive: it need no more be "obeyed" than a categorical imperative need be obeyed; it merely ought to be "obeyed"—that is, it ought to be seen for what it is and expressed clearly by the rational agent. On any of the accounts of cause and effect that are seriously entertained today by philosophers of science, it would not normally be called a cause from which effects follow. Accordingly, the rational agent who sees it and expresses it would not normally be called without qualification a cause (or causal power) from which effects follow. The rational agent ought to see things as they are and express them clearly, but the nature of this obligation carries with it the possibility of its being ignored. Any sense in which a rational agent is called a causal power must take account of this.

That this is felt by philosophers to be an important issue, we know from the extensive debate on the relations between reasons and causes in the recent literature.[3] It will be seen at once, however, that the debate has not focused clearly on just the point I am trying to make. It has instead centered so much on the reasons that may exist for an act that attention has been diverted from the important role reasons play in certain acts. It is a role in which the articulation of reasons is scarcely to be distinguished from the dynamism of the act itself—the acts being, after all, prima facie acts of reasoning. I shall return to this matter at several points in the course of this book. Here it is important to say again that the rational acts that went into the writing of Planck's 1900 paper were pervaded by the reasons articulated in it and in the prior work; and that their being so pervaded by an acquiescence in reasons is part, but by no means all, of what we mean when we say of a responsible rational agent like Planck that he could have acted in some respects otherwise than he did. In this preliminary survey there is nothing more important and more obscure than this point that the standards to which reason is receptive oblige but do not compel—that our openness to them includes the possibility of ignoring them; that seeing what thus obliges may in some circumstances also be an obligation, but again one that can be ignored.

The conviction that the *prima facie* features of rational agency we have looked at so far are indeed what they appear to be is identical with the conviction of the authenticity of responsible rational action. Although I have deliberately chosen examples outside the field of morals, it is obvious that what has been said so far applies there as well: the reasons *in* a practical action in the moral sphere, for instance, will be as important as the reasons *for* it, and reasons in both senses will qualify any causal power exercised in the act even as they do in the case of the examples just considered. In both spheres the notion of responsible rational action is a rich one—precisely how rich we shall see in some detail in chapter 2. It includes the themes of causality, of explanation, of the appropriateness of praise or blame; and it includes the theme of freedom as well, but qualified in ways of which the preceding remarks about obligation give some hint. Within it the subordinate notions "responsibility" and "rational action" are in such intimate mutual support that it will be convenient to shorten our formula to either "the authenticity of rational action" or "the authenticity of responsibility" as the occasion demands.

The interdependence of the notions of responsibility, causation, explanation, and reward or punishment is an ancient one. It is even more striking in the philosophical mother tongue of the west than in the languages in which most philosophy is carried on today. In classical Greek the usual word for "cause" is the feminine noun "*aitia*," but its appearance in philosophy with that sense is preceded by its use to ascribe responsibility to a person, and this appears to be its root sense. In those early appearances it usually has a negative sense—"charge," "accusation," "blame," "fault"—and more rarely the positive sense "credit." There is also an adjective "*aitios, a, on*," which as early as Homer has the sense "culpable," "blameworthy," and which has the secondary sense "being the cause," "responsible for." Plato often uses the neuter noun "*aition*," which is formed from this adjective, in philosophical contexts that require the translation "cause."[4] Both this noun and the more usual philosophical noun for "cause," "*aitia*," have overtones of our word "explanation"; these overtones are often sup-

pressed in the way we use the word "cause" today, although they are
heard in the term "aetiology" and in related technical terms. All this
tells us that our notions of causation and explanation are in their ori-
gins closely related to the notion of an action performed by an agent.[5]
The notion of responsibility is of course a richer one today than it was
in antiquity. Despite the great precedent of Aristotle,[6] we are probably more conscious than the Greeks were that we can not take the rational agent seriously as an ultimate explanatory factor unless it could
have acted differently from the way it did. We also place more emphasis on subjectivity than they did; we think, for instance, that the rational agent should acknowledge all this—that some of the complexity
of the notion of responsibility should be before one's mind when one
feels responsible for one's actions; but there are complexities about
feeling responsible that we must set aside for the moment.

2

Contemporary Doubts about the Authenticity
of Responsibility

It is often felt nowadays that this complex conviction that we are responsible rational agents is not justified. Human nature is hard to
know as it is: though it seems to express itself in action, though we
have a way of "knowing" ourselves in which experience and words
seem to conspire to give us the very presence of ourselves in action,
there may be some illusion in this. Profound operative principles at
work in our bodies—structures of incredible intricacy, of which so far
our science provides us only a glimpse—may carry out the real work in
ways that make the notion of responsible rational action wholly superfluous, something tossed up, along with our consciousness itself, as a
curious and irrelevant disturbance in it that hides the real truth from
us. The doubt about the authenticity of responsibility is very pervasive. In its most common form it is no more than the assumption that
the hidden truth is whatever science is competent to tell us about the
microstructure of the *prima facie* agent's body—the assumption that
the action is a mere appearance. In a positive sense the doubt about
action is the disposition to take science as a cognitive ideal. It is a disposition by no means limited to scientists and certain influential philosophers of science. It is shared by every child of this century, and
even those of us who think it is a mistake are under the influence of a

constant flow of information that is colored by it. It unites a variety of philosophers who disagree about the structure of science and about the kind of epistemology that is needed to undergird it: it is shared, for instance, by some writers who are phenomenalists and some writers who are realists about the objects science deals with. We shall look, in chapters 5 and 6, at idealized forms of the two most influential contemporary metaphysical versions of this disposition, but for the moment I want to deal with it not as a highly structured metaphysical doctrine but only as a widespread prejudice about how *prima facie* rational agents fit into the scheme of things. Viewed as a general disposition that cuts across many party lines, it goes a long way to explain why so many philosophers who are struck by the resistance *prima facie* rational action offers to explanation in conventional scientific terms have nonetheless been reluctant to take the radical and risky conceptual steps that are necessary to do justice to it.

If one were to frame an account of rational action consistent with this pervasive disposition, it would maintain that the notion of the agent-in-act explains nothing: it is a name, a symbolic place-holder, something that merely draws our attention at the commonsense level to a complex physical event that awaits explanation. For science rational action is not something that should be invoked to explain states of affairs but rather something that needs to be explained—it is not an *explicans* but an *explicandum*. When we do offer a rational act as an explanation for a state of affairs and thus take the rational agent to be *responsible* for it, we do so only because the setting in which the explanation is put forward is a gross and unexacting one. In a more demanding setting, we turn at once to science for an explanation of the act, hence for the state of affairs. Although those who hold this view will concede that science is not able to oblige us immediately, they point out that it is gradually providing explanations for important features of action; and that a projection of this gradual success makes it plausible that a complete explanation will be available some time in the future.

It is clear that one can hold a position like this without also having a well-developed philosophy of science, let alone a systematic metaphysics. There is, however, a dominant version of scientific explanation that cuts across disagreements between philosophers of science, and it dictates a certain familiar way of dealing with supposed rational agents. Science forms a complex epistemic system, in which the laws of nature, or if not the laws of nature, then supposed nomic universals that do service for them,[7] play the controlling role. Statements like "Planck discovered the quantum principle," "Hume wrote the *Treatise*," "David caused the cue ball to move by striking it with his cue stick," and similar statements that seem to express some power, or force, peculiar to the agent must give way to a more complex expression of the same matters in the language of the sciences. Instead of talking of the agent, we should talk of physical entities, physical events, and physical states of the kind a physiologist—or better, a physicist—works with. These should be of a fine-grained sort—ideally, as fine-grained as physics needs. Though entities of some sort are usually assumed to be present, they are not the focus of metaphysical interest but are regarded merely as things within and between which events can take place and which can themselves be in physical states. There would even appear to be a preference, not universal but probably dominant, to think of the category of event as more fundamental than that of entity. But let us set that ontological question aside for a moment in favor of a statement that covers as much ground as possible. A body of laws, postulates, definitions, semantic rules, transformation rules, and so on (for short "body of theory") stands in such a relation to the entities, events, and states into which we resolve the agent that certain kinds of statements about them can be regarded as instantiations of the body of theory. In particular, statements about an entity, event, or state regarded as a cause, when joined with the body of theory, entail statements about an entity, event, or state regarded as its effect. The explanatory power of this procedure is inseparable from prediction: what is explained could have been predicted; and there is as much determinism in this view as the correlation of explanation and prediction requires. As the categories usually associated with action have no place in such explanations, rational agents (persons, subjects) are not conceived of as entities endowed with the ontological capacity for producing action but rather as pseudoentities to whose supposed efficacy we attribute what we do not yet understand but can in principle discover. Where the physiology, for instance, is still obscure enough to make it impossible to identify all the factors in what is properly a complex physiological event, we fall back on traditional terminology and speak of an act that springs from the power of an agent. Although, as we saw, it would be an exaggeration to say that this view of science eliminates the notion of entity in favor of the notion of event, it is quite clear that it prefers to replace the notion of an agent, regarded as an entity, with that of events taking place in a physically defined context that includes other sorts of entities. The *prima facie* status of the rational agent as an entity that acts is regarded as inauthentic: the agent is held to be an appearance whose corresponding reality is disclosed by the kind of scientific explanation of which I have given a rough sketch.

The view that the rational agent is an ultimate explanatory factor, which we may take for a while as roughly equivalent to the view that rational agency is authentic, must certainly be reconciled with the plain fact that science also explains what it deals with and explains it well. One way to do it is to think of science as amplifying our understanding of action by taking account of such matters as the physiological conditions that contribute to it. No violence need be done to the explanatory category of rational action so long as an analysis of its conditions is not held to replace that category without loss. But the view of science we have just looked at has worked against any such irenic outcome in two fields in which many philosophers have been notably busy for the last two decades—philosophy of mind and action theory. The two topics are obviously closely related, especially so where rational action is our theme, and a theory in one of them usually has resonance in the other.

In philosophy of mind the situation is rather too complex for us to attribute the lack of a reconciliation just to a dominant attitude towards scientific explanation. There are also present there some longstanding epistemological prejudices that are shared by many philosophers whose work is not closely related to science. The greatest obstacle to a reconciliation has been the assumption that if one were able to give an account of mind that was in some measure distinguishable from a physiological account—something that the authenticity of responsibility evidently requires—it would have to take the following form. Mind, mentality, or consciousness is patently distinguishable from the physical by the character of the events that take place there. What one means by "there" in an ontological sense is often left open, but it is usually supposed that there is in any case a class of items— impressions, ideas, feelings, sense-data, raw feels, volitions, intentions and the like[8]—that is ontologically suited for residence "there." These are the things that mind first attends to, or is immediately aware of, and from the point of view of mind so regarded, the physical world accordingly becomes a problem. Though noncommittal about, or hostile to, the notion of substance, this attitude towards mind is obviously heavily, though indirectly, in debt to Descartes' third meditation, and the problematic nature of the physical world is an echo of his own problem about the external world in the sixth meditation. The concern with mental events is, however, definitive in this contemporary doctrine of mind. Mental events that have some analogy in their sequence to physical events are thought of either as occurring in mind or as definitive of it. Thus the appearance *within* mind of one of the class of items mentioned above would be an example of a mental event on one interpretation; on another, mind would *consist in* the occurrence of mental events defined by the successive appearance within them (as part of them) of such items, the question of what the items appeared *to* being either set aside or considered meaningless. Something very like this view of mind—there are many individual refinements and variations—is widely held among philosophers who are not physicalists. It is also held by some writers who wish to combine physicalism, however paradoxically, with some form of phenomenalism.[9] Although we can scarcely say it is held by physicalists, it is what they think mind would be like if there really were a mind; for their defense of physicalism consists in part in trying to purge the language of science from any dependence on it. It is, in any case, difficult to accommodate science within such a view of mind and also difficult to accommodate responsible rational action there. It is accordingly unlikely that we shall get from it any reconciliation between the explanatory power of science and the *prima facie* explanatory value of rational agency. But it is not the only nonphysicalist theory of mind, as I shall try to show in the course of this book. There is a genuine mind-body problem, but it is not located precisely where this view of mind would have it.

The pervasive view that takes science as its cognitive ideal has also affected philosophical study of action in a variety of ways. The most important influence appears in the theory of causality—some intimation of it was given in our sketch of scientific explanation—that has become almost canonical in action studies. The theory, which is probably impossible to reconcile with the authenticity of responsibility, is a modern version of Hume's doctrine, though there are modifications in it he would not have tolerated. Since it must cut across fundamental doctrinal differences between philosophers of science, it is sometimes couched in almost commonsense terms. It is commonly expressed as a relation between events or states, and as the events are thought of as physical ones, the doctrine is Humean only in the sense that it has the form it might well have been given by him if he had supposed himself to be dealing with a sequence of patently physical events rather than with a stream of impressions. A compact expression of it will always be open to challenge and qualification, but it is usually said that one event or state is the cause of another if its occurrence is necessary and sufficient for the occurrence of the other. If it is events rather than states that are at issue, the event that is the cause must be temporally prior to the one that is the effect. In an earlier book I therefore called this version of causality c→e causality.[10] The determination of just when such a relation exists between two events is a more difficult matter. As we saw earlier, it is usually said that the existence of the causal relation is best expressed in terms of the laws— more generally, the body of theory—that it instantiates. In a strict Humean formulation, laws are observed regularities, and the necessity and sufficiency of one event for another therefore implies no power in the cause that necessarily produces the effect. In some recent anti-Humean versions, and certainly in common sense, that latter productive necessity and power are held to be real, although I do not detect in these versions any disposition to exempt a causal power that necessarily produces some state of affairs from the fate of having itself been necessarily produced ("power" and all) by some other causal power or powers—a fate that cancels, it would seem, the status of that "causal power" and any earlier ones as well.[11] Any authentic causal power of an agent would have to be exempted from such a fate in some such way as the one I shall sketch in section 4 and develop further in the rest of the book. Because the strict Humean version of c→e causality has until recently been the dominant one in English-speaking philosophy, I called it in my earlier treatment of it the official view of c→e causality; the view that attributes power and necessary production to the cause I called the working view,[12] because of its association with common sense and because it is detectable in both the off-duty Humean philosopher and the on-duty scientist. Since event-language is so often used in philosophic discussions of action, c→e causality is sometimes simply called event-causality.

This version of causality has become so canonical in contemporary action theory that other versions more easily reconcilable with the authenticity of responsibility have not found wide acceptance. The most well-known alternative versions are those of Chisholm, Von Wright, and Taylor; and what they have in common is sometimes called agent causation—more rarely immanent causation.[13] Discussions by the originators and their critics appear to envision two sorts of agent causation. (a) The agent, regarded as an entity, acts as a causal power and causes either a state of affairs external to it or an event distinguishable from it, as a writer causes ink marks on a page or as a player in some ball game causes the movement of a ball through the air. (b) The agent, still regarded as an entity, causes something within itself—indeed something that appears to be within its action, or to be part of its action—as I might be said to cause certain neurons to fire or certain muscles to contract by my writing. Both sorts have seemed implausible to critics,[14] because they have come at agent causality with c→e causality as their only model for the kind of power an agent could exercise if it were in fact a causal power. The originators of these versions of causality have provided, as far as I can tell, no alternative to c→e causality, except in the sense that they have insisted that the agent, regarded as an entity rather than an event, can be the c in an instance of it. In the above sorts of agent causality (a) is intuitively easier than (b), but one still wonders why the agent-entity can not just as easily be regarded as a complex of c→e events, and its "causal power" status accordingly dismissed. As for (b), if we have the c→e model before us, we look for some event-like nexus running from an act to an event that can be regarded as part of it, which sometimes requires us to suppose that the normal temporal order of c and e has been violated. This is not the place to review agent causality and its difficulties in more detail, as it is one subordinate purpose of this book to present a more developed statement of yet another alternative version—I will not say of agent causality, but of the agent's involvement with the problem of causality—that I have given on earlier occasions. As it does not use the c→e model, except in case (a), and then only in a highly restricted form, I think it avoids the difficulties found in Chisholm, Taylor, and von Wright. But it is so distant from event-causality and from the c→e model it is no wonder that those who are committed to the cognitive ideal of science and to the canonical view of causality have not seriously considered it. It is part of the purpose of this book to show that some alternative version of causality is necessary, not only to reconcile the explanatory power of science with our intuitions of the explanatory value of rational acts, but even to make sense out of the creative production by scientists of more and more powerful scientific explanations.

The view that rational action is properly an *explicandum* and not an *explicans* is often more than a prejudice permeating large parts of the scientific community, the philosophic community, and the educated community in general. It is sometimes clearly and systematically expressed as a metaphysical doctrine—that is, one that claims that the entities, principles, and explanatory methods it recognizes are the only authentic ones; and that all other entities and principles are inauthentic in the sense of being disguised versions of the others and thus dispensable without loss in a truly rational discourse. When explicitly put forward as a metaphysics, the doctrine is usually called materialism or physicalism, and there are today many sophisticated, detailed, and influential versions of it. The *raison d'être* of most of them has been the need to understand not the nature of action but rather the relation between mind and body. Of these the most influential by far has been the identity theory of mind and body.[15] But some versions of this theory are readily generalizable to a theory of rational action; in at least one case—Edgar Wilson's *The Mental as Physical*—the author has in effect already generalized it, despite the title.[16] Taking advantage of the closeness of the topics of mind and action, I myself construct and undertake to refute, in chapter 6, an ideal theory of the identity of rational action with its physiological basis.

The influence of the physicalist view of human nature grows daily, both in the number that give it allegiance by propounding or accepting an explicit metaphysics and in the vaster number that simply operate on the assumption that the rational agent is never an *explicans* in any profound sense but only an *explicandum* for science. It is by way of becoming the dominant account of human nature and its place in nature in general. Pressed to its conclusion, it denies the authenticity of responsibility, not just because it is deterministic, but for the deeper reason that it regards the very category of action as spurious. Agent-formulas like those mentioned awhile ago are not in fact explanatory as they appear to be, because the "agent" does not in fact have the status it appears to have. The notion of appearance is of fundamental importance throughout the range of physicalist attitudes, even though it is not mentioned explicitly in the identity theory. There are first of all explicit epiphenomenalist positions on mind. Epiphenomenalism does not seem to be a popular position among philosophers nowadays,[17] although it turns up from time to time in the writing of scientists— especially those who are much impressed by analogies between the computer and the brain.[18] Writers on action do not usually adopt an explicitly epiphenomenalist view of it, for reasons I take up in chapter 5, but it is not uncommon for them to take what they call the phenomenal or phenomenological features of action to be appearances of which the physiological events that underlie them are the corresponding realities. Chapter 5 is devoted to a consideration of an ideal version

of an appearance doctrine of that kind, which I have called, drawing
upon the expression "manifest image," which some writings of Sellars
in the sixties made current, the *physicalist manifest image* (PMI) doctrine. Although the ideal doctrine I construct is not an epiphenomenalism with respect to rational action, it has much in common with
epiphenomenalism. It should be noted, incidentally, that when I use
the expression "*prima facie* rational action" I am *not* calling action a
manifest image. The identity theory in its pure form is almost always
directed towards the mind-body problem. Its extension to action, as
noted before, is natural enough. One would suppose that such an extension would so insist that action is not something distinct from the
physical that the question of an appearance-status would not arise at
all. Nonetheless it does; Danto's position, for instance, fails of being a
physicalist identity theory only because he takes the phenomenology of
action into consideration.[19] Indeed if it did not arise it would be hard
to see why ingenious writers would take the trouble to try to demonstrate (in the mind-body case) that there are not two ontological items
but one. (This is considered in some detail in chapter 6.)

It would seem, then, no exaggeration to say that the denial of the
authenticity of responsibility, with the consequent relegation of the rational agent to the status of *explicandum*, always carries with it the
attribution of an appearance-status to the agent. Although the rational
agent-in-act has a *prima facie* status as an operative power, that is said
to be just because the true operative powers, which demand to be conceived of in quite different terms, appear to us in that way. The agent,
then, is claimed to be phenomenal in the sense of not being authentically what it appears to be; consequently, any explanatory value we
attribute to it will not stand up to serious inquiry. Agent-explanations
will one day be replaced by proper explanations, and these will be as
complete as any explanations can be. In their light it will be seen that
the traditional attribution of power to an agent is dispensable without
any explanatory loss.

3

*Two Ways of Settling the Question
and a Via Media*

It would at first appear that there are only two ways of settling the
question: we can appeal to the authenticity of *prima facie* rational

agency or to the authority of science. Each way has difficulties. An appeal to *prima facie* rational agency invites the charge of circularity. About the appeal to science there is a preliminary difficulty before we come to the real one, for no one seems to think that there is any prospect of some empirical discovery—about the structure of the brain, for instance—that would settle the matter once and for all. It is rather the general movement of science that is appealed to: its competence in dealing successively with whatever issues come up; its failure to encounter so far any decisive lacunae in nature that could not be filled up except by recourse to the explanatory value of agency. And in this gradual progress it is not at all clear what would finally settle the issue, short perhaps of complete and detailed prediction of the future—a thing generally agreed to be not only practically impossible but fraught with all sorts of logical difficulties as well. But beyond this there is the more troubling difficulty that the work of scientists consists in *prima facie* rational acts. Indeed, the work of Thomas Kuhn[20] has persuaded many readers that scientific truth itself is defined by what the community of scientists—a community of *prima facie* rational agents—accepts in a given epoch. If the appeal to science is not precisely circular, it can plausibly be called self-subverting to just the extent it questions the authenticity of those *prima facie* agents who discover, accept, and reject paradigms. Similar difficulties can be put forward from the point of view of phenomenology—not the point of view, I should say at once, from which this book is written.

The appeal to *prima facie* rational action is never an appeal just to that, but rather to a whole world understood to be congruent with it— an appeal to the world, or to the nature of things, as seen by a *prima facie* rational agent; a world understood to contain rational agents who are at home in it and not anomalous presences. Most traditional philosophy has "appealed" to *prima facie* rational agency in that broad sense. Often enough in the past, then, the appeal to *prima facie* rational action has meant the systematic elaboration of a philosophical system in which rational action is accorded a place; the shaper of the system takes for granted his rational capacity as shaper, forms the system in accordance with it, and finds a place for agency within it. If such an exercise is carried out today, a place must also be found for science and for the findings of science about the world and ourselves. This compounds an ancient difficulty: the inconclusive competitiveness of a large number of philosophic systems.

That sort of appeal to *prima facie* rational action has been made implausible by the dominant view in the English-speaking philosophical world about the nature of philosophy itself. It is a view that cuts across the debate about the authenticity of responsibility, since it has been held, or at least affirmed in their practice, by certain philosophers—for instance, Kenny, Hampshire, and Strawson[21]—who incline to think it authentic and by numerous others—certainly many of those who once adhered to logical positivism—who do not. It is the view that philosophy does not provide us with any first-order knowledge about either ourselves or the world but only with a second-order knowledge of the logical structure of our languages, conceptual frameworks, language games, and so on—the terminology depends upon what particular path one enters after having made the linguistic turn. The prevailing dogma—or rather the one that used to prevail, for its influence is waning—has it that we can know the world in only two ways: that of the scientist and that defined by common sense—by our everyday attitude expressed in the structure of our language. The latter way is hospitable enough to *prima facie* rational agency, but it affords no more knowledge of it than what is already implicit in the linguistic-conceptual framework of ordinary life. In that arena the confrontation of linguistic analysis with the findings of science has remained philosophically inconclusive, although all the while discussion goes on the steady advance of science gradually erodes the prestige of our ordinary conceptual framework. At any rate, the circularity we have already noticed in the appeal to *prima facie* rational agency is even more salient in linguistic analysis than in the older "systematic" kind of philosophy.

Is it possible to find some third point of vantage from which all those difficulties vanish? It is impossible even to put that question without making an appeal that begins, at least, with the authority of *prima facie* rational agency itself. But if we do so I do not think we are then constrained to choose between old-fashioned system-building on the one hand and a second-order analysis of the logic of languages or of concepts on the other. There is a *via media*, and it is not the "rigorous science" of phenomenology, which itself leads us either to some variant of an idealistic system, or else—if we fasten on the last phase of Husserl's career, the phase that produced *Krisis*[22]—to something very like the authority of the world of common sense and ordinary language. The *via media* I have in mind presupposes in the first place an empirical engagement of philosophy with the world. It is a kind of engagement that is difficult to characterize because of a fallacy about the nature of knowledge—not just philosophical knowledge, but knowledge of all kinds—that has dominated epistemological theory at least since the time of Descartes. It has many varieties, and as I do not wish to do history of philosophy just here, I shall invent a term for it and say that it is the fallacy of the *cognitive intermediary*: it supposes that, whatever one wishes to know—oneself, some physical thing, the physical world in general, God—can not be known directly but only through some intermediary that one does know directly. The intermediaries are given various names in accordance with either the particular slant or the momentary purpose of the writer. They are called impressions, ideas, images, concepts, representations, and so on; what they have in common is the supposed possibility of being known directly, which used to be thought of as the possibility of existing in the mind. Most of the contemporary victims of the fallacy prefer to dispense with the notion of a mind, and so today the intermediaries are usually taken to be linguistic items. That proposed simplification actually produces complications, and as the whole matter is dealt with in some detail in chapter 3, I shall be brief here. However the mediators are to be understood, they need only mediate. They need not be *what* we know; they need not be known as they mediate; and they need not necessarily conspire with our sensory roots in the world to produce experiential surrogates that are other than what our interest is ultimately directed upon. If nonphilosophical knowledge is at issue, we are not constrained to know only mental intermediaries, linguistic intermediaries, or language-structured sensory intermediaries. As for philosophical knowledge, that it should be linguistically creative and creative of heightened awareness in a direct, or first-order, engagement with the real requires only that it should share this birthright of nonphilosophic knowledge. Though philosophy is often and profitably directed towards the structure of cognitive-linguistic intermediaries, that second-order activity is not its only and not its most important vocation.

The *via media* I propose, then, is an empirically engaged reflection that begins with the point of view of the *prima facie* rational agent and attempts to transform it. This reflective task is by design a linguistically creative one; and in the epistemological view here adumbrated, and developed in more detail in chapters 3 and 4, linguistic creativity on an empirically engaged base can make more adequate our (not indirect) cognitive grasp of ourselves as rational agents. The role theory plays in all this is minimal, if by "theory" one means the contriving of a theoretic structure, which then becomes the sole object of our cognitive attention. (There is of course a kinship between a theoretic structure and what I have called cognitive intermediaries in general; they are, like at least some of the latter, things we can know as "directly" as we can know any commonsense object, even though there are profound differences between the status of the two kinds of objects. That possibility of "direct" knowledge of the intermediaries is one of the reasons for the strength of the fallacy of the cognitive intermediary.) For better or worse, chapters 3 and 4 are not put forward as a theory about rational action. Such theories have their use, but I think the chief one is in bringing our concrete knowledge of rational action, after transformation by reflection, into harmony with the domain of scientific theory.

4

An Anticipatory Supposition: The Nature
of Rational Action

Before turning to the reflection promised in the last section, two digressions are in order. The longer is the one embarked on in the next chapter. It deals with the metaphysical conditions of responsible rational action—that is, with what features the rational agent and the nature of things of which it is part must have if the rational agent is authentically what its *prima facie* nature lays claim to being. And for this task we need no more than a faithful adherence, I will not say to the concept of the rational agent, but to what the *prima facie* rational agent is concretely experienced and known to be, in an equally *prima facie* sense of "experience" and "know," as we ourselves carry out what purport to be our own rational acts.

A shorter digression precedes it and begins just here. It is designed to suggest to the reader the main outlines of a view of action that I hope the rest of the book will justify. Confronted without that preparation, it will have something of the look of a theory about rational action, and surely any reader who tends to look towards science for a cognitive ideal is justified in taking it so. I shall in any event state it roundly and without argument, as a supposition to be entertained as a kind of telos for what follows. If the reader should be able to suspend disbelief about it, the goal of the rather intricate course of the rest of the book will at least be in view as a guide.

The supposition I offer will be clearer if I first make one or two preliminary observations. Acts, it would appear, can be analyzed in at least two ways. In one way, we find no elements that are themselves acts, but only items that have a different ontological status. They may be events or entities or states of entities: events like the contraction of a muscle or the firing of a neuron, entities like muscle cells or neurons or macromolecules, states of entities like the oxygen level in a muscle cell or the electric potential at a given place and time in the axon of a neuron. Whatever they are, science and philosophers of science agree in telling us that they are linked in a causal order under laws that science is concerned to formulate. Our supposition will require us to say that this mode of analysis is concerned with the *infrastructure of the act*. This implies that analysis of this sort does not yield an account that is fully equivalent to the *analysandum*.

In the other kind of analysis we find items that are ontologically on much the same level as the act itself. If, for instance, we begin by considering the act of speaking a paragraph, analysis will reveal several acts of speaking sentences, and analysis of these in turn will reveal several acts of speaking words. Let us call them all sub-acts. Sub-acts are perplexing things, for it would seem that they have all the marks that their superordinate act has, except that they are subordinate and it superordinate. In a *prima facie* sense acts do not succeed each other in a causal order, or at least not in the same kind of causal order in which infrastructure items are thought to succeed each other. An act of a given rank does not cause the next one, and no sub-act of a given superordinate act can be adequately understood as a mere effect of the preceding sub-act. Any sub-act is an act and not merely a causal consequence of an earlier act or acts. Sub-acts, indeed, are just as amenable as superordinate acts are to the two kinds of analysis I have just mentioned: they have infrastructures, and, though sub-acts, they themselves ramify in other sub-acts of a lower rank. This kind of analysis, then, purports to reveal a nested hierarchy of acts, but it neither reduces an act to an equivalent set of sub-acts nor sees any sub-act as a mere abstraction from its superordinate act. Our supposition will require us to say that this way of analyzing action claims the ontological authenticity of each act in a hierarchy of acts. The claim is the obverse of the restriction we have already placed on the first kind of analysis.

The supposition about which I ask the reader to suspend disbelief may now be stated: an act is precisely what it purports to be to the intelligent and articulate awareness of the agent who performs it. By this I mean that when one experiences an act of one's own—alternatively when one is aware of acting—and articulates, or could articulate, one's experience in language, the *prima facie* reality thus experienced and rationally acknowledged is an authentic reality. The old-fashioned expression "authentic reality" is deliberate: it expresses the claim that the concrete grasp of the world within which the most abstract proceedings of science go on does not in principle miss what is the case. The linking of experience, or awareness, on the one hand and its expression in language on the other is equally deliberate. It is a way of calling attention to a mode of knowledge that, although not theoretical-empirical in the sense in which science is, has nonetheless both a theoretical (more properly rational) and an empirical component. Though one is tempted to think of it as prerational, pretheoretic, or even primordial, that temptation should be resisted. What is important about this mode of knowledge is that its rational and empirical components are fused in a sense in which they are not fused in science. Here we can not isolate a theoretic structure from the empirical situation in which, on the analogy of science, the theory should be put to the test. And this is not a defect in this mode of knowledge but rather its peculiar excellence: what is rationally articulated is precisely that which is also empirically present, and that presence enters into and becomes part of the rational articulation; what is empirically present is present in virtue of just that rational articulation—present with a completeness it would not otherwise have. Rational articulation here comes into its own only by articulating empirical presence; empirical presence in turn is presence to an awareness that realizes itself in rational articulation. And the concomitant development of those two factors can not be adequately modeled in terms of a speculative-empirical cycle in which theories are first developed and then put to the test in an experience that can be had independently of the theory. All this implies a realist epistemology whose ramifications we shall explore later.

Our supposition requires the rejection of another one—the supposition, very common nowadays, that what one experiences as present in the above *prima facie* way is phenomenal, and phenomenal not merely in the straightforward and unexceptionable sense that it is something that appears to a subject but also in the sense that it is either entirely derivative from or else identical with some true reality or complex of realities that does not normally appear. An experienced macrostructure or macroevent is interpreted as the appearance of microstructures or microevents that are the true operative realities, and what one takes oneself to be aware of and to grasp articulately with one's intelligence is not in fact the operative power it appears to be. We shall suppose instead that the *prima facie* act, manifest to one's normal intelligent awareness of oneself and of others, *is* the reality: in this case it is indeed the exercise of the power of speaking a sentence or a paragraph.

Our supposition does not, however, require us to postulate an independence of the act from its infrastructure. On the contrary, when we attend to the act itself we also attend to all the elements of the infrastructure—not severally, to be sure, not with a direct appreciation of each of them, but rather in the guise of their total contribution to the act as conditions for it. Scrutiny of the infrastructure in our first mode of analysis discloses a multiplicity of other entities and events—for instance, the firing of a complex sequence of a multitude of neurons in the speech centers while a paragraph is spoken. The reality of this multiplicity is authentic enough, and the ontological status of each item in it is not called in question by our attending to the act. Indeed, there is no reason why we should not think of infrastructure elements as secret powers, so long as we do not think of them as powers that in their aggregate cancel out that of the act itself, giving it the status of a mere appearance that is unqualifiedly identical with the aggregate. The reality of the act embraces, makes use of, even in some measure dominates the realities of the infrastructure, but neither act nor infrastructure cancels the authenticity of the other. The apprehension of an act by an agent is not exhaustive, because the agent's involvement in it precludes simultaneous apprehension of the complexity that contributes to it. On the other hand, only an agent can experience and be rationally aware of an act, and what it then experiences is not an ontological deception. It may well be that behind every apparent reality, from the action of a person to the career of the most evanescent particle, there lurks a reality that is the true secret power that never appears—call it Being, or the One, or *Deus sive Natura*. But if that should be so, it raises no special problem for action, for any secret powers established by observation or theory would suffer the same fate.

Although I seemed to concede awhile ago that an act is a macrostructure, or a macroevent, there are certain features of certain actions that are not very precisely described either by these terms or by the related term "macroscopic." Consider once again the act of speaking a paragraph. If a person articulates some line of reasonable argument in a paragraph, the linking of the words just so and the marshaling of the reasons just so are constituents of the *prima facie* power exercised by that agent. They are as much a part of the texture of the act as are the movement of the lips or the gestures of the hands. The power of speaking a paragraph includes the power of the reasons articulated in the paragraph. To put it another way: the compelling power of the reasons or their failure to compel is part of the so-called macroscopic reality, part of the total phenomenon we call the act itself. They are not so much reasons *for* the act as they are reasons *in* the act: the *prima facie* power of the agent appears impossible to extricate from the *prima facie* power of the reasons themselves. Indeed the power of the agent is in one sense an acquiescence in the power of the reasons expressed and assented to. The point is not weakened just because the agent can act only in and with an infrastructure.

It is usually taken for granted in contemporary discussion that action requires explanation, if not by philosophy, then at least by science. From that point of view our supposition is heretical enough, since it establishes an in-principle limitation for the predictive features of scientific explanation. Theory and observation appropriate to the infrastructure permit no complete prediction of the act itself. Thus the physiological state at time t_0 is of no help in establishing the *prima facie* reality of the act (including the speaking of certain words) at time t_1. More than that, the physiological state at time t_0 is not even adequate to establish the complete physiological state at time t_1, for the latter will be a function of the words spoken at time t_1, no less than a condition for the speaking of them.

This is less of an oddity, however, if we regard an act as having a quantum-like feature. As a quantum of energy has a temporal component that confers upon it an inner unity that forbids an internal analysis of it in the causal terms of prequantum physics, so it may be with an act. While it is the prevailing view today that quanta of energy are basic to nature in the sense that we can not explain why they have the kind of integrity they do have and must therefore make all other explanations conform with that integrity, nature may also be conceived of as a nested system of quanta, the higher levels of which exhibit in their own way this essential feature of the simplest level. Acts—and many levels between acts and the simplest quanta of energy—may live their undivided power-time units by virtue of embracing, and being supported by, those of lower levels, which, taken as an assemblage, they may place under some restraints. A unit of higher order would thus realize itself not precisely in independence of units of lower order, but nonetheless with a unity of power over time that would be distinct from the assemblage of units of lower order in the sense that it could not be fully accounted for in terms of them. This would be a correlative of the fact that a unit of higher order not only can not be experienced as an assemblage of those of lower order, but also can not even be understood in those terms. It would follow that there is in principle something inexplicable about an act—inexplicable in the sense that an account of everything that is happening in what science might prefer to regard as simply a certain space-time "region" can be adequate only if it involves directly or indirectly the category of action itself.

From the perspective of the persistent notion that we ought to act more justly, more rationally, more effectively, with more dignity and responsibility, it is not in the least strange to regard action as not wholly explicable. Indeed one then calls attention to action as a way of *explaining* certain very complex happenings—those that are the concern of morals, of art, and of history, including the history of science itself. The explanatory value of invoking action in this way has as its complement the opacity of action to complete explanation by any other mode of explanation.

II

The Metaphysical Conditions of
Ontic Responsibility

1

Ontic Responsibility, Moral Responsibility,
Social Responsibility, and Legal Responsibility

Legal responsibility in the sense of *de facto* accountability offers in itself no philosophical problems: the citizens of a political community are made responsible in that sense by what linguistic philosophers call the performatory utterance of the lawmaking body of that community; which means that they are subject to whatever sanctions the law lays down. Legal responsibility of this kind is one instance—no doubt the most important one—of a general social responsibility that may also be interpreted in terms of *de facto* accountability. Society holds us responsible for our actions under a variety of codes for behavior, some of which, like the rules of a school or profession or like the law itself, are relatively stable and formalized; and some of which are as informal and evanescent as the perception by a given social set of what is or is not done by those who run with it. In thinking about the law one thinks first of the sanctions that go with *de facto* accountability, but conformity with this or that code of the many interlocking groups that are pervaded by social responsibility can bring substantial rewards as well.

It is much harder to give a plausible account of moral responsibility by confining ourselves to *de facto* accountability. Most societies do indeed take certain standards for behavior to be of such peculiar force that they override all other standards, and sometimes their sanctions coincide with those of *de facto* social accountability. Murder is regarded as immoral, is punished by the law, and will not usually advance you in the eyes of fellow parishioners or fellow club members. On the other hand, many of us treat other persons not as ends in themselves but as means to some end and yet manage to escape all serious sanctions, despite the common view that we are morally responsible to do otherwise. Someone who wished nonetheless to insist that moral responsibility is a kind of *de facto* accountability might reply that the rewards and sanctions of morality are chiefly internal—a *de facto* internal accountability to the standards society lays down in all of us. The moral authority of the Freudian superego is said to be of this kind. But whether we regard these demands of society as a set of rules implicit in the internal operations of each member of society or as a set of feelings that will inevitably manifest themselves when certain actions are performed or observed to be performed, the case is not persuasive. What purports to be the voice of moral responsibility often puts forward a new rule or maxim whose authority was not theretofore acknowledged or calls upon us to feel a feeling that was not theretofore felt. Indeed, even those who labor to provide a naturalistic account of morality sometimes show a disposition to believe that even if there is no pervasive set of rules or feelings definitive of our common humanity—a set beyond any set inculcated by some particular society— then there *ought* to be. It is just this "ought" that makes it implausible that moral responsibility should consist in a mere *de facto* accountability. Nowhere does it have so odd and paradoxical a force as when someone claims that responsibility under the law is immoral and ought to be done away with because nobody is a responsible rational agent in the sense legal responsibility seems to require.

This is not the place to consider that paradox, but it will be convenient to use that "ought" to introduce our main topic. There are many practical problems about social responsibility in general and its most important particular instance, legal responsibility, but philosophical problems do not ordinarily arise until we ask whether some person ought to be held responsible in some particular case or raise the more difficult question whether anyone ought to be held responsible in any circumstances. The latter question is most often raised about legal responsibility, partly because accountability of almost everyone to the law seems necessary for the preservation of order, and partly because the sanctions of the law are more dire than those of other social codes. When we then try to decide whether people in general should be held legally responsible by determining whether or not they are in general responsible rational agents, the word "responsible" has shifted meaning between its first and its second appearance. In the latter it no longer means "*de facto* accountable" but rather "so constituted in its ontological nature as to make accountability appropriate, just, and seemly." The focus has shifted from the calling of persons to account to the ontological justification for doing so: agents are appropriately responsible (sense 1) because they are in fact responsible (sense 2); and the latter sense must then be amplified by reference to one or more of a number of familiar philosophical criteria: the presence of free choice, the capacity to do otherwise than one in fact does, the capacity to be governed by reasons instead of causes, and so on. It is clear then that responsibility (sense 2) is inseparable from the status of rational agency itself. To say that persons have responsibility (sense 2) is to say that they have authentically the status of rational agent they seem to have.[1]

In this essay I shall assume that all well-developed discussions of the authenticity of responsibility (sense 2) are metaphysical ones. But as I intend to make use of the notion of being at a number of crucial points in the course of this book, I shall call responsibility (sense 2) *ontic responsibility* rather than metaphysical responsibility. If ontic responsibility should be authentic, both social responsibility and its most important particular instance, legal responsibility, will be qualified by it, and we shall not be able to capture their full meaning in terms of *de facto* accountability. As for moral responsibility, its status will also depend upon whether or not ontic responsibility is authentic. Indeed, many readers might prefer to say that "ontic responsibility" is simply another name for moral responsibility—that the question whether we are so constituted in our ontological natures as to make accountability appropriate, just, and seemly is merely the question whether moral responsibility is authentic. But there are some grounds for thinking that ontic responsibility is a wider category and that, if it is authentic, moral responsibility is a special case of it—ontic responsibility exercised in certain well-defined and very important circumstances. It is clear, for instance, that ontic responsibility covers all acts whatsoever, or at least all acts that admit of degree of excellence, so that all our work in science, in the arts, and indeed in the entire practical-productive sphere comes under it. Thus, all Max Planck's work in science from his 1879 doctoral dissertation to his famous 1900 paper would exemplify it. But we should probably want to say that only some of the ontically responsible acts performed in the course of his scientific work were also instances of moral responsibility—perhaps only those of his acts that involved relations with other persons. Still, certain impressive arguments suggest that moral responsibility is almost as extensive as ontic responsibility itself. If all the acts a scientist performs in the interest of science are qualified by a felt moral obligation to find the "objective" truth about nature, most and perhaps all of Planck's acts that led up to the 1900 paper might well be regarded as morally responsible. The extreme case is established by Platonic arguments in which the Good is sovereign—to use Iris Murdoch's term—in both the ontological and the moral sense.[2] In this book, however, we shall say that if ontic responsibility is authentic, then moral responsibility is a special case of it. It will be clear, then, that we want the notion of ontic responsibility to function in many of the ways in which the notion of free will functions in other settings. We shall see that there is some advantage in thus avoiding that vexed notion in what follows.

2

Prima Facie Rational Action and the Conditions of Ontic Responsibility

The traditional justification for applying the sanctions and rewards that go with most kinds of social responsibility and for applying the sanctions that go with its most important instance, legal responsibility, is that we are responsible rational agents and therefore just the sort of beings that should be held responsible (de facto accountable). The traditional reason for holding us responsible (sense 1) is that we are responsible (sense 2)—in our present terminology, that we are ontically responsible and therefore also morally responsible in a sense not reducible to de facto accountability. The corresponding justification for suspending the sanctions of the law or of some other code in certain circumstances is that ontic responsibility can sometimes be diminished or canceled entirely. Either external circumstances or some internal flaw—temporary or permanent—in the structure of certain persons can diminish or preclude entirely the capacity for rational action. Although the authenticity of ontic responsibility is under heavy attack, belief in it persists as the foundation of law and social custom. It is a belief that sometimes continues to work even in those who accept the philosophical arguments that purport to show that there is no justification for it.

Any well-developed denial of ontic responsibility must rest on the claim that reality in general has a structure that makes that instance of it we call rational human action not what it appears to be. Any well-developed defense of it must make its own appropriate claims about the nature of reality. In this chapter I do not mean to defend the authenticity of ontic responsibility, but simply to state, as precisely as I can, what conditions must be fulfilled, not only in the agent but besides in "the nature of things," if it should indeed be authentic. To lay down the conditions for ontic responsibility is no light matter: the universe in which one envisions them as holding is radically different from one in which other conditions are in their places. Whether or not they do hold, it is worth confronting them in all their difficulty, for there is no other way to see how profoundly important a claim we make when we say that we are ontically responsible.

Our guide in determining what conditions must hold is a familiar one: it is nothing more than the rational awareness—an articulated, linguistic matter no less than an empirical one—we have of our own *prima facie* rational actions. It is, however, an odd and ambiguous guide, for the conditions are not immediately obvious, and as we try to state them we find that we can not do so without bringing that rational awareness to a sharper focus. The fully articulated conditions constitute a fully articulated definition of what rational action qualified by ontic responsibility purports to be. Two familiar difficulties stand in the way of a project that is by design both rational-linguistic and empirical. For one thing, a good deal of writing and talking about rational action stands in our way. There are *concepts* about such matters as free will, volition, motivation, intentions, reasons, causes, and all the other things that turn up in such discussions; and these stand so much in our way that with the best will in the world it is hard to see through them to the concrete reality of our own supposed rational acts. For another, there is an influential dogma about philosophy for which the clamor of these concepts for our attention is the insufficient justification: the dogma that when engaged in philosophy we can not possibly be dealing with the concrete but only with the concepts some nonphilosophic attitude has won from experience or brought to experience. I shall assume here that that dogma is false. If there is any justification for my assumption, the reader will find it in the persuasiveness of the conditions that come out of these investigations.

3

The Conditions of Ontic Dependence, Causal Power,
and Ontic Power

The condition of *ontic dependence* concerns the relation between act and agent: if ontic responsibility is authentic we must exclude an ontology of acts whose occurrence need not be referred to an entity that acts. Indeed, ontic responsibility requires that the being of the agent and the being of the act should be inseparable: the agent must be the source of the act and must become permanently qualified by it. If, for instance, I were now speaking directly to you rather than writing, my speaking would be one significant way in which my presence as a *prima facie* entity would manifest itself to you. The power exercised in the act would manifest itself as my power, so much a function of my presence that if called upon to identify me you might well say, "he is the one who just said such and such." Whatever the *I* may be upon which the act depends, if *I* am the rational agent responsible for it, then we can not do justice to the fact with an act-ontology in which the occurrence of an act requires no reference of it to an agent-entity.

What the dependence of an act on an agent consists in is hard to say. Certainly the unity of the act and the power exercised in it must depend on the unity and power of the agent. No doubt it would be excessive to say that while the rational agent is acting it is identical with its act, because the totality of what the agent is *as* it acts seems to exceed the content of the act. But at any rate the tie between agent and act must be closer than that between cause and effect, or at least closer than that tie is usually taken to be in contemporary discussion of the causal relation. One might hazard the thought that ontically responsible agents must be efficient causes of their acts, although in an older sense of "efficient cause" than the sense now limited to the notion of antecedent event. But even that, as we shall see, will not quite do. As for the notion of antecedent event, it has very little application here. Since acts, though no doubt not entirely captured in the notion of an event, are *also* events, we may perhaps regard my speaking these words as an event antecedent to and sufficient for the event of your hearing them. But the dependence of the act of speaking on the entity who speaks is not that of consequent event on antecedent event, or at least it is not if the entity so originates the act as to be responsible for it. If I am indeed the rational agent responsible for this little speech, I was present sustaining it at its beginning, at its middle, and at its end—simultaneous with the whole of the act rather than before it, and persisting, though not unchanged, after the end of the act. In one sense, I was indeed before the act, in that I was identifiable then as the person who later spoke those words; but on the other hand, my coming into being did not end with what it was before my act. It is continuous with the new act and indeed continues to happen as the act itself happens.

This is enough to tell us that we are not efficient causes of our acts in the sense in which an older tradition supposed God to be the efficient cause of the world. The dependence of act upon agent has no doubt something in common with causal dependence, and some light may be cast upon it by what is said about causation in our discussion of the second and third conditions. But the kind of dependence we require is *sui generis*, for if I am responsible now for the act, so responsible that you can call me to task for it, the act must have qualified me. If I am the cause for the act I am also its effect: the development of the act is my development as well, and I am now what I was not before, the person who spoke just those words. By the development of the act I mean the development of the act in its full concreteness, just as I experienced it in one way and you in another: the development includes the meaningful succession of words; and not only the succession and the physical movements that produce them, but also the complex subjective pattern that is my awareness not just of the occurrence of the words, but of my intending to say something of the kind and in the event doing so. And if I am ontically responsible for it, all this development depends upon me, and yet is so much a part of my development that what I am now depends upon it.

The second condition, that of *causal power*, requires that the agent-in-act should be able to exert causal power on something other than itself. It might be more cautiously expressed as the condition of the capacity for exercising causal power, because it is not immediately clear that all rational acts include the direct exercise of causal power in the world about us. Silent thinking to some purpose, for instance, would appear to be a rational act without immediate effects outside the agent. But in the case of speaking it is clear that causal power is being exercised in a *prima facie* sense. Though so much a part of my development that if regarded as an event it must also be regarded as part of the longer event that is my history, the act nonetheless reverberates in the world about me. It appears to be my power exercised in the first instance on your ears; and it must be authentically that if the present condition is to be fulfilled: that is, it purports to occur before your hearing, and in the obtaining of certain necessary conditions it appears to be sufficient for your hearing. What purports to be ontically dependent upon me also purports to be an exercise of power upon you and to bring about certain effects in you; and this we may express equally well in terms of two features for which Hume claimed we have no evidence whatsoever: given certain conditions in you, my speaking purports to produce effects in you and also to necessitate those effects. And unless it in fact does so, there is something inauthentic about the ontic responsibility I appear to exercise.

Causal power must of course *originate* in the entity that acts. A number of the later conditions will address the positive content of the notion of origination, and so here we may content ourselves with some negative remarks. In the first place, if causal power is authentic, then the notion of cause is not exhausted by the relativized sense in which any cause may with equal justice be considered an effect. If that were so, the agent's "power" could be said to be entirely an effect of other entities or other events prior to it. Alternatively, its "power" could first be made equivalent to the "power" of entities in its infrastructure, or else to a multiplicity of events in its infrastructure, and any of these could then in turn be regarded as wholly caused by entities or events of the same kind, and thus eventually by entities or events prior to the agent. Such a view of causation recognizes no causal power of any kind and hence none in the agent. Chisholm's revival of an older terminology tempts us to say that that view tolerates no causal power because it recognizes no immanent causes but only transeunt ones. But that unfortunately distorts the original force of the old contrast between "immanent" and "transeunt," even if it should not seriously distort the sense of "immanent" in that contrast. In the original sense, which was applied chiefly to God, a transeunt cause was not merely a cause in the relativized sense just mentioned, for it was precisely by virtue of an immanent power that a cause was said to be able to operate transeuntly: immanent power was the source of transeunt power and transeunt power the sign of the presence of immanent power.[3] Let us say, then, that a cause in the relativized sense is a *transmitted* cause; that a merely transmitted cause exercises no authentic causal power; and that authentic causal power is in some measure an *originative* cause.

Among contemporary doctrines the best example of the merely

transmitted cause is to be found in any version of physical determinism that regards any event or state in a given region at time t_n as the cause of an event or state in the same region at time t_{n+1} and the effect of an event or state in the same region at time t_{n-1}. In the extreme case, the word "cause" itself is dispensed with, as in a well-known paper of Bertrand Russell in which he claims that "in a sufficiently advanced science, the word 'cause' will not occur in any statement of invariable laws."[4] An earlier version of the paper puts the matter even more strongly: the word "cause" should be eliminated from philosophy as it already has been from physics, which, because "in fact, there are no such things," has ceased looking for causes.[5] Russell advocates our speaking instead of "causal laws,"[6] or "scientific laws,"[7] and he so generalizes this notion that it makes reference—as indeed it should—to the whole universe rather than to some local region, and besides is not limited, as the notion sometimes is, to the matter of prediction: "There are such invariable relations between different events at the same or different times that, given the state of the whole universe throughout any finite time, however short, every previous and subsequent event can theoretically be determined as a function of the given events during that time."[8] In that paper, written many years ago, Russell was not defending physical determinism so much as he was defining it, but more recent definitions do not differ from his in any essential way, except that most determinists want to insist only on predictability, and so usually retain the term "cause" and let it refer to the earlier of two temporally adjacent events in any discriminated sequence. A cause in that future-oriented sense is still merely a transmitted cause. The image of a great tenseless, or static, physical field, of which physical time is one dimension like any other is, however, a recurrent one, and it is often the object of an ontological, rather than a merely methodological, commitment. A physicalist Parmenidean monism of that kind obviously excludes authentic causal power whether or not the term "causal power" is retained for some methodological purpose.[9] The same thing can, of course, also be said for any Parmenidean or Spinozistic monism that is not physicalistic in intent.

One more negative remark may elucidate the "originative" nature of the causal power required by the second condition. Even if causal power should be recognized in some nondeterministic setting, the term "agent" must not be regarded as merely a commonsense way of referring to the aggregate of a multiplicity of events some of which might be the result of causal powers. There are certainly reductionist doctrines that are less steadfastly deterministic than those just described, and some of them may leave open the possibility that some entities have causal power, while still refusing to attribute it to an agent. This can be done by way of a resolution of what common sense might call the power of an agent into a multiplicity of c→E events within what I have called the infrastructure of the act. By "resolution" I do not mean only such an analysis itself, but rather that analysis supplemented by the claim that it can replace without significant explanatory loss the notion of causal power in the *analysandum*. In such a resolution the "causal power" of an agent becomes a mere appearance, the real causal powers, if any, residing somewhere in that multiplicity.

Needless to say, the other conditions flesh out this rather skeletal expression of the notion of causal power. The third condition is that of *ontic power*. It concerns the relation between the causal power I claimed to exercise awhile ago and the multiplicity of other entities and events—for instance, neural nets, neurons, and macromolecules, as well as events taking place within and between them—that seemed to contribute to it. The condition of ontic power lays down the negative requirement that the causal power the agent exercises should not be exhaustively analyzable into a multiplicity of contributory powers simultaneous with it. With this goes a positive requirement: that in the exercise of its causal power the rational agent must exercise a power of a different sort over these contributory powers—a power that makes them genuinely contributory to it rather than in their assemblage so identical with it that any reference to its power would be superfluous. Ontic power is not yet clearly recognized in contemporary discussion in the way in which causal power is beginning to be recognized, but it is vital to the originative feature of causal power and hence to that in it which can be said authentically to produce or to affect something else. If we were to accept the revival of "immanent" while setting aside the new sense given "transeunt" in contrasting it with "immanent," we might go on to say that ontic power may be regarded as the ground of the agent's immanence in its causal power. But I think it is less confusing to say that it is the ground of the origination of causal power in the agent. It is, in any case, the power that must pervade the inner complexity of an act—must, that is, pervade its infrastructure— if the act is to be capable of producing or necessitating something distinct from itself in the way the concept of causal power calls for. Otherwise the action appears to be resolvable without loss into a multiplicity of c→E transactions within the infrastructure, and as we shall have no more reason to ascribe an originative causal power to any entity within that multiplicity than we have to ascribe it to the act as a whole, those transactions will presumably be instances of relativized, or merely transmitted, causality. Being in that case identical with a multiplicity of instances of transmitted causality, the "agent-in-act" becomes itself an instance of transmitted causality.

It seems appropriate to call this power an ontic one because it is plain that if the condition of ontic power should be fulfilled, what we are calling attention to with the help of it would not be wholly intelligible in terms of the notion of causality, or at least not wholly intelligible in terms of what that notion has come to mean in modern times. We are calling attention instead to the being of the act regarded as not completely analyzable into a multiplicity of components, or to the being of the agent regarded as immanent in the act and itself not analyzable into a multiplicity. If the condition of ontic power should hold, the relation between the totality of an act and its components can not be expressed in terms of cause and effect in any sense dominated by the $c \rightarrow e$ image. It might be said in reply that the "relation" is one of identity—that we can therefore dispense with all talk about a relation between an act and its components. The condition of ontic power, however, is in effect the condition that the totality of an act should not be identical, in the sense intended by physicalists, with whatever components a scientific analysis might resolve it into.

If causal power is authentic, then I do in fact produce, or necessitate, certain effects in you by my speaking, and the effects are truly the effects of my act. But if in the act of speaking I act authentically then the persistent thought that in doing so I also do something either to or by means of the components of my nervous system must have something to it, though surely something that demands that it be expressed in some other way: that there should be a causal relation (in the $c \rightarrow e$ sense) between the I-in-act and some neuron seems, and probably is, preposterous. The I-in-act is not after all exhaustively described if we do not bring in just those neurons that fire in the course of it. That the condition of ontic power should hold requires no causal relation in any sense congruent with the $c \rightarrow e$ image, though there are older senses of "cause" that might well be invoked to illuminate the notion of ontic power. But it does require that the unit of power that is the I-in-act should in some sense dominate, influence, or qualify such units of power as single neurons, neural complexes, and so on; and it therefore requires more distinction between the being of the

I-in-act and the being of the physical multiplicity that subserves it than physicalist identity theories tolerate. The condition of ontic power calls for the ontic distinctness from an infrastructure of the entity that is said to exercise it.

4

The Conditions of Explanatory Ultimacy and Explanatory Opacity

We must now consider two conditions so complementary that we might well comprise them in a wider condition of explanatory adequacy. The fourth condition is that of *explanatory ultimacy*: the acts in which (as we still imagine) I spoke the preceding words may be offered in partial explanation of the state of affairs that is your entertaining whatever it is you are now entertaining. Such an explanatory account is adequate, so far as it goes, and it is also indispensable in the sense that any other account that might be offered to enrich your understanding of the complex intersubjective situation in which we find ourselves as I speak to you—and surely physiological accounts of what is happening in our central nervous systems already do enrich it and promise to do so even more in the future—would leave that state of affairs incompletely explained if it left out the commonplace but nevertheless momentous fact that some rational agent spoke such and such words. I do not mean just that the alternative explanation would be incomplete in some *prima facie*, commonsense, or everyday way that can be dismissed as belonging to the archaic language in which we have heretofore carried on our intellectual business. I mean that, however interesting and illuminating it might be, it would nevertheless be seriously incomplete when judged by the standards of strict rationality, in that it would fail to include a complex power truly operative in the situation; for that power would be no less operative for being conditioned by, supported by, intimately entangled with, a host of other powers that our alternative account may indeed seriously and profoundly address.

If this is true it will also follow that the power of the rational agent so qualifies the other powers that support or condition it that our alternative explanation will leave something quite obscure even in the subject matter for which it was first devised. This does not mean just that a perfected physiology would be unable to give an exhaustive explanation of the speaking or writing of a paragraph—including one's intending to speak, one's awareness of speaking, and one's sense of having managed to say more or less what one had intended to say. The condition does indeed require that any truly adequate explanation of speaking or writing should include reference to the power of the agent—include it not just as a concession to common sense but as a response to a demand of rationality more authoritative than that of science itself. But beyond all that, the condition requires that the physiology itself should be incompletable in at least this sense, that a brain-state at a time t_0, just before the speaking of some words, is in principle not adequate to establish the state at time t_1, after the speaking of some words, because the latter brain-state will be a function of the words spoken no less than the transition from the first brain-state to the second will be a condition for the speaking of the words.

The fifth condition is that of *explanatory opacity*. It is the obverse of the condition of explanatory ultimacy: whatever functions in explanation in a way not reducible to or replaceable by other explanatory categories is an explanatory ultimate, and what is thus ultimate can not itself be explained. It is clear that in an overwhelmingly monistic and deterministic system there will be only one explanatory ultimate, only one thing that is opaque to explanation. Influential statements of such monisms in the past have been theological more often than not: one thinks of Parmenides' One, about which no more need be said than "It is," or of Spinoza's God (Substance, Nature), of which the only explanation is that He, or It, necessarily exists, is *causa sui*. But something just as absolute, necessary, and arbitrary lies behind contemporary monisms of a physicalist sort. It is the mass-energy system that an ideal statement of the laws of nature would completely characterize. It is envisioned in various ways, the most persistent recent image being that of a unified field—the one great tenseless singularity of which all other apparent singularities—including those of experienced time—would be merely functions. If that were indeed the ultimate structure of reality, its explanatory power would be complemented by its own absolute opacity to explanation. And nothing whatever that was in any sense distinguishable as an item within such a reality could be said in its turn to be opaque to explanation, for as soon as it was distinguished it would at once have been so explained.

A radical pluralism of acts would give us the necessary explanatory opacity and indeed as good a model for explanatory ultimacy as one could wish for. Such acts, insofar as they sprang from agent-entities,

would reshape them: an agent capable of such acts would be to that
extent *causa sui*. But it has been noticed often enough that this still
leaves us with the initial character (or nature) of the agent to whom
we attribute the capacity for such acts. I know of no pluralism so radical as to make each agent *causa sui* with respect to that initial character. And so we are back with something or other out of which agents
spring and upon which, for all their explanatory ultimacy and explanatory opacity, they must be dependent.

What would prevent our condition from being fulfilled is not so
much a source of agents, and hence indirectly of acts, that is absolutely opaque to explanation, but rather one whose opaqueness is coupled with a monistic feature that tolerates no explanatory opacity in
any finite particular. And from this perspective, if there is no explanatory opacity in the particular, then there is no authenticity in it either.
If rational agents-in-act are to be in any sense opaque to explanation,
the background against which we distinguish them can not be of a
monistic sort. To distinguish the rational agent at all *within* the background is of course already to concede that its explanatory opacity is
not absolute, for its existence in that case is not absolutely necessary
but contingent in the sense of being necessitated by whatever it is dependent upon. But an explanatory opacity may be no less opaque for
being derivative. We shall suppose that if the explanatory opacity of
the source instantiates itself in the particularity of the rational agent-
in-act the condition shall have been fulfilled. This, at least, is what we
have in mind when we call the rational agent an act-source without intending to say that it is its own source. A pluralism of this kind is
plainly no radical pluralism, but neither is it a deceptive appearance of
pluralism. If the nature of things is *causa sui*, then it must be also
causa sui authentically instantiated here in the particular agent-in-act,
if the agent is to have the explanatory opacity the condition calls for.

Although conceding, then, that the agent exists against an explanatory background of some power, a background that may illuminate in
various ways its capacity for rational action, the condition nevertheless
lays it down that something in the development and activity of the
agent should be inexplicable except by calling attention to the fact
that the agent indeed did thus and so. After all details of the infrastructure have been given in partial explanation; after a causal analysis
in terms of all the powers that condition it or otherwise contribute to
it has been given; after all causal influences from the physical environment, from society, and from training have been considered; after all

theological underpinnings have been explored and allowance made for them; after all these things have been done, there must remain some features of the agent-in-act that are inexplicable in the sense that no explanatory technique can further illuminate what is expressed in the statement that the agent indeed acted in just that way. Otherwise agency is inauthentic in the sense that it is not what it purports to be.

5

The Conditions of Partial Determinateness and Positive Indeterminateness (Ontic Potentiality)

The sixth condition is the condition of *partial determinateness*: the rational agent-in-act must have something determinate about it and something indeterminate as well, so that the development of an act can begin in partial determinateness, gradually resolve what is indeterminate, and end in full determinateness. The agent poised before a rational act is already determinate in important respects; indeed, some degree of determinateness would appear to be essential to our willingness to consider it ontically responsible. At least from the time of Aristotle it has been taken for granted that it is appropriate to consider an agent ontically responsible only if its acts spring from something determinate and settled in its nature. Aristotle's term for it was "*ēthos*," which we translate as "character"; we might well have gone on to translate his expression "*ēthikē aretē*" as "virtue of character," although in fact we usually translate it as "moral virtue." A moral virtue he thinks of as a settled disposition (*hexis*) to a certain kind of act. Since both character and settled dispositions are determinate features, his moral ideal might be said to be to *determine* oneself to have a certain kind of *determinate* nature.[10] The context is of course that of moral responsibility, but the point about the need for determination is readily generalizable to ontic responsibility: capacity as a scientist, scholar, artist, or practical man of action is no less tied to determinateness of character and disposition than capacity for moral choice is.

The other side of our insistence upon some determinateness is our unwillingness to regard any act that appears to be done by an agent, yet seems to have no precedent whatever in past acts and therefore no apparent connection with something determinate in its nature, as one for which the agent is truly responsible. We immediately suppose some unusual circumstance—drugs, compulsion, madness—that takes

the act out of the realm of ontic responsibility. The act is so uncharac-
teristic—the word itself makes our point for us—that we feel that it
can not really be attributed to the person whom we know to have a
different sort of character. Whatever its origin, it does not flow from
the power of that agent, who is therefore not responsible for it. There
are, of course, circumstances that could make us change our minds,
but they are circumstances having to do with some defect in our
knowledge of our agent's nature—we might for instance be ignorant
of similar things the person had done in the past—and they would
only restore the point about the need for some determinateness.

It is also important that, whatever "freedom" may characterize the
act of a rational agent as it develops, a completed act is nonetheless a
fully determinate thing. It is finished and settled: whatever it could
have been, now that it is ended it is forever determinately what it in
fact was. Any careful analysis of what this means will lead us to the
conclusion that the act has left behind determinate traces in the world.
We may interpret these traces in various ways and may disagree about
them in accordance with our metaphysics—for instance about whether
a psychological trace is identical with a physiological trace—but we
shall probably agree that there are traces of some sort both in the environment and in the agent; and that they are now determinate features of whatever they are traces in. We may sum up the point about
determinateness in this way: whatever pattern of determinateness and
indeterminateness may be found in a developing act, it would appear
that the agent so acts that the act has at the end this rather than that
determinate structure; and that this goes back in some measure to
what was already determinate in the agent. We might even say that
the agent determines its act to have this rather than that structure, so
long as we do not mean by this that it performed some other act to determine what the new act should be. Thus it was Planck, a man with
a determinate history that included the writing of a doctoral dissertation on the second law of thermodynamics, who performed in the
nineties of the last century those acts of reasoning about the distribu-
tion of energy within an ideal black body that led to the final act in
which he expressed the quantum principle. The earlier determinate
features of the late seventies—among them the determinate feature of
having written *Über den zweiten Hauptsatz der mechanischen Wärmetheorie* by 1879—contributed to the power he then exercised in the
crucial cognitive acts of the nineties. We admire Planck for these determinate things, early and late; and we even have a word, "determina-

tion," that draws attention to the importance of a goal-directed and
settled character. And in the moral sphere one of the most important
ideals is to so determine our characters that they shall have that determinate feature called goodness.

But the condition is one of partial determinateness, and it requires
that the determinateness be no more than that. If the agent were
wholly determinate in the sense a determinist would demand, it would
be impossible for us to think of it as a *source* of acts, for our *prima
facie* rational awareness of action forbids the emergence of an act de-
terministically from a wholly determinate structure. In a well-known
article by Dickenson Miller—one of the two he wrote under the
pseudonym R. E. Hobart—the need for partial determinateness in an
act-source is distorted into the claim that there is no free will without
determinism.[11] But our own condition of partial determinateness forbids a complete determinateness in the agent; we are very far from
compatibilism of any kind. Determinateness of character—the determinateness of an act-source—is only whatever determinateness is appropriate to an authentic act-source. It implies no deterministic emergence
from a wholly determinate "agent" of what would in effect be a
non-act.

No ontically responsible act emerges from a wholly determinate
source as a consequence of its determinateness only. If an act or acts
flowed from that determinate system either with logical necessity or
with some other kind of necessity that would make the act or acts
wholly explainable or predictable to someone who had some appropriate knowledge of the determinate features of that system, there would
be entirely too much determinateness to sustain authentic ontic responsibility. The appropriate knowledge of the determinate system
would vary with the metaphysical structure of the universe within
which we are visualizing our rational "agent," but otherwise it does
not matter what kind of universe we are proposing: there would always be an excess of determinateness in it. A thoroughly determinate
"agent" predestined in some theological perspective to salvation or
damnation would "act" only as a function of its given nature and the
law that established its fate. A Leibnizian monad, or substance, thought
of as a subject created with a determinate set of predicates specifying
its history in the finest detail will "act" in accordance with those predicates; and all Leibniz's ingenuity will not persuade us that it acts out
of an authentic ontic responsibility. An "agent" having a determinate
psychological structure subject to determinate psychological laws (if

there are such structures not reducible to physiological structures) will "act" only in the sense that apparent acts will follow from its determinate structure with the necessity appropriate to the status psychological laws might have. An "agent" identical in an unqualified sense with a determinate physiological system governed by covering physiological laws will be explicable-predictable by those laws, and its "acts" will be merely *prima facie* acts that in fact display a development that is necessary with whatever kind of necessity the laws express. If physiological laws are in fact reducible to physical ones, then we can rewrite the previous sentence so as to make no difference for the status of the "acts" so envisioned.

Because a nonreductionist view of science is sometimes thought to yield a world view more hospitable to such notions as responsibility, it should perhaps be said that this point holds not just for the variety of determinism that maintains that the laws of nature are reducible to those that govern microstructures. It holds also for any hierarchic view of the laws of nature that envisions deterministic "higher level" transformation laws that come into play only at a certain level of complexity. As long as the laws predicted the flow of one wholly determinate mass-energy system into another, something perfectly determinate would have been succeeded by something equally determinate, and so succeeded that a statement of the parameters of the first appropriately conjoined with a statement of these laws of nature would have entailed the parameters of the second. Whether philosophers of science called this a matter of logical necessity, physical necessity, or natural necessity, or preferred to avoid the notion of necessity entirely, there would be no room for an agent conceived of as an entity that determines anything, either itself at some later time or something in the world about it.

The seventh condition may be called either the condition of *positive indeterminateness* or the condition of *ontic potentiality*. Together with the previous condition it provides a sense in which the ontically responsible agent should at least partially determine itself. And that is to say that it provides a radical, or categorical, sense in which the agent could have done otherwise, for to have been able to do otherwise not only if circumstances had permitted, or if one had wanted to do otherwise, or if one had chosen to do otherwise is tantamount to having been able to *be* otherwise.[12] That it is a paradox to determine oneself, to make oneself *be* other than what one *is* goes without saying, and we can say in advance that these two conditions can be fulfilled only if

the self has a status somewhat different from what it is commonly supposed to have.

The condition assumes that the agent is an act-source in some ways
determinate and in some ways indeterminate, and it requires that in
acting it should determine itself in respects in which it was indeterminate. What is wanted is that in the development of an act that is authentic something should be at issue in any phase of its temporal span:
it is a movement towards full determination in which indeterminations
are successively resolved—as when, for instance, in the speaking of a
sentence, the beginning lays down a certain syntactic direction that excludes certain terminal words as ungrammatical but leaves open precisely what word may end it. But it will not do that in this movement
the *determining* feature of the agent should be what was *wholly* determinate in it, and that the *determined* feature should be that which
was *merely* indeterminate, for the indetermination in that case would
only be apparent. It is difficult to say what this necessary lack of determinateness would be, either in the agent poised before the act or in
the agent-in-act. The difficulty is an ancient one: the notion that what
has being is something that *determinately is* defines the tradition that
begins in Parmenides, is refined by Plato, and then persists as the
strongest stream in Western philosophy. One sees it not just in obvious
Platonic places but also in all those analytic and phenomenological enterprises in which philosophic discussion revolves around the status of
such "things" as properties, predicates, classes, propositions, natural
kinds, nomic universals, essences and other items of which it can be
more easily said that they are determinate than that they have this or
that ontological status.

As to the agent, we can say such noncommittal things as that if it
does act authentically it will become determinate in respects in which
it was not determinate before the act; that its acting will have brought
this about—that is, will have determined it; and that something indeterminate in it will have played a role no less positive than its determinate features. This means we must reject the view that insofar as the
agent is determinate before the act it is a rigid structure set in the
equally rigid structure of its universe; and that insofar as the agent is
indeterminate there is a blank and featureless aspect to it and its universe that is the matrix of what is commonly called chance.

It is an old enough difficulty to find ourselves caught between these
two extremes as we try to express the nature of an act-source that must

be truly altered by its acts. Insist that the agent in its determinate particularity is truly the source of some act—is truly the being that accounts wholly for just that act, and it seems that the act can not produce any genuine alteration in the source. The act now seems wholly the creature of the source: the finitude and particularity of the latter then represent themselves as features of a wholly determinate thing that is productive of wholly determinate acts. As a source of that kind did not in the first instance make itself by its acts and does not now remake itself by them, praise and blame are diverted to the real source—the one that made what from this perspective we now see to be a merely apparent act-source. Far from being *causa sui*, the agent does not now seem to deserve to be considered even the authentic cause of its own acts. Indeed, from this perspective we might well conclude that talk of *acts* is no longer appropriate. Emphasize, on the other hand, the originative nature of an act, make it into a creative thing that fundamentally alters its own source, and we seem to be saying that the source was not really the source after all, and that we should therefore not give it the praise or blame hitherto thought appropriate. Press on with this thought, and we find ourselves saying that insofar as the act is something radically new that springs up, there is nothing whatever to praise or blame: though we might celebrate or deplore the coming of the new thing, the reason for its coming seems to be indistinguishable from chance. It seems that every time we try to characterize some finite particular as *causa sui* we run the risk of merely giving an honorific title to chance.

Both of these extremes forbid the authenticity of ontic responsibility. The present condition requires instead (a) that the agent-in-act should have so presided over any completed act as to have determined what was at the outset indeterminate; (b) that what was indeterminate in the agent should have played some positive role in the completion of the act along with what was determinate; (c) that in the course of acting the agent should have further determined something that was indeterminate in itself qua agent. This mingling of determinateness with a positive indeterminateness in the power of the rational agent should be part of what we mean when we say that it could have done otherwise, if we intend that claim in the categorical sense that ontic responsibility requires, and not in one of the trivial hypothetical senses that compatibilists put forward. This leaves open many things about the nature of that power: we have so far only the negative requirement that the indeterminate positive power working within the determinate-ness of the agent must be bound and limited by that determinateness but not wholly determined by it.

Evidently if the rational agent really could have done otherwise than it did do, it must have had associated with it a power superabundant in respect of what it actually did. Something *wholly* determinate in the agent, operating determinately, will not do, for there will be no authentic *determining* brought about by the agent; nor will something *merely* indeterminate in the agent do, for in that case there will be no authentic *self*-determination. There must be courses of action open to the agent other than the one taken, and they must be real possibilities, not merely logical ones; there must be ways in which the agent becomes further determinate, and there must be some sense in which this is the result of *self*-determination. Some other self that did not come to pass must have been a real possibility before the course of action that excluded it.

The condition of ontic potentiality, then, is a momentous one: there must be a feature of the agent that in terms of power and not mere logical possibility exceeds any actual exercise of power that brings about one possibility and excludes another. It is also paradoxical, because in one sense it must belong to the agent—the agent's ontic status must somehow include it; and in another sense not belong to it—an account of what the agent determinately is, as this rather than that individual, must not include it. The self-identity of an agent that really could have done otherwise than it did do must include more than the determinate features of the identity of some particular self. Our self must *be* its determinate self and it must *not be* it, and its not-being must not merely be the "hole in þeing" Sartre had in mind, but a merely relative not-being. Our self *is not* its determinate self in the sense that *what it is* is not wholly captured in an account of that determinateness. We are of course talking about self-transcendence, and a self that transcends itself in that sense exercises a power that is not radically isolated from what its existence is dependent upon.

We can not therefore do full justice to the particular individual who really did have a certain potentiality that was not actualized, if we try to capture it entirely in terms of the category of particularity or individuality, as a truly radical pluralism might understand it. Characterize our agent-in-act at the beginning of the act as exhaustively as the nature of it allows, and we produce only an abstraction of a truly authentic self that is capable of going on to act and determine itself further.

The "it" we speak of has indeterminations left present in its nature by
the determination already present there, but if it is free to determine itself further, then whatever makes it possible for it to do so can not be
unambiguously its own private possession. If it were its own, and only
its own; if it could be characterized, described, or identified as such,
it would in fact be a determinate particular power—as indeed a Leib-
nizean *haecceitas* is determinate and particular. The alternative is to
think of it as a nonparticular power that the individual agent participates in, depends on, or instantiates as it moves in a series of determining acts towards its own complete particularity.

By identifying some particular agent-in-act, then, we do not also
identify a radically particular power that makes it ontically responsible.
If it is in some respects free—if it could categorically have done otherwise—we do not account for that freedom by citing a determinate and
particular power as the reason for it. It is, to be sure, just this being
that did this or that, that became this or that; it is indeed just this being that could have done something, could have become something, a
little different; but it is also Being, instantiated in that particular, that is
to blame or to praise. That is not to say that there is some other particular there, distinct from the individual, that could serve as an "it";
the point is rather that the individual that is ontically responsible participates in something that is not an "it" to be so. The category of
mere particularity, of mere individuality, is inadequate to express the
nature of ontic responsibility if there are indeed ontically responsible
rational agents.

The condition of ontic potentiality is a pluralistic one in that the
entity in question must have the power to come-into-being in alternative ways, and the power must be in some sense its power. But the
condition does not require a radically pluralistic universe, and indeed
it is not entirely clear that a pluralism of radically self-determining particular powers—each power self-contained, each entirely self-sufficient,
each wholly particular, each nonetheless determining itself to be this
rather than that—is an intelligible notion. A self-determination of particulars that falls short of that radical autonomy because of a dependence upon what all particulars participate in to be particulars is of
course as inscrutable as the notion of coming-into-being has always
been. We shall accept this inscrutability and say that the condition of
ontic potentiality would be satisfied by a self-determination that rested
upon a tie between the individual and "the nature of things" that
qualified the wholly particular, the wholly individual status of the self

that is said to determine itself. Our condition need not require that
the feat of coming-into-being—alternatively, both possessing and ac-
tualizing a potential order—should be accomplished by a multiplicity
of particular beings each utterly on its own. Few pluralisms are so radically pluralistic as to neglect the sense in which such a particular accomplishment is also an instantiation of the unity of things, of "the
nature of things." The condition that follows should make it clear, in
any case, that such a modification of an utterly radical pluralism is
necessary if our authentic agent is to be in any sense a rational one.

                                     6

The Condition of Rational Obligation

The eighth condition is the condition of rational obligation. Together
with the preceding two, it carries the principal import of our account
of "being able to do otherwise than one in fact does," and with them
it makes it clear how inappropriate it is to call this capacity "freedom
of indifference." It is all too easy to oversimplify this condition by supposing it concerns only the traditional opposition usually expressed in
terms of wants, needs, passions, or inclinations on the one hand and
conscience, obligation, or duty on the other. It is true enough that,
from the perspective of the rational agent who is ontically responsible,
certain actions ought to be performed and certain others ought not to
be performed. But rational obligation does not come into play only
after the course of duty has been ascertained and the agent stands bal-
anced between its call and that of inclination. We are talking about
ontic responsibility and not just about its instantiation in moral responsibility, and so the "ought" that goes with it is not something appropriate just to moral crises. To put the matter more precisely, rational obligation is not merely something that is felt *before* an action
as one of the factors that lead us to act in this or that way: it must
qualify the entire development of rational acts that are ontically responsible.

   This consideration will, I think, lead us eventually to a subtle ad-
justment in our views about the role of obligation in the sphere of
morals, but before we turn to that there are some more obvious things
that can be said about rational obligation. It is something that must
qualify any goal-directed enterprise in which truth or at least excel-

lence is part of the goal that is sought. Returning to our earlier example, we notice that if the acts Planck performed in the realm of mathematical physics before 1900 were qualified by ontic responsibility, then he was indeed obligated not to rest until he had sorted out all that tangle of data, known laws, and conflicting theories about radiant energy and could express, as he did at last, a view of it that henceforward must always be taken into account. There are parallel obligations in other fields if ontic responsibility is authentic. An artist ought not merely reiterate conventions received from the past. Art, though rooted in one's life, ought not be self-indulgent. One ought to write sentences that get to the root of the matter and are easy to understand. One ought to prune one's fruit trees before the sap rises.

We need not, I think, concern ourselves just here with the Kantian distinction between hypothetical and categorical imperatives, for it is not necessary that our views on obligation should conform with those laid down by a theory of knowledge that loses much of its force if we do not regard the premises that dominated theory of knowledge from Descartes through Hume as the only truly rational ones. An obligation need not be in flat opposition to inclination to be taken seriously; and it need not be formulable in the lawlike form of a maxim or an imperative to be rationally effective. A particular obligation that is felt by Max Planck and has an independent and nonparticular correlative that justifies it may be said to be rational (and thus directed towards the universal and necessary) even though it is not felt by, say, Virginia Woolf, and even though that correlative may not demand that she should feel that same particular obligation. A correlative that remains the same for her but exacts something different from her will be no less "universal" for that. What the condition of rational obligation requires is, first, that something in "the nature of things" that is independent of a person's wishes and inclinations, and, more generally, independent of everything in the person that is particular and determinate in the sense discussed under the rubric of the sixth condition, should make rational demands appropriate to the particularity of the person in the particularity of its situation; and, second, that what makes the demands should be the same for all persons despite all the variation in the particular exactions it makes and the particular situations in which they are made.

Moral responsibility, being an instance of ontic responsibility, will exemplify this tension between universality and particularity in its own way, though its exactions are familiar to all of us in a way in which the exactions felt by the scientist or the artist are not. Whatever the particularity of Planck or of Woolf, there were situations for each of them in which the obligation to respect their fellow human beings and to act with justice towards them would have been felt. Once again we need not suppose either that it need be formulable in a categorical imperative or that it must inevitably be in conflict with inclinations.

Ontic responsibility, in any event, is not a matter of merely feeling obligated. If Planck was indeed ontically responsible, it was not just a feeling on his part that he was rationally obliged to understand the way radiant energy is lost or gained, although we may probably assume that the feeling was there. And if Virginia Woolf was indeed ontically responsible, then her felt obligation to turn her memories of her parents and of her childhood summers in St. Ives—memories that were deeply felt and deeply personal—into the impersonality of *To the Lighthouse*, was an obligation to the nature of things. As it happens, she seems not only to have felt that obligation but even to have interpreted it in some such way.[13] If ontic obligation is authentic, then it is sometimes good, in a sense not reducible to the necessitations of some undiscovered but determinate and determining power or powers, that this rather than that should happen. And the correlative of that in the agent may be a felt obligation that is a genuine one. The feeling in that case would be the subjective correlative of a self-determining power that might act on the obligation but could in fact do otherwise. The source of the obligation, understood to qualify the power the agent participates in as it exercises ontic potentiality, would be one, but I suspect not the only, positive feature of the indeterminateness discussed under the seventh condition. It would be, to be sure, something that obliged but did not compel. One supposes that, to an agent participating in it, the positive but indeterminate power would be fully available only when recognized as not compulsive in the self-determination of the individual but rather as merely offering to it the power to take the form it ought to take. The Platonic tradition deals with all this in terms of the power of the Form of the Good.

The awareness of ontic responsibility in the form of a felt obligation brings us to a most important feature of the rational agent—the involvement of mind in its actions. I use that vague word "involvement" deliberately, for the term "rational act" covers a spectrum of acts from

those—like pruning a fruit-tree properly—that are intelligent and pur-
poseful without being highly articulate to those—like Planck's acts
mentioned earlier—in which every expressive faculty is at the stretch.
For involvement in this very broad sense we may perhaps recapture
the root sense of *mens rea*. The expression has been used so long in the
law to deal with the alleged responsibility of a defendant for an illegal
act that it is usually translated as "guilty mind," and there is ample
precedent in classical Latin for at least the association of the notion of
mens rea with that of a defendant or accused. But the root sense of the
adjective *reus* is "concerned in a thing, party to an action," and it
should serve to remind us that ontic responsibility, which applies to
so many kinds of acts not directly concerned with moral issues let
alone legal ones, is a thing in which the mind of the rational agent is
vitally concerned. Some element of *mens rea*—thus broadly interpreted—enters into every ontically responsible rational act.

But just as there is a range of rational acts running through theoretical, artistic, practical (in the nonmoral sense), and practical (in the
moral sense), so there is a range of intensity with respect to *mens rea*.
Sometimes it coincides with the distinction between practical and
theoretic, as in the contrast in mental intensity between the work of
tree pruning and the work of Planck; sometimes it does not. The case
of intensely theoretical acts is somewhat overlooked in contemporary
discussion of reasons and causes, which tends to revolve around the
question of the reasons *for* acts. Reasons no doubt qualify the power
exercised in acts in that way, but it is just as important to notice that
there are reasons *in* acts; that acts themselves can *consist* in reasoning,
or at least partly so—as the writing of a good sentence or paragraph or
the propounding of a theory like Planck's are both ways of reasoning.
That is tantamount to saying that rational obligation characterizes the
very development of acts of that kind. This brings us back to an
earlier point: rational obligation does not come into play only before
an action, making this act one we ought to avoid and that act one we
ought to perform. It is part of the very texture of a rational act.

In the moral sphere, then, the burden of rational obligation is upon
us not just after we have determined what our duty is and are trying to
do it. If ontic responsibility is authentic, then the burden is upon us
throughout every act of articulate reasoning we engage in to reach that
point, and the burden is there whether or not our reasoning successfully
carries out what is enjoined. The call of this "duty" of reason dominates

all reasoning about particular duties, all reasoning about duty in general, and indeed even all metaethical reasoning, in which, sometimes, the very meaning and usefulness of the notion of duty might be at issue. Ontic responsibility, if authentic, is exercised in all acts of thought, whether silent or overt.

In the range of rational acts mentioned a moment ago the power of reasons *in* the acts—hence of rational obligation interior to the acts— is so salient that it suggests another way of conceiving of the positive indetermination that forms the seventh condition. The rational agent-in-act holds itself indeterminate in the sense that it holds itself open to the power of reasons so that it may be determined by them; and although these do not inevitably determine it, they ought to. From this perspective the agent's indeterminateness is no *mere* indeterminateness, for its potentiality to act includes at least one instance of a non-determining but by no means random power—that of truth. Nowhere is this more obvious and important than in those acts of rational attentiveness in which the status of ontic responsibility itself is what the agent is concerned with. We are then not only under the general rational obligation that characterizes all rational acts but besides under the particular obligation to understand and account for obligation itself. If we are indeed ontically responsible, our responsibility does not appear in its most developed form until this reflexive problem of the nature and status of ontic responsibility arises for us.

It is not immediately clear to *what* we have the varied rational obligation envisioned under the rubric of the eighth condition, nor is it clear what sanctions it lays down. Felt obligations that are only that are perhaps not too difficult to account for. Even if legal responsibility and the wider social responsibility that enframes it were as arbitrarily grounded as we have assumed they would be if ontic responsibility were unreal, the business of having to give an account of one's actions to some group of people making up the family, church, company, college, profession, or political community generates in itself a *feeling* of obligation. No doubt the sanctions that may follow play some role in generating that feeling. At the least, the counterpart obligation in the case of an ontic responsibility understood to be authentic is to an independent "universal" correlative that justifies the feeling of obligation. The feeling manifests itself in the need of one aspect of oneself to come to terms with another aspect of oneself; but the latter purports to be more than that and more than the disguised voice of society. And so we call it conscience, or duty, or self-control, or the voice of God. No doubt we are not so clear about it as we should like to be. But even if we can not be any clearer just now, it is still intelligible to say that sometimes one was able to and ought to have become something other than what one has become. This saying, though dark enough, may still express an objective feature of things. Indeed, the obligation to become clearer about *what* we are obliged to is perfectly consistent with our still being very unclear about it.

As to sanctions, there is the pragmatic one of what one becomes in part because of one's practical actions and in part because of the degree of intensity and honesty of one's thought; and what one becomes is always qualified, if ontic responsibility is real, by the consideration just mentioned, that one could have become someone somewhat different. That consideration alone is often sanction enough. Whatever other sanctions might conceivably lie at the meeting point of the person and "the nature of things" certainly lie beyond the scope of this essay. Religion and some kinds of art deal with them, and for some readers this may well mean that they are mere mythical echoes of more down-to-earth sanctions we know well enough from various forms of social responsibility. But it would be premature to call the power of religion and art a mere archaic survival. The mention of intensity of thought, however, reminds us that not all of our ontic responsibility can be exhausted in terms of practical action. One profound feeling of rational obligation is the one that moves us to replace one version of the truth with a more adequate one, and to do so for no other reason than that it seems we ought to. It presents itself as a duty not to be (causally) determined to think in a certain way about the way things are but rather to so move within determinations that really do determine (e.g., physiological facts of the central nervous system) as to make use of them to submit, as we ought to, to the order of the way things are.

7

The Condition of Ontically Significant Appearance

The ninth condition is the condition of *ontically significant appearance*. Before philosophic criticism coming either from reflection upon science or from some other quarter, we assume that our cognitive response to a rational agent-in-act (which may of course be oneself) places us in the presence of something that is what it purports to be. Though it may be significant of something else as well, it is, we think, a positive appearance—not just an appearance of something else but an appearance of what is in fact the case. We assume the presence of an infrastructure that could itself be made to appear, or at least could be made to appear within the limits laid down by our sensory modalities, but we do not assume that the appearance of the full concreteness of the agent-in-act is only an appearance of the operative powers within the infrastructure—that if we were in principle able to inspect the infrastructure in detail we should then be in the presence of everything that is of any ontic significance. If the condition of ontically significant appearance holds, then the agent-in-act, appearing to us in all its concreteness, and so appearing that it masks the appearance of infrastructure elements, is not deceiving us. It does not *merely* appear, and its appearance is not *merely the way in which the true infrastructure powers appear in the distorting medium of subjectivity*. The rational agent-in-act is authentically what (from another perspective) it "appears-in-the-guise-of"; its appearing is its being present to a subjectivity authentically capable of the correlative epistemic achievement of attaining the presence of what is ontically the case.

If the present condition is fulfilled, the appearance to itself of the rational agent in its full concreteness is the reflexive achievement of an epistemic capacity it exercises in many ways. From this angle we come around again to the conditions of explanatory ultimacy and explanatory opacity, for in making itself appear authentically to itself rational agency would have affirmed its own self-explanatory character and thus its status as the ontic ground of all explanation. After all relevant scientific explanations directed to the infrastructure had been propounded and had explained what they could explain, there would have remained something about the agent-in-act, precisely as it appeared to itself, that was effective, operative, powerful, yet nonetheless opaque to scientific explanation. In attending to our own rational agency in its full concreteness our proper contrast would in that case not be appearance-reality but rather concrete-abstract. The agent-in-act, if authentic, is not merely the appearance of a hidden reality: it is the fully concrete reality of which the detailed analysis of the infrastructure yields an abstract model; the appearance to itself as that reality is an ontically significant appearance.

8

Degree of Ontic Responsibility

If all these conditions must hold for the rational agent to be ontically responsible it is no wonder that responsibility of that kind is now widely regarded as an illusion. But it is well to be clear about what a momentous thing it is, if it should indeed be real, and how paradoxical and disquieting a thing. A mode of action in which some self determines itself *to be* something other than what it now *is* does not comfort us about the status of our selves considered as particulars. The more individual, the more a particular, the more a *this* one takes one's self to be, the less suited it seems to determine itself to be something other than that. The more we conceive of the self as suited to such a task, the more its powerful and operative side takes on a general, or universal, aspect in which one finds it harder and harder to recognize one's particular self. Nor in that guise of self-shaper can it be a mere transcendental ego regarded as either a neutral spectator or as a logically necessary "I" that appears in linguistically articulated knowledge but has no further status. If authentic, it must rather be a self that, not being exhausted by what is particular and determinate in it, can powerfully reshape itself.

Momentous as ontic responsibility may be, we must be wary of making it too momentous. Our nine conditions may well hold, but hold in so minimal a way that the responsibility whose shape they prescribe may also be minimal. It would appear that all of the conditions may admit of degree. Some of us—perhaps most of us—may display in most of our occasions an explanatory adequacy of minimal import: though it may be a necessary and irreducible explanatory factor in an ideal and complete explanation that an action is yours or mine—that you or I *did* it—that factor may nonetheless be negligible in weight over against all of the conditions of heredity and environment. Those conditions, expressed either in a pure infrastructure analysis carried out by some perfected physics of the future, or in that more complex and less tidy way, involving the cooperation of many sciences, that prevails today, may include what we now think of as the whole weight of physical, psychological, and cultural conditioning. They may accordingly explain so much in the case of certain persons that it may seem to add very little to say, yes, whatever else that event was, it was also a rational act. Though each of the conditions may be fulfilled in varying degrees, the matter of degree is especially obvious in the conditions of partial determinateness, positive indeterminateness (ontic potentiality), and rational obligation, which, taken together, are more obviously related to the notion of freedom—so often supposed to be a matter of degree—than the others are. Caught in the massive determinateness of a self shaped by physical inheritance, by physical and social circumstances, we may be scarcely open to that paradoxical feature of the same self—its positive indeterminateness that can determine; straitened in a narrow actuality, we may scarcely leave room for a power that is ours, without yet being actual in us, to prise us open; moving to the compelling power of received doctrine and opinion, we may perceive in only the dimmest way our obligation to a truth not yet successfully expressed, to an ideal for action manifestly at odds with the way we act.

That ontic responsibility should admit of degree is, however, just what we should expect if human beings do indeed have, what the law, at least, still insists they have, an intrinsic responsibility that can in some cases be diminished. For it is not the diminishment of responsibility in the extrinsic case of physical duress that gives us the most conceptual trouble in the sphere of legal thought, but rather those cases in which our perception of the very make-up—the very character—of the defendant tells us that it is unjust to hold that person as fully responsible as we might have held some other.

9

*Social Consequences of the Rejection
of Ontic Responsibility*

The conditions for the authenticity of ontic responsibility sketch out a universe so much at odds with the common perception of what science requires the universe to be that it is not at all surprising that it is widely believed to be unreal. The feeling that one is ontically responsible persists nevertheless, and persists, commonly enough, even among those who hold that belief. In such circles the feeling is sometimes explained as a subjective phenomenon having the same inauthentic status as the *prima facie* knowledge of ourselves and our world of which it is an aspect. In this section I do not mean to argue that matter directly but to look instead at an assumption that sometimes goes with it—that the question whether or not ontic responsibility is authentic is irrelevant to the status of legal responsibility and the wider social responsibility of which it is the most important instance. The assumption might be expressed in this way: the question of the authenticity of ontic responsibility, and consequently of moral responsibility, is a metaphysical one, and metaphysical questions are notoriously difficult to settle, if indeed they can be settled at all. Whether or not they are authentic, legal responsibility is as real as the sanctions that go with it; and this is true of social responsibility in general, for the reprobation of any social unit—family, church, company, college, or profession—carries sanctions quite as effective, if not so dire, as those of the law. Even if there is no ontic responsibility and therefore no moral responsibility grounded upon it, general social responsibility (de facto accountability) and its instantiation in legal responsibility belong to the texture of appearance that provides the ineluctable arena within which we behave towards one another.

I am sure that arena is ineluctable in the sense that we shall continue to apprehend it through the same sensory modalities and respond to it with the same affective capacities—both things that are deeply woven into our bodies. But the way we conceive of and value an affective complex like feeling oneself responsible to some social unit is, I suspect, not nearly so ineluctable as the general cognitive framework within which we now experience it. The replacement of a legal system based upon the notion of responsibility by some form of social engineering has been advocated in social-science circles for some years. It has long since found its way into the wider intellectual community to which propaganda like Skinner's *Walden Two* and *Beyond Freedom and Dignity* is directed: *Walden Two* is now as common in the high-school reading of Americans as its apotropaic counterpart, *Brave New World*. But conceptual attacks directed against ontic responsibility can be much more sweeping than that of behaviorism, which after all never had an explicit metaphysics, for all that it had an implicit one. Truly metaphysical attacks, like that of physicalism, are no respecters of a behaviorist scientific preserve within the area of studies devoted to human nature. Although some physicalists who hold the identity theory of mind and body make common cause with behaviorism, and although Skinner himself appears to have been moving towards identity theory in recent years,[14] any determined and well-thought-out physicalism will include a reductive program sweeping enough to demand the reduction of even such categories as "behavior," "stimulus," and "response" to a physicalist language. Edgar Wilson's *The Mental as Physical* is a recent case in point. It advocates, though not always with complete consistency, the identity of mind and body, but the argument is sufficiently general to be considered also an argument for the identity of a rational action with its physiological basis—a kind of identity against which chapter 6 of this book is directed. It is thoroughgoing, openly metaphysical in its physicalist principles, and, consistently enough, it is critical of behaviorism.[15] It is clear that although Wilson does not use the labels I am using here, he thinks we hold people legally responsible only because of our ancient and mistaken conviction that they are ontically responsible. He argues, it seems to me consistently with his physicalist principles, that legal responsibility, and with it the authority of the courts to punish, should be abolished. Something like the present legal system would persist, but the sole function of the courts would be to decide such questions of fact as whether a person had done something (in the normal *prima facie* sense) that was in conflict with the law's expression of the norms for behavior within the society in question. The law, whether so called or given a different name, would by intent embody those norms and only those norms: that is to say, the *de facto* existence of those norms within the society would be the only reason for the existence of the law.

Presumably, as now, one could quarrel with some existing law because it failed to conform with morality—where "morality" meant the most important and general norms pervasive of society, and thus the norms definitive of social responsibility. (The argument of course requires the elimination of social responsibility along with its instance in legal responsibility.) But failure of a given law or code of law to conform with "morality" could only mean either failure to express some norm that the society in question in fact accepted, or else failure to express precisely what kind of behavior did not in fact conform with the law. As "morality" could only mean the *de facto* structure of the norms, there would be no ground whatever for claiming that the norms themselves were somehow in conflict with some "higher" set of norms, accessible perhaps to one's moral sense, one's practical reason, one's conscience, or whatever faculty one might take to be capable of pronouncing upon moral responsibility understood as an instance of ontic responsibility.

Once *de facto* conflict with the law's formulation of the norms had been established, the role of the courts would end. No punishment would ensue, as none would be appropriate: the person's actions were predictable-explicable and in that sense were necessitated, or caused. The person could not have done otherwise. Nor could the norms within society—whatever they may be—have been otherwise, for they too are caused and caused in the same sense. There would, however, be a new species of tribunal, whose job would begin when that of the courts ended. It would be made up of scientific, not legal, experts, and would prescribe some course of training, conditioning, or other procedure designed to bring about conformity with the norms.[16] The program is an extreme one, but it is not without precedent in the annals of contemporary jurisprudence, for instance in the suggestion of the (British) National Association for Mental Health, made to the Butler Committee in the course of the latter's inquiry into the treatment of mentally retarded offenders, that the concept of *mens rea* and criminal responsibility should be dispensed with in favor of the concept of strict accountability coupled with a sentencing procedure conducted under professional-scientific guidance; it is quoted and discussed by Anthony Kenny in a defense of the notion of *mens rea*.[17]

It is easy to find persuasive arguments against such a program, provided one takes for granted a moral responsibility, grounded upon ontic responsibility, in terms of which any *de facto* set of norms can be criticized. But once we dismiss that, programs like Wilson's seem almost impregnable. If, for instance, someone who has dismissed ontic responsibility should still insist that *mens rea* is important, if only to determine whether a defendant has in fact done (in the normal *prima facie* sense) what the law forbids, physicalism has a ready response: it can incorporate *mens rea* provisions (again in the normal *prima facie* sense) by simply reinterpreting any "mental" state in terms of some physiological state it takes it to be identical with. To protest that social engineering that proceeds in the way Wilson recommends may sometimes produce unjust treatment of a defendant is unreasonable unless one is willing to make a case for ontic responsibility. Many of us are still willing to do so. But those who are not—and their number is growing—can indulge their "higher moral sense" only at the expense of knowing themselves to be exhibiting an archaic feature of human nature that their own principles are designed to eliminate. Certainly our present system, in which the utter relativity of moral standards to a given society is maintained by so many who bring an evangelical fervor to pointing out the moral shortcomings of any given society, works only in the sense that people refuse to think the matter through. It is common to find intelligent people adopting at one time a position that is tantamount to saying that we are morally responsible (in the sense grounded on ontic responsibility) and at another a position whose central doctrine is that whatever one does one could not have done otherwise. Circumstances bring out one or the other ephemeral and blurred conviction.

Still, the viewpoint that rejects ontic responsibility and then goes on with clear-sighted consistency to something like the two-tribunal system has its own pragmatic inconsistency built into it, since it is unlikely that any society that held this view of the matter could maintain for long the norms towards which this social engineering was directed; for the feeling that they are norms and that one ought to live in accord with them seems tied to the conviction that it is in our power to do so. One suggestion for preserving the power of these norms occurs to me, one that is not without precedent: in addition to the two-tribunal system, let us have two levels of education for two kinds of citizens—one for those who are to accept the norms without question as definitive of "good citizen," "good person," and ideals of that kind; one for those guardians who are to settle upon the norms and oversee the social engineering that inculcates them and then insures their continued sway.

III

The Foundation Question Reopened:
The Circle of Action and Knowledge

1

*The Ineluctable Circle: Prima Facie Rational Action
and Our Prima Facie Knowledge of It*

From the perspective of a philosophy that takes science as its cognitive
ideal, the nine conditions for ontic responsibility define a strange
enough world. It is no wonder that responsibility should seem an illusion from that perspective. Still, if it is an illusion, it is one that is extraordinarily hard to get rid of; for if we are to understand human nature more adequately, we must act to do so, deploying, as I now do,
the words of our natural language; perhaps deploying as well one of
the many other symbol systems we have created and embedded in our
natural language. It does not matter what direction our efforts take:
the situation will be precisely the same whether we set out to show
that human nature is perfectly intelligible in terms of physicalism or to
show that it is not. We have only to attend to what we are up to, and
it will still seem, in the face of all the doubts we have looked at, that
something comes into being: in the first place, our act itself, in the
second place, whatever body of theory or doctrine we put forward;
and, in the third place now, but no less important for that, ourselves,
for in some measure we seem to come into being—become what we
can be—in virtue of the way we understand things or think we understand things.

So, in any case, it seems; and this is to say that as we act in a *prima
facie* sense, our acts are qualified by an awareness, or experience, of
acting. There are good grounds for not calling that experience, in its
usual form, a *prima facie* knowledge. When we act we usually attend

to the task itself, whether it is a practical rational one like pruning a fruit tree, or a theoretical one like expressing ourselves in language about some difficult scientific or philosophic issue. Our attention to the act itself is accordingly peripheral, and so is our awareness, or experience, of acting: the concrete texture of the act merely enframes our practical or theoretical doing, making, or knowing; we submit to the texture of the act to accomplish our task and so do not focus with full cognitive attention on the act as such, which means that we do not articulate it rationally in language. This peripheral awareness, or experience, is nonetheless of great importance. There is no way of knowing anything else with full rational articulation without relying on it. Even if we are intent on expressing only the most abstract and formal truths, we can not avoid experiencing peripherally the qualifying presence of the *prima facie* rational acts in which we do so. It is true that we can be so intent on what we are doing or saying that we may for the moment fail to notice that peripheral experience: mathematicians, for instance, sometimes talk about the structures they are developing as though those formal entities were utterly independent of the acts that develop them.

The reader and I are in a different position. We have already made a reflexive turn together and can thus consider whether or not there is a peripheral experience of action as the mathematician carries on the business of developing a proof or as we ourselves engage in the acts that make up our imagined conversation. Indeed, by articulating the question in language we immediately make our position different from that of our hypothetical mathematician. Once we make the reflexive turn, once we make the act as such the focus of our cognitive attention and articulate it in language, what was a peripheral experience of acting now becomes a *prima facie* knowledge. To put it differently, the question whether there was in the first instance a peripheral awareness, or experience, of action upon which every theoretical structure depended is now a matter for rational assessment of the facts of the case. If our mathematician should challenge us, protesting that there is no peripheral awareness of acting as one defines certain mathematical objects or demonstrates some theorem about them, we insist upon another look; which means that we ask the mathematician to take the reflexive turn with us and *attend* to those actions. Reflection, we say, will reveal that a peripheral awareness was indeed present in them; that one can never move to some ideal world that is free from the concrete though peripheral presence of our own enframing rational acts;

that each move to do so but reinforces the enframing authority we had not attended to, had not taken seriously.

Prima facie knowledge of prima facie rational action is, then, nothing more than the latter reflexively attended to and given rational expression in language. It is therefore our reflexive thesis about it that even when we do not attend to it deliberately and reflexively, our peripheral awareness, or experience, of it is essential to whatever we are doing or saying. By having come so far we do not eliminate the qualifier "prima facie," which still attaches both to the action itself and to this reflexive, language-saturated way of knowing it. At this point we have no way of demonstrating that both are not mere seemings—the one not authentically what it appears to be, the other no true knowledge when judged by rigorous standards.

On the other hand, neither do we have any way of demonstrating that they are in fact mere seemings. Words like "seeming," "appearance," "phenomenon," "phenomenological," and even "illusion" do, however, come insistently to mind, just as all of them can be found in the literature about action. Not all of them are inevitably disparaging; indeed, from the beginning the various words based on the Greek verb "φαίνω" have carried some positive overtones,[1] if only because the root active sense was "to bring to light" and the root passive sense "to come to light" or "to be seen"; we shall look at some of those positive senses in chapter 5. Still, as used in current discussions of action and mind, "phenomenon" and "phenomenological" do have negative overtones, except in the work of committed phenomenologists, who are more likely to be accused of idealism than of physicalism. To say that something is an appearance or phenomenon, that it has a phenomenological status, is usually to be disposed to hold it in some ontological disesteem, to suspect it of being inauthentic. Since we have so far no conclusive reason for thinking that of prima facie rational action, or for that matter of our prima facie knowledge of it, let us simply say that the prima facie status of these things is of profound importance and persuasiveness; and let us entertain the possibility that it may turn out to be their true ontological status. Rational action may be precisely what it appears to be to the rational agent that acts and reflects about its action; and the prima facie knowledge of it and of the world in which we appear to act, though it is neither scientific nor, as yet, philosophic, may not be doomed in principle to miss what is ontologically the case. This suggestion does not require us to suppose that the prima facie knowledge we now have of our action as we reflect upon it is completely adequate to what action is in fact; only that whatever advances we might make in understanding it, either in the mode of science or in any other mode, should not cancel its *prima facie* status but simply display it as an authentic glimpse of what we should then understand more clearly.

There is one good reason for taking *prima facie* rational action and our *prima facie* knowledge of it seriously: the two link together to form a circle that is ineluctable in the sense that there is no experiential way in which we can step outside it. One acts to know anything whatever and in any sense whatever of "to know," not excepting any of the senses that find place in the epistemic structure of science; one acts even to muster all the complex scientific and philosophic argument that goes into a physicalist attack on the authenticity of responsible rational action. As it enframes all such cognitive efforts, *prima facie* rational action is itself enframed by an articulated cognitive grasp of the world within which the action takes place; and this grasp is exactly the one that we shall make use of if we bring our peripheral awareness of the enframing texture of action into the focus of our cognitive attention.

This brings us to the most important sense in which the circle of rational action and our knowledge of it is experientially fundamental: if we can not step outside it when we are dealing with things other than action, neither can we step outside it when we are dealing with action itself. Thus, although it is always open to us to theorize about action so as to represent it as quite different from our *prima facie* cognitive grasp of it, *prima facie* rational action will enframe this act of theory as well, still peripherally present, still potentially the focus of the agent's cognitive attention. Even if we should grant that our knowledge of it and of the world in which it takes place is questionable and should then put it to the question, we must act to find out the real status of that knowledge, so that we are back where we started. *Prima facie* rational action returns upon itself by way of *prima facie* knowledge; *prima facie* knowledge returns upon and criticizes itself by way of *prima facie* rational action.

2

Towards a Reflexive Exploitation of the Circle

A physicalist account of rational action purports to show that it is not what it appears to be and that ontic responsibility is therefore not au-

thentic. If I am right about our circle, there will be something paradoxical about the physicalist enterprise, since it will have to rely on
the texture of *prima facie* acts to propound its doctrine. I consider this
paradoxical feature in chapters 5 and 6. There is however no such paradox in the attempt to show that *prima facie* rational action is precisely
what it purports to be. Because there is no escape from the circle, we
must all rely on the texture of *prima facie* action; and there is nothing
paradoxical about claiming that what one relies on is authentic. One
might well be wrong about the authenticity, but there is nothing paradoxical about making the claim.

If our attempt consisted only in the attempt to frame arguments
there would be another danger, for an argument designed to show
that we are ontically responsible might covertly assume that rational
action is what it purports to be—no paradox indeed, but plainly a circle in the argument. It is exceedingly hard to proceed in a merely argumentative way without doing something of that sort. Arguments
that appeal to the logic of the language in which we ordinarily talk
about action will I think founder in that way. By merely appealing to
our *prima facie* rational action as we habitually exercise it and habitually speak about it—by merely taking for granted our *prima facie*
knowledge of it—they invite us to accept what is in question. We are,
to be sure, pent in the circle, but we shall not persuade anybody that
what we find there is authentic if we do no more than acknowledge
our confinement.

I propose to work within the circle in a different spirit: acknowl-
edging that it is ineluctable, I propose that we undertake a reflection
on *prima facie* rational action for the purpose of making our *prima
facie* knowledge of it more intense and clear. I do not mean that we
should frame theories about rational action—theories that *ex hypothesi*
would be philosophic rather than scientific ones—and then bring these
to the test by somehow confronting them with our pretheoretic awareness, or experience, of action. That way of putting it suggests that our
awareness of action is a given thing, not to be altered by any rational
effort; that any change in our understanding of it would come about
by way of our constructing and understanding a theory about action.
But if on the contrary the character of our concrete awareness, or experience, of action should change with the intensity of the cognitive
glance we cast upon it, the matter would be quite different. "Cognitive glance" is of course metaphorical; we may bring it down to earth
by noting that there is no true cognitive glance that does not complete

itself in the development of language and the other symbols embedded in our natural language. But, this being understood, it becomes clear at once that we need not think of *prima facie* rational action as something we are aware of, or experience, once and for all—an unalterable experiential *donnée*. It is, perhaps, never less than what it is experienced to be as we express it in everyday language, but as we sharpen our rational focus we also break out of our customary linguistic habits. From this common beginning in what purports to be a rational experience of action expressed in everyday language we may hope to go on to a deeper and more intense rational experience, whose depth and intensity will manifest itself in part in the more complete presence of action in our awareness and in part in the more adequate language in which it comes to pass.

So too with the *prima facie* knowledge we bring to it: as we reflexively focus upon it with the same rational-empirical intent we bring to action itself, our grasp of it may also intensify and deepen. Contemporary philosophers are almost unanimous in thinking that there is no such possibility. I hope to show that this conviction is based on an inappropriate model for knowing—more precisely, that it is based on the inappropriate notion that *any* model can illuminate a power that is ontologically prior to the making and knowing of models. Whether or not I am right about this, I must concede at once that our cognitive engagement with the real is experientially much more elusive than whatever object or objects we know by virtue of it; it is clearly not a *thing*, to be known like any other. But many epistemological traditions that have little else in common will agree that knowledge has bodily roots and that in some ways it manages to transcend them. If they are right, it is an activity no more outside our experiential ken than is the body itself; and this raises the possibility that it is there at the reflexive focus, waiting only for our expressive powers to disclose it. Lest this should suggest some paradoxical physical achievement like seeing one's eye without the help of a mirror, let me say that reflexive seeing, though no doubt also rooted in the body, also a matter of experience, or awareness, completes itself in language just as the nonreflexive kind does. Though we put the emphasis in the wrong place when we identify awareness with the use of language, both nonreflexive and reflexive cognitive "seeing" is qualified by the language it gives rise to. The intent of this part of our reflection, then, is to so focus upon our cognitive engagement with the real as to bring that engagement before us as a rationally articulated empirical presence. The precise role of language in that engagement is, then, part of what we shall be trying to articulate in this chapter. The way I have already expressed the matter will warn the reader that I take it to be a mistake to make very much of the obvious social nature of language. Adequate language emerges from an adequate encounter with the real; but both adequate and inadequate language are social. As for *how* adequate language emerges, we do not yet have adequate language for that; and that, I suspect, means merely that we have not yet had an adequate cognitive encounter with the reality of our own cognitive engagement with the real.

In this chapter and the next I intend to work within the circle of action and knowledge, focusing in the rest of this chapter on our *prima facie* knowledge, which purports on occasion to be knowledge of rational action, and in the next chapter on our *prima facie* rational action itself. The reflection is empirical in intent in that it is meant to provide an awareness, or experience, of these two things; but the awareness sought for is understood not as a *donnée* but as the result of an active penetration of the real that is more revelatory of what is the case than our habitual awareness is. The reflection is in that sense intended to be a transformation of *prima facie* knowledge. This concedes that awareness, or experience, is indeed a *donnée* from the point of view of any received attitude, but insists that it is not essentially a *donnée*: in its time what is now habitual may have been an achievement that overcame an earlier habit. The reflection is, on the other hand, theoretic—more accurately, rational—in the sense that it is meant to articulate in more adequate language, in more adequate categoreal schemes, what is the case about those two things.

The enterprise consists of a series of *prima facie* rational actions, and its experiential and theoretic-rational poles are understood to be interdependent in a sense the reflection itself will disclose. We may anticipate the main lines of it in this way: the penetration to a level of awareness that is more adequate to what is the case is presumed to take place only in and with the rational articulation of that feature of the real of which we have awareness, or experience. We suppose ourselves to prise open the real with the help of language, making it show itself, making it appear as it is. But that phrase "with the help of language" is not quite right. It suggests an instrument or apparatus that we manipulate until the falling into place of certain words tells us something about what we are intent on becoming aware of. As we shall see later, it is just as important to notice that the words fall into place as a consequence of heightened awareness. Though our primary concern in this book is to bring about a heightened and articulate awareness of rational action, our reflection must deal with our *prima facie* knowledge of it as well. Our *prima facie* cognitive power must be taken as part of the real—as part of what is the case—and made to appear as it is. The question whether in attending to *prima facie* rational action with our *prima facie* cognitive grasp we are attending to an ontically significant appearance or merely to a deceptive and inauthentic one can not be settled without settling also the question of the status of our *prima facie* cognitive powers.

All this means that we are to try again—though I hope with a difference—a kind of philosophical reflection that has been notably inconclusive in the past and is certainly now out of favor. I mean that kind of philosophy that develops by way of an intense, concrete, and not merely argumentative look at the foundations of knowledge itself. This time, however, the enterprise is fruitfully complicated by the involvement of the topic of rational action with that of knowledge, and I think we shall find that this will keep it from being foundational in the sense that has recently been under attack. Our enterprise itself purports to proceed by way of a series of rational acts. There will in fact be something in common with that remodeling of an epistemic ship in full sail that has seemed to recent epistemologists so satisfactory an image for their calling—except that here the ship is taken to be that of rationality in general rather than of science. Nevertheless, given the prevailing winds of doctrine, it is no light matter to try to reopen the question of a foundation for knowledge. A digression to look at how the question now stands will in the long run make it easier to see what I am trying to do in this chapter and the next, and may even help make the doing of it seem worthwhile.

3

The Question of a Foundation for Knowledge

Knowledge, it is now widely believed, needs no foundation. With one form of this belief few would disagree, for although knowledge has had no foundation—has had none in at least the sense that there has been no generally agreed upon account of it since the very beginnings of Western philosophy, knowledge itself has indeed existed and prospered. Commonsense knowledge ramifying in practical techniques is coextensive with human culture itself; and scientific knowledge, though no doubt much transformed in its recent exponential growth, is by no means entirely new in human affairs. It is one purpose of this section to show that this pragmatic reason for dispensing with a foundational approach will not stand up to close examination. Before turning to that, however, we must distinguish this reason from another and more parochial one for repudiating the foundational approach: a confusion of the bankruptcy of a particular foundational tradition with the bankruptcy of epistemology in general.

Two bankrupt foundational traditions, frequently but not necessarily allied, come to mind. The first is the one to which the notion of representation is central. It is true that most practitioners of foundational epistemology from Descartes to the contemporary epigoni of Hume and Kant have been dominated by this or that version of the representative theory of ideas, or at least by one premise that it shares with certain related theories, namely, that *what* one knows directly *when* one knows is some item ontologically suited for residence in a region sometimes called mind but also known as consciousness, mentality, awareness, experience, subjectivity, intentionality, and so on. The various names stress different aspects of the same supposed region; and the various names for items that reside there—impressions, sensations, perceptions, representations, ideas, concepts, propositions, and so on—show them to have this family resemblance, that they require for their existence the sustaining air of just that ontological region and no other. It is also true that there is something fundamentally wrong with that premise—something so obviously wrong that those who never felt the force of it can only wonder why it took empirical philosophers so long to notice it.[2]

The second bankrupt foundational tradition is much older, and though since Descartes it has often been allied with the representative theory, it is not logically tied either to that theory or to the premise just mentioned. Indeed, those who discovered the principle that defines the tradition—Plato and Aristotle—specifically reject that premise, although failure to attend to the difference in meaning between the Cartesian term "idea" and the Platonic term it transliterates seems to have led one contemporary expositor to suggest that Plato is somehow responsible for that premise.[3] I mean the foundational tradition in which a deductive relation is asserted to hold between that which is known directly and, in being known, is also *known to be the foundation* and other things that are seen to be dependent upon it. Drawing upon the category of explanation, we may sum up the tradition in this way: the foundation when found needs no explanation; it has no merely premise-like (or axiom-like) status, and other things are explained by having their explanatory principles deduced from it. The principle of deductive unification, which is the principle of the unity of any particular science and of the ideal of the unity of science in general, obviously comes out of this tradition. It is now taken for granted that it is a mistake to look for an absolute deductive foundation for science, and so the basic propositions of a science are assumed to have the status of premises, or axioms, that may or may not be true. It is also presumably a mistake to look for an absolute deductive foundation for rationality in general. If so, those bred in these enlightened times should forgive their great ancestors for these mistakes, and for the further mistake of confusing science and philosophy in the course of the search, for the principle of deductive unity discovered along the way has been of immense importance for science.

Despite the bankruptcy of these foundational traditions, and despite our pragmatic ability to get along without a foundation for science, the need for a foundation of some kind for rationality in general continues. The symptom of the need is a familiar one, and if we attend to it we may use it to define the great schism in modern philosophy more effectively than we can do by stating it in terms of the stock contrast between analytic philosophers and all the others. The symptom is the confrontation of two treasured attitudes, neither of which we would willingly give up, and one of which we are simply in no logical position to give up even if we were willing to. In this book I have expressed the opposition as one between the authority of science and the authority of our *prima facie* status as responsible rational agents, but I think a new foundational approach is needed even when the problem of responsibility is not under consideration, and so, just here, it may be wise to give the confrontation a somewhat more general statement.

As soon as we do so, we find that the notion of two well-defined and treasured attitudes in confrontation is far too simple, and that the very fact of a confrontation means that a third attitude has begun to emerge. Things are further complicated because one of the two original attitudes has historical priority, the other having developed out of it as a modification of it. Common sense, if I may call it by the most neutral of the several names available, came first, and science arose out of it. There are philosophers who feel that this gives common sense no privileged status, and that it might in due course be utterly superseded by some scientific attitude of the future; but for the moment even the most abstruse kind of science is carried on within the framework of common sense. And this means that any third attitude that should arise will arise out of the world of common sense in the same way. In that sense any third attitude, whether it should purport to be an utterly new one, or to develop out of science, or to develop out of common sense itself, will still, genetically speaking, be a development out of common sense.

When the third attitude is acknowledged for what it is, an attitude in which some perspective is sought from which the other two may be fairly assessed, it is perceived as being foundational and therefore philosophical, and the risk of making philosophical judgments is consciously taken. The reasons given for the judgments that in due course are made purport to be reasons seen from a vantage point from which they can legitimately be made. The claim to have found one's way there is presumptuous enough, and it is usually found to be unjustified after a while, so that explicitly foundational efforts have fallen into disrepute. Philosophic hubris, however, takes many forms. Some philosophers contrive to pronounce philosophical judgments of a foundational kind while protesting that it is illegitimate to do so. They presume to set our intellectual world in order with all the certitude of having reached a vantage point from which this can be done, all the while they insist that there is no such vantage point and that only someone in the grip of philosophic hubris would pretend that there was. We shall look a little later at a cryptofoundational attitude of this kind.

Turning now to the first of our two attitudes, we find that before it is placed in confrontation with the second attitude to generate a third, it is nothing more than the practice of science in accordance with the standards of the age. When it is explicitly opposed to the second one, it becomes that version of the scientific attitude which claims that science is not just an important mode of explanation but the very paradigm of explanation and therefore of rationality in general. In this guise it is a third attitude, one that purports to show that the findings of science make available something ontologically more fundamental than common sense can provide. Those who adopt it speak not as scientists but as physicalist (materialist) philosophers—as when, for instance, Sellars says, "science is the measure of all things, of what is that it is, and of what is not that it is not."[4]

The second attitude, the one I have called common sense, is sometimes also called the attitude of ordinary language; sometimes the phe-

nomenological or phenomenal one; sometimes that of the manifest
image, of the natural standpoint, or of the life-world. It makes a great
deal of difference what we call it, for these ways of characterizing it
have different overtones—of approval, of neutrality, of suspicion—and
the overtones themselves change in subtle ways in the mouths of different speakers. The attitude of common sense is a paradigm of rationality for Thomas Reid or for G. E. Moore, so much so that the third
attitude consists, so to speak, in our *using* common sense in such a way
as to see its own commanding authority. But it is treated with some
ontological disdain by a physicalist like Quine,[5] or, for that matter, by
an idealist like F. H. Bradley, and it is given a subordinate role by Descartes. Sellars, though sensitive to its magisterial appeal, puts it in what
he conceives to be its ontological place by calling it the attitude of the
manifest image.[6] This overtone of an appearance that is not to be relied upon by any truly reasonable person is also present when the expression "phenomenal" is used, used not so much for the attitude as
for the world correlative with it; this is such a widespread use among
physicalists that it needs no further comment. Much the same thing
can be said of "phenomenological" when that is used not as a phe-
nomenologist would use it but somewhat as "phenomenal" is generally
used.

   The same attitude regarded as the one ordinary language expresses
has had its philosophic ups and downs in this century. It meant little
enough to Russell and Wittgenstein in the days when they thought
they understood each other—meant only an attitude awaiting replacement by a more adequate one.[7] But to English and American analytic
orthodoxy from the time of Wittgenstein's recantation of that earlier
position[8] until the last *Zettel* of his *Nachlass* had been piously edited,
translated, and conveyed (German and English on facing pages) to
the libraries, it meant a good deal—meant that the most rarefied kind
of rationality was about to emerge from it. In one sense the world of
ordinary language *was* that most rarefied kind of rationality; in another,
its privileged status could not legitimately be demonstrated by a *saying*, but had to be *shown* to initiates, so that this showing, which took
place *within* ordinary language, was that true rarefied kind of rationality—was, that is, the third attitude we have been talking about. Now,
it appears, the attitude of ordinary language means little enough again.
Analytic orthodoxy is now different. For the moment, at least, the
American wing of it is in the ascendant, and Americans who belong to
it really do believe, for the most part, that science is the measure of all

things; and they do take more seriously what can be done with formal language than what can be done with ordinary language, for the construction and study of artifacts of that kind in the pursuit of "results" seem to them activities as close to those of the scientist as any philosopher can ever aspire to. Little is left of the consensus brought about after his recantation by Wittgenstein's masterful personality but the conviction in some quarters that the intellectual life is best expressed in the metaphor of the language-game.

When the second attitude is called that of the natural standpoint or that of the life-world,[9] it is plain enough that a third attitude is already in view: the explicitly foundational one of phenomenology. The term "natural standpoint" invites us to depart from the second attitude (without ever quite losing sight of it) to take up a sounder position. The term "life-world" brings with it a different nuance, suggesting as it does how important the position we depart from remains even after the phenomenological *epochē* has opened up the way to a new, more secure, and more comprehensive perspective. When I called the second attitude one in which we take our *prima facie* action seriously, and then went on to extend an invitation to enter the *via media* I spoke of in the first chapter, the invitation was also explicitly foundational, although there is little else it has in common with phenomenology.

The two attitudes are not inevitably in the kind of competitive confrontation that generates a third. Most people move back and forth between them, pragmatically affirming each as the occasion demands. But it is a fact of our contemporary intellectual life that they are often in competitive confrontation, and I shall not trouble to argue it further. I do want to insist, though, that if we recognize a confrontation and take some steps to settle it, we have already adopted an attitude distinct from the ones we are comparing. Whether we then go on to look for a compromise or to bring the matter to an unrelenting conflict does not seem to matter much. In either case we are looking for a foundation—a viewpoint, an attitude, a perspective—from which we can judge the nature of the confrontation and the relative worth of the two attitudes. It may well be that not all philosophy is foundational in this sense, but it seems clear enough that a foundational move of this kind is philosophical. At least it seems a reasonable claim that once we recognize the confrontation, make the recognition articulate, and then set about laying down some judgment about it, we are already talking or writing philosophy. To do all this and still insist that we are

not engaged in an enterprise that has much in common with earlier and
openly foundational ones is disingenuous.

Foundational judgments of this kind are not the special prerogative
of those who belong to the profession of academic philosophy. They
may be made by someone in any line of work who is competent to deal
with such matters. But if professional philosophers in general should
come to feel that such judgments are either unnecessary or impossible,
and that they do not really have the traditional task they supposed
they had, it is open to them to abolish their profession. I doubt whether
Richard Rorty, who disparages professionalization in *Philosophy and
the Mirror of Nature*,[10] really expects that to happen; certainly it will
not happen if the movement to disband must originate in that part of
the profession in whose idiom he speaks. There are, to be sure, sound
objections to the professionalization of philosophy, and a few of the
best of them have been around a long while: many of the men who
first began to define the Western philosophical tradition were repelled
by the professionalization of philosophy in the hands of the Sophists. I
raised the issue of professionalization myself some years ago;[11] but it is
a separate issue. The emergence of foundational judgments of this
kind—judgments to be sure different from Descartes' or Kant's, or, for
that matter, Plato's—is perennial. They go a long way towards defining
philosophy, and they will continue to emerge—perhaps from scientists
or poets acting qua philosophers—even in the unlikely event that the
American Philosophical Association should decide to call it a day.

Foundational attitudes are philosophical, and philosophy at its most
searching is foundational. It is best that it should be openly so. Its mistakes will then be plainly in view, and they can be judged and either
set aside or modified by subsequent foundational efforts. To put it this
way is to suggest that a foundation for knowledge is no utterly permanent thing. Should we then discard the very notion of a foundation as
containing an inappropriate metaphor? I do not think so, for though
foundations are to build upon, buildings themselves are not for all
eternity. What is rightly objected to in the foundational tradition is
the claim sometimes made within it to have found something more
permanent than the foundation of a human building. If the third attitude is not explicitly but implicitly foundational, there is no great
harm done. We can see the foundational intent of, say, the reasons
G. E. Moore puts forward in defense of common sense[12] and can see
also that they contradict not only the positions they are aimed at but
also the Cartesian foundations upon which those positions ultimately

rest. If, however, the third attitude is represented as nonfoundational, and if it is maintained besides that no foundation is needed, we may suspect the presence of a hidden foundation that is taken for granted. It will be no less hidden for being also hidden from those who build upon it. This, I think, will be true of that piecemeal remodeling in mid-voyage of the epistemic raft of science that is so often thought to be preferable to the old-fashioned foundational enterprise it replaces. There, as elsewhere, a deep-seated professional prejudice serves as the true foundation. It is not surprising that in much of contemporary philosophy the hidden prejudice has to do with the status of language.

4

The Cryptofoundational Consensus about Language

A powerful professional consensus about the status of language has dominated much of American and English philosophy for a long time now. I will call it the consensus of linguistic enclosure, and I will say that it is cryptofoundational because in many ways it serves in place of a more traditional epistemological foundation, and because reliance upon it is often coupled with the explicit denial of the need for any such foundation. The consensus embraces a number of related views that are probably not all consistent with one another, but the way in which all of them are expressed reveals yet another implicit doctrine that is at odds with most of what is explicit in the consensus. This doctrine I will call the repressed doctrine. I hope the presence of those two terms "cryptofoundational" and "repressed," which might well seem to reinforce each other, will not lead the reader astray. The doctrine I call the repressed one I conceive of as canceling the cryptofoundational doctrine by implicitly relying on a more natural, less obsessive, and, I think, entirely more accurate view about our relation to reality and the role language plays in that relation. The repressed doctrine is the one I think the reader and I share when we are using language to some first-order purpose without supposing ourselves to be confined in language. To call it a repressed doctrine is to say that those who labor under the obsession of the linguistic consensus share it too— that they must, moreover, rely on it to express the fundamental claims of the consensus. I want, in due course, to uncover the repressed claim, to turn it against the consensus, and then to use it to lead the reader

into the explicitly foundational attitude that will dominate this and
the next chapter.

My reason for this rather intricate prelude is that our *prima facie*
knowledge of action—and of the many other important things that also
came under its glance—is, after all, linguistic in some very important
and fundamental sense. That sense, I contend, is radically different
from what the consensus explicitly says about our involvement with
language. I think it will be liberating if I manage to express that
difference.

Before turning to the consensus itself, I must note (at least for those
nonspecialist readers one always hopes to have) that two quite distinct
kinds of language play roles in the linguistic consensus. One is so-called
natural language: the human language which, in its thousands of forms—
English, French, Swahili, Chinese, and so on—all of us speak. It is in
an important sense *one* language, though its local forms differ in development. Within these languages, or at least within the ones used by
groups that have produced important amounts of literature and science, there can be found specialized vocabularies not understood by
all speakers of natural language, so that we may safely distinguish two
kinds of natural language—ordinary and technical. They are, however,
not distinct languages but rather distinct regions of one natural language. The other kind of "language" is, however, radically different,
different enough to deserve those quotation marks. It consists of a
great variety of language-like objects that have been devised for special
purposes. The clearest examples are the formal "languages," more accurately formal systems, constructed for axiomatizing this or that
branch of logic or mathematics. What distinguishes all of them from
natural language is that they can not function. in the limited "linguistic" sense that tempts us to call them languages rather than "languages," unless they are embedded either in natural language or in
some other "language" that is ultimately so embedded. Let us speak of
natural language as language$_1$ and of the many "languages" as lan-
guage$_2$. Few of those who work with language$_2$ would accept my account, and so when I speak of language$_2$ in discussing some doctrine in
what follows, my label may challenge the doctrine's explicit content.

The study of both language$_1$ and language$_2$ is monumentally complex and I hope to say here only some things that should be obvious
but, I think, have not always been so. Languages$_2$ are best seen, one
would suppose, as theoretic objects not radically distinct from mathematical objects; indeed, some languages$_2$ are clearly mathematical ob-

jects and are so treated. (That may not help much, because it is by no means clear what the ontological status of mathematical objects is.) Besides being interesting for their structures, as all such objects are, they could then be regarded as symbolic instruments that were parts of language₁ in the sense that they amplified its capacity by allowing us to use it to talk with precision about things that we could ordinarily deal with only in an inexact way. Certain languages₂ of that kind have permitted gifted people to grasp certain principles of logic that would have been missed without them. So viewed, they appear, like the technical vocabulary and the theoretic structures of the sciences, and like the symbolism of mathematics, to be part of the technical language that is itself an extension of natural language. There are many metaphorical uses of the term "language" (e.g., computer "language," the "language" of DNA) that obscure this perhaps commonsensical point.

However that may be, the point has sometimes been well hidden in this century, and language₂ has sometimes been regarded as something that could in principle, and should, if properly devised, supersede language₁. One such "ideal" language was the language₂ of the pure logician that Wittgenstein proposed in the *Tractatus*. He did not, evidently, mean to say that our natural language is somehow incorrect or mistaken; the ideal language was in fact thought to be entailed by the structure of our natural language in the sense that the rightness of natural language in dealing with the gross, complex, and *prima facie* features of the world required that there should be a certain language₂ capable of expressing the hidden simplicities that gave ontological support to this *prima facie* complexity. The ideal language, as he saw it, had a form for which the extensional language₂ used in the logical system of Russell and Whitehead's *Principia Mathematica*[13] provides at least an adumbration. Wittgenstein's point was that an ideal language of that kind, when fully developed, would have the structure that logic requires. Such a language₂ would represent reality by being isomorphic with it, and though Wittgenstein seems to have been puzzled by just how the ultimate units of the language₂ would fit with the ultimate units of an (equally idealized) experience, it also seems that the question was not of final importance to him. What was important was the capacity of the language₂ for representing the structure of reality; the content, or matter, as it might be in some ideal experience, could be dismissed. For him, in those early days, it was logic that was isomorphic with reality—it was perhaps logic that *was* reality—so that if we were to develop and perfect its structure from within, unfolding logic, as it were, by unfolding the ideal language, we should discern at last, in that linguistic$_2$ structure, the lineaments of things as they really are. As logic differs from physics, so will the structure of reality also differ: it will have only that spare, bony, and indeed static structure that logic requires. That is, at least, the general telos of the *Tractatus*; it is where its author was tending, although there are remarks here and there in it that can be given a more conventional positivistic setting. This telos of the *Tractatus* is often misunderstood, even by those of a physicalist or positivist bent who have drawn upon it for their own versions of language$_2$.

The second ideal language was that of logical positivism[14] itself, which of course owed a good deal to Wittgenstein's precedent. It is dominated by two premises. (1) An ideal language$_2$, though it will have a bony structure for which extensional logic supplies the model, must be what an ideal physics rather than an ideal formal logic requires. (2) Physics, however, is an empirical study, and the structure of experience is roughly what Hume said it was. An ideal language$_2$, then, must be capable of accommodating whatever theoretical entities a perfected physics requires, and it must be capable of reducing both expressions about such entities and the expressions of language$_1$ (more precisely, only the meaningful expressions of language$_1$) to those of a very spare sensory vocabulary. At the overt level, the thought that language$_2$ should represent *reality* is dismissed, for this purports to be an empirical language$_2$ rather than a metaphysical one, and this means that in the long run its expressions should be verifiable in empirical encounters. The supposed nature of these encounters is, however, so subrational and mute that I venture to say that the theme of linguistic enclosure here takes the form of the supposition that rationality, at least, is so enclosed, and that an empirical awareness escapes that enclosure only at the expense of being subrational and inarticulate. The ideal encounter of language$_2$ and experience was thought to be signalized in expressions of minimal and atomistic empirical import, like "this green now" or "here, now, red," expressions of such minimal import and so ontologically noncommittal that for the most part theorists were reluctant to regard them as statements. In one of the several senses of "phenomenal," the language$_2$ of logical positivism is a phenomenal one. The standard historical account of this movement—it has been given often enough—is that its reductionist ambitions could not be realized, and that, moreover, it could be shown that in principle they were not realizable.

This is by now an old story, and I sketch it only to be able to make the point that the theme of the supersession of language$_1$ by language$_2$ has been an important one within the linguistic consensus. Though the project has been dropped, at least in the extreme form of it I have described, it is worth noting that it was doomed from the start in the sense that even if some language$_2$ could supersede language$_1$, it could do so only by absorbing into itself all those features of language$_1$ that make it possible for us to use it in our ordinary intersubjective discourse, and use it, moreover, to embed in it various useful kinds of language$_2$. A language$_2$ can supersede language$_1$ only by becoming language$_1$—language$_1$ modified, to be sure, in some technical direction. There are influential members of the consensus of linguistic enclosure—Quine and Sellars, for instance—who still propose an ideal scientific language as a desirable philosophic objective, though not, as we shall see, an ideal language$_2$.[15] Each of the two mentioned has in his own way transformed the unacknowledged metaphysical faith of the positivists into an open metaphysical doctrine. Quine, for instance, claimed as early as 1948, in the well-known article "On What There Is," that to be is to be the value of a bound variable—that is, that we presuppose any alleged entity to be if, and only if, it must be reckoned among the entities over which what modern logic calls the variables of quantification—"something," "nothing," "everything"—range in order to make one of our assertions true.[16] The point can be more perspicuously stated in logical notation, and when it is so stated, it becomes plain that the most likely candidates for inclusion in the catalogue of what is are those that can be accommodated within an extensional language$_2$ as values of its bound variables. The claim is, then, both logical and metaphysical in its bearings, and it brings with it at least a distant echo of the Wittgenstein of the *Tractatus*. There are many languages$_2$ and many theories, and what Quine calls our ontological commitments will vary depending on which ones we adopt for our various purposes. For much of that essay he is concerned only to offer a "standard whereby to decide what the ontological commitments of a theory are," the question of which ontology to adopt being left open. But the essay carries with it what appears to be Quine's own ontological commitment, for what is left open seems to be left open under the general assumption that the ontology ultimately to be accepted is whatever one the over-all development of science (in the broadest sense) ultimately requires; and Quine's later work bears this interpretation out.[17] Seen in that light, the claim is clearly a metaphysical one. As for Sellars, the motto I quoted earlier seems downright enough: "science is the measure of all things, of what is that it is, and of what is not that it is not."

For both writers, and for a large number of other American writers who either never followed Wittgenstein when he turned in his later years to ordinary language or, if they did, have changed their minds, science is both a linguistic matter and the metaphysical measure. The theme of the supersession of one language by another is a continuing one, although the objective is less extreme than the one the positivists had in mind. But the point about the relation between language$_1$ and language$_2$ still applies: an ideal physical language$_2$, being necessarily ultimately embedded in language$_1$, can only supersede it by taking on just those features that allow language$_1$ to function without being embedded in yet another language. Quine, Sellars, and related writers are therefore best understood as trying to modify language$_1$ in a desired technical direction by embedding in it an array of epistemic artifacts that would include among other things some appropriate languages$_2$. That, I take it, is what science is always doing, and there is no doubt that the embedded languages$_2$ gradually modify the sense of quite ordinary and nontechnical usage in language$_1$. Quine and Sellars are not scientists, however, but philosophers, and the technical direction in which they wish to modify language$_1$ is in the interest of metaphysics rather than science. Thus, in Sellars's view, concepts now proper to language$_1$ when we talk about such matters as *prima facie* rational action would have "successor concepts" in the modified language (on my interpretation, modified language$_1$) that would supersede it.[18] Although expressions like "rational action" would be correlated with their successor concepts and so would not be utterly eliminated, they would nevertheless be relegated to the status of an archaic dialect.

A somewhat different view of the status of language$_1$ that can still be found within the linguistic consensus is the one developed by Wittgenstein in the latter part of his career. Its monument is the posthumous *Philosophical Investigations*, completed in 1945 but not published until 1953. The book is the result of Wittgenstein's repudiation of the possibility of an ideal language$_2$, and in it Wittgenstein explores the perfectly satisfactory texture of that kind of language$_1$ for which the term "ordinary language" has become standard. It is often said that in the *Investigations* Wittgenstein also repudiates the notion, expressed in the 1922 *Tractatus*, that language represents, pictures, or maps the structure of reality. But a close look at the continuity of doctrine in the *Tractatus* and the *Investigations* suggests that this conventional view needs to be qualified. It seems to me more accurate to say that Wittgenstein is telling us, from beginning to end, that anyone enclosed in a given language (either language₁ or some language₂) can not stand outside that language and determine how accurately it represents or fails to represent whatever we use it to talk about. And that point is consistent enough with his continuing to be obsessed with the thought that language *is*, after all, representative. We shall, a little later on, look at two distinct senses of "representative," one of which would be consistent with what Wittgenstein was saying in the *Investigations*.

One continuity that bears upon this point is the distinction between saying and showing, made first in the *Tractatus*, and there used to make the point that only natural science is a genuine first-order discipline that can actually be used to *say* things. Philosophy—especially metaphysical philosophy—that tries to say things is meaningless, and the true method of philosophy consists only in showing the meaninglessness of metaphysical philosophy. One common metaphysical urge is to try to say something about the fit of language to the real. Though there is a good deal of that sort of thing in the *Tractatus* itself, philosophy of that kind is, Wittgenstein thinks, always nonsense: it tries to represent logical form by placing itself outside logic, and this can not be done. Logical form does represent reality, and philosophy may concern itself with this representative feature of language, but it can express its concern only by the second-order activity of *showing* the logical form of language as it uses that form to *say* things.[19] The difficulty all this poses for the metaphysical claims of the *Tractatus* about the form of reality as represented in the ideal language₂ is familiar. Wittgenstein tried to outface it in the famous ladder image of *Tractatus* 6.54, in which he defends it as useful nonsense: we must climb out through the propositions of that book—climb on them, over them; only when we have surmounted them can we see the world properly.

For Wittgenstein, the prospect was wide and free; it appears that for a while he even found himself free, as he so much wished to be, from that most troubling thing, philosophy itself. *There was to be no more philosophy.* The matter was closed and the problem solved. For a while he gave up philosophy entirely, and returned to it later and with reluctance only when it appeared that the theory of meaning upon which the *Tractatus* was based would not do. *Philosophical Investigations* replaces the notion of meaning with that of use, and the center of philosophic attention is language₁ rather than an ideal language₂. Philosophy now has the job of showing by multifarious examples, discovered or invented, how satisfying the logic of ordinary language is. But we still can not say things in philosophy. It is still *showing* that is its proper vocation; and as it shows the amenities of the logical form of our everyday language₁ it exorcises the mistaken urge to speak about things in ways that are forbidden by the limits, i.e., the logical form, of ordinary language. The traditional philosophical part of language₁, or at least the metaphysical-epistemological part of it, lies outside the limits of that logical form. The words in which Wittgenstein makes points of this kind now have a somewhat more Kantian ring to them; "phenomena" turns up where in the *Tractatus* "reality" might have been used; but it is clear enough that philosophy must still *show* rather than *say*. What we want to understand is not hidden but in plain view, even though we seem not to understand this. Our real job is not to "penetrate phenomena" but to attend to "the 'possibilities' of phenomena"; and these possibilities can be shown by reminding ourselves "of the *kind of statement* that we make about phenomena. . . ."[20] Though it lies open before us, there is the urge to misunderstand the logic of ordinary language (or, as some might prefer to say, the non-technical part of language₁), an urge caused, he tells us, by analogies between forms of expression in different regions of language; and it is precisely such misunderstandings that cause us to think we are making empirical assertions when we philosophize in the traditional metaphysical-epistemological way. But we are not, and the philosophical problems that arise out of the effort are not empirical problems. We may solve them not by trying to give new information but by so displaying the workings of our language as to make us recognize those workings. We can not in philosophy get a view either of the nature of things or of our cognitive engagement with the nature of things, but only of the "entanglement in our (linguistic) rules" that had first persuaded us that we were getting a view of the nature of things. According to the Wittgenstein of the *Investigations*, philosophy can say nothing foundational about the way language₁ engages with reality, and when it tries to do so it produces nonsense.[21]

One reason for this might well be that the logical form of language₁ prescribes the form of phenomena, and we may carry this Kantian thought further by supposing that the form of language therefore "represents" reality in the sense that these language-saturated phenomena "stand for," or "stand in place of" a reality that can not in principle be captured "in itself." (The mysticism of the later Wittgenstein—a matter of saying, showing, and silence—is often reminiscent of what Kant would be without the second and third critiques and without the "metaphysical" portions of the latter part of the first critique.) The notion of representation is, after all, common enough in Kant himself, even though the sense he gives it, which is certainly not Descartes' sense, forbids the thought of an isomorphism between the representation and the thing-in-itself. At any rate, it seems fair to say that Wittgenstein was dominated throughout his career by the notion that the only way language could engage with the real was by either representing it as an isomorph of it (*Tractatus*) or "representing" it in the sense of prescribing a phenomenal substitute for it (*Investigations*). Wittgenstein, I think, had by no means freed himself from the representative doctrine in the latter part of his career, and I suspect the very metaphor of language-game is evidence for it. And I am not so sure that Rorty, for all his criticism of the representative doctrine, is quite free of it in following Wittgenstein.

After this extended preliminary, we may now set about defining the consensus of linguistic enclosure. One thing that stands in the way of a tidy definition is the disagreement within the consensus on questions of some moment. This should not surprise us, for the two philosophers of the great epistemological tradition to whom the members of the consensus are most in debt—Hume and Kant—are in sharp opposition on matters of some importance. Things are further complicated by some movement within the careers of certain influential writers from a more or less Humean position to a more or less Kantian one. As this book is not designed to explore the details of controversies that go on within the consensus, the two distinct anticipations of linguistic enclosure in those two great creditors of the consensus should be kept in mind as defining the two poles of the consensus. The first is Hume's doctrine of Relations of Ideas, in which our rationality, deployed in such relations, is effectively divided from Matter of Fact, which then becomes the arena of both experience and belief. The second is Kant's doctrine of the phenomenal character of experience, a character derivative from the formgiving, or constitutive, function of our understanding: we have only to think of the understanding as proliferating linguistic structures in general, rather than prescribing some particular set of categories, to make experience itself a linguistic matter. In the one case we are enclosed in a (linguistic) rationality effectively divided from experience, with which it makes only enigmatic contact; in the other, we are enclosed in a language-saturated experience effectively divided from what is truly the case.

It is important to see at once that the notions of representing, picturing, and mirroring do not define the consensus. In an earlier attempt to disrupt it, I deprecated the use of those notions (they are not precisely the same) to talk about knowledge,[22] and it is true that they have played an important role in the consensus. Still, it is possible to repudiate the representative doctrine (at least in its Cartesian or Lockean form) while nonetheless exemplifying acceptance of linguistic enclosure. Richard Rorty does this in *Philosophy and the Mirror of Nature*, and the importance in his work of Wittgenstein's revealing metaphor of the language-game is evidence of it. It is as though beyond the game were something not a game—something about which only silence is appropriate; something we could only attain by leaving the game we can not leave. And, to be sure, we can not leave off expressing in language what we are aware of; yet the metaphor of the game may make us express *this* activity—the very activity of expressing awareness—in a way that encloses us in error, an error that is no less so for being a subtle distortion of the truth. Nor does it help much that we are invited to think of the game not as showing the logical form of our languages but as showing the ultimately social nature of truth.

To define the consensus we shall do better to look first not at the representative theory but at that premise I spoke of awhile ago as being common to Descartes' representative theory of ideas and to certain related theories, namely that *what* one knows directly *when* one knows is some item ontologically suited for residence in a region often called mind but also known as consciousness, mentality, awareness, experience, subjectivity, intentionality, and so on. In that form, of course, it will not do to define the consensus. Even as a preliminary, it is a surprising premise to look to, for if there is any explicit metaphysical view that one tends to attribute to the members of the consensus, it is that the ontological region called by such names—except, perhaps, "experience," which may or may not be used to denote an ontological region—does not exist. It is less surprising if we rehearse the variety of items that were thought to be suited for residence there by the earlier consensus of which the linguistic one is a direct descendant. That consensus was more "idealist," "mentalist," or at least "dualist" than the present one, and its list, which included impressions, sensations, perceptions, and ideas, also included items that could be given a linguistic interpretation, like representations, concepts, propositions, judgments, and so on. The regnant consensus of linguistic enclosure takes seriously only items of the latter kind, and it supplements them by such related items as seem needed to serve as a base for both natural language and formal languages—items like predicates, sets, rules of logic and semantics—and by other items, more complex than these and in some sense formed out of them—items like theories, arguments, and even languages$_2$. For some, items like meanings were also once countenanced; for others, especially those of very strict nominalist views, interest focuses on the symbols we deal with in talking about some of these things. It is, obviously, possible to suppose that *what* one knows *when* one knows is a set of symbols in relationship with one another, and to leave open the question whether one knows anything else in knowing them. It is a very disparate list, and, having in mind the ontological controversy that can swirl around any one of them, I shall call them only supposed linguistic entities (or objects).

We may now state the central doctrines of the consensus of linguistic enclosure. Oversimplifying, and neglecting some borderline cases, I will reduce the doctrine to two.

The *first doctrine* is that *what* we know *when* we know is a supposed linguistic entity, or a structure of such entities, that is *true*. It is obvious, then, that linguistic entities that are not true may be entertained. It is also obvious that the notion of truth has a good deal of relativity built into it, since determining the truth of some simple proposition may seem relatively easy and determining the truth of some complex theory, very hard. But we shall not turn aside to consider that question here. Another question—what it is that entertains linguistic structures, true or otherwise—is not an unimportant one within the consensus, but it seems to be regarded as an unsafe one in the sense that consideration of it threatens the purely linguistic nature of the consensus. For those who belong to it, entertaining linguistic structures is dealt with in a noncommittal way by simply regarding it as what we do when we use and understand language—speak and hear it, read and write it, or otherwise cope with it (for there are also languages$_2$ to consider).

We are, however, talking about a consensus among *empirical* philosophers, and, because for them experience must exercise some sort of control, however puzzling, on the development of language, it seems odd to speak of linguistic *enclosure*. If, however, we look at the way experience is thought to be related to language, the metaphor of enclosure seems justified. Here there is some disagreement within the consensus, the poles of the disagreement being roughly Humean and Kantian, with, as we saw, some tendency for Kant's influence to increase as time goes on. The utter dominance of the consensus by the ideal of the natural sciences means, of course, that the Kantian spirit is considerably modified, even as its influence increases. Despite the disagreement about experience there appears to be one overriding agreement: what we *experience* is not what we *know*—it is not even what we *rationally* entertain.

From the Humean pole we have the image of a subrational and atomistic "real" experience to which, in our pursuit of the scientific ideal, language adjusts as something external to it, and over against which common experience is somehow deficient. It is the extreme of phenomenalism and conventionalism, and it works, or rather worked, with various sophisticated modern versions of Hume's radical separation of Relations of Ideas and Matters of Fact. That wing of the consensus has not been quite the same since the appearance of Quine's "Two Dogmas of Empiricism."

From the Kantian pole we have the notion that what we experience is not what we *know*, but rather that our *experiencing in just that way* is a function of linguistic structures some of which meet the ideal for knowledge and some of which do not. Thus, the linguistic structures in virtue of which we experience ourselves as rational agents may be deficient over against the evolving linguistic structures of science. As we learn to use these latter structures with confidence we begin to learn to "experience" ourselves also in terms of the concepts that are part of them, the two modes of experiencing being in some competition for a while. What happens in the long run we need not venture to say. It is enough to make the drift of the consensus clear.

Within this "Kantian" wing (we may suppose that, if there is any unhappiness in Elysium, Kant might be unhappy if we did not put in the quotation marks), we may detect two tendencies. One grasps the nettle of the thing-in-itself doctrine and says that the language of science tells us what things *really* are. This brings with it a certain difficulty. On the one hand, the experience-mediating function of this language is sufficient to interpose, in the sense just noticed, an "experiential" veil between ourselves and ordinary experience that discredits the way we experience things like action with the help of our ordinary language. On the other hand, its experience-mediating function is insufficient to give us any direct experience of the *concrete* theoretic entities (e.g., fundamental particles) it propounds, so that in using the language we seem more directly in touch with theoretic entities that are *linguistic* ones. It is only "Kantian," but it is sufficiently like Kant's own position to make us find extravagant any claim that science lays hands upon the thing-in-itself. The other tendency within the "Kantian" wing stresses the *variety* of the languages we develop and the various correlate modes of experience we have by virtue of those languages. In the case of those faithful to Wittgenstein, all this is expressed in terms of the language-games we play. In the case of Nelson Goodman, where the influence of Kant comes down through figures like Cassirer, we have instead the notion that we make a number of distinct worlds by virtue of our different languages.[23] But one outside the consensus receives the impression that among the worlds made and the games played, the world or game defined by the evolving language of science has a privileged status.

There is one problem with the "Kantian" form of the doctrine that is especially troubling, one much discussed these days. There is no access to an experience not already structured by language; how therefore does language change, as for empiricists it should, under the stimulus of experience? How do we determine truth in some way that brings in *experience*? Language being in the long run a social matter, linguistic enclosure appears to be social enclosure, and in the long run the determinant of truth, and perhaps the very definition of truth as well, seems to be merely the agreement of a community of language-users. The question has been debated since Peirce and hotly debated since Kuhn's *The Structure of Scientific Revolutions*. It will, one hopes, be debated even more vigorously. Meanwhile, it is a view of truth all too convenient for those who hold positions of power in any intellectual establishment.

So much for the first doctrine of the consensus. It would be interesting to say more about the role the representative theory of ideas has played in it. It is obvious that any member of the consensus working either consciously or unconsciously with the representative theme will exemplify enclosure in a very clear-cut way. But as I said earlier, the consensus of linguistic enclosure is not defined by the representative doctrine, and one does not leave the consensus just by denouncing that doctrine. It should be added, in any case, that the notion of representation does harm only when it is applied to our basic cognitive engagement with the real. Given a first-order, *sui generis* rational engagement with the real—one, therefore, not defined by the representative theory or by linguistic enclosure—we may clearly use that capacity to inspect theories, models, and linguistic$_2$ objects in general and see some representative relation they may bear to other things. The familiar double helix made of plastic and wire does really represent, in a perfectly straightforward fashion, the structure of DNA as that is inferred from a complex of empirical and theoretic data. The details of the data, the details of the model, and the isomorphism itself we may grasp in a first-order, *sui generis* way that breeds no paradoxes. But to say more about representation just here would only extend an already long argument which is in any case intended only to set the stage for an alternative to the consensus. We return a little later to a brief further consideration of the question of representation.

The *second doctrine* of the consensus lays down a still more extreme linguistic enclosure for philosophy, one that is without even that enigmatic relation with experience conceded by the consensus for nonphilosophic knowledge. Philosophy is a second-order, linguistically oriented discipline; it is not only enclosed in language, it is also exclusively concerned with language. It can say nothing about the empirical, either in the ways common sense and science do or in the way art perhaps does. In particular, it can say nothing about the relation between the knower and the real—can say, that is, nothing foundational about our engagement with the real. To do so would violate the principle expressed in the first doctrine, a thing philosophy is unfortunately often tempted to do. Here our preliminaries about Wittgenstein come to mind again. He is not the only one to place such restrictions on philosophy, but his is an extreme case, and what has already been said about it should help to define a view that is expressed in a number of different ways throughout the consensus.

Although these are the two controlling doctrines of the consensus, it does take many forms. Let us now rehearse in a summary way some of the forms already touched upon and add one or two others. All of them are familiar enough in "analytic" philosophy, some of them being very generally diffused, some of them being especially associated with certain writers or their followers. We shall then be ready to offer an alternative.

—The topic of reality and the topic of language are inseparable, and ontological distinctions are therefore linguistic ones.

—Epistemological distinctions are linguistic ones, and the old discipline of epistemology (or rather, whatever is worth saving in it) must become a linguistic discipline; though language has an empirical obligation, it is best dealt with by assimilating it under the rubric of the semantics of either language$_1$ or language$_2$; the old epistemological foundational nisus should be domesticated within the safe confines of a language study.

—We live our rational and affective lives within a web of linguistic structures. As we gradually perfect one of them—that of science—we can use it to predict and control sensory experience, and so it is rational. As for sensory experience itself, it is otherwise enigmatic and subrational. Certain linguistic structures can be profitably and rationally considered apart from any connection with experience. Certain other linguistic structures are either emotional in their use or else downright nonsensical and useless.

—We live our rational and affective lives within a web, or under the net, of linguistic structures. We can use ordinary linguistic structures as a logical guide to ideal ones. These latter will isomorphically represent reality as it is, but we can not confront that reality directly. There is, however, something paradoxical about this claim; no matter, the paradox must be lived with.

—As we use our ordinary linguistic forms, which are not to be set aside in favor of ideal ones, they prescribe the forms phenomena must have. These forms permit a variety of linguistic games, but in none of them do we penetrate behind phenomena. Phenomena "represent" reality only insofar as they stand in place of it; we could not determine an isomorphism even if there should be one. We must be silent except as we use these linguistic forms for their proper purpose, which is that of speaking about those phenomena.

—All awareness is linguistic, so much so that we can not intelligibly express the relation between language and any extralinguistic reality it purports to express. Some of our linguistic representations prescribe the form of *prima facie* empirical "realities" that are in fact mere phe-

nomena that "represent" reality only by standing in place of it rather
than by being isomorphic with it; they thus misrepresent it. Other
linguistic representations—those that science is gradually perfecting—
give us as it really is an authentic reality that is not itself empirically
accessible.

—The intellectual enterprise consists in the playing of language-
games in accordance with rules inherent in each of them; if we are
dissatisfied with all of the games we can do no more than invent some
new one, which will then have its own rules. The forms of our various
language-games are determined by rules that are social in their origin
(alternatively, the forms are determined by an inner coherence evolved
in pragmatic social enterprises). These forms, in turn, determine how
the particulars of experience are to be taken up into a general linguistic truth. There is no other awareness of these particulars. So there is
no reality (thing-in-itself) alternative to the linguistic one. This version of the status of language, moreover, must be the right one, because to assert any other would be to assume that linguistic structures
were representative and that there was a thing-in-itself either adequately or inadequately represented by them. Nonetheless, some languages are better than others, and no doubt we shall one day learn to
speak an especially respectable one—the language$_1$, incorporating a
variety of languages$_2$, prescribed by an ideal science. That will be in-
structive, and it will also remove some present philosophical confusions. But we shall continue to play at other language-games anyway,
and some of these may edify us, even if they do not instruct us.

The observer of the consensus, even though mindful that it is a
consensus of empirical philosophers, is driven to the desperate conclusion—no doubt an overstatement, but one with some truth in it—that
the consensus holds that we can not express in language what is extralinguistically the case. And it is certainly not an overstatement to say
that the consensus holds that philosophy, at least, can not express in
language what is extralinguistically the case. What is lost in all this is
the naive, but powerful and salubrious, objective of managing to retain
in the very use of language an awareness of the extralinguistic reso-
nating in it; for of our rational awareness it is only a half-truth to say
that it is linguistic. Before all the professional authority of the consensus one can only stand, abashed but obdurate, in the naive conviction
that it is precisely the vocation of language to express what is extralinguistically the case—that this, moreover, is the vocation of the philosopher as well.

We must now see whether we can use the cryptofoundational consensus to suggest a new approach to the question of a philosophic foundation for knowledge. Although the consensus already provides a kind of foundation, I have not of course meant to imply that it is a sound one, and that its only defect is that it has simply not been acknowledged as a foundation. Beneath the obvious claim about language there lies a suppressed claim of a different sort that is in fact in conflict with the obvious one. "Suppressed" is not quite the precise word, for it suggests a deliberation about the matter that is no part of the consensus. Call it, then, a repressed one. It is a most important claim, and when it is made explicit it will be seen to undermine what the consensus says about language. When properly understood, it will turn out to be sound and to provide us with an unexpectedly rich foundational resource.

The repressed foundational claim is that we know what the status of language—its epistemic, its ontological status—in fact is; that we know what is the case about language; that we know what the truth of the matter is. The repressed claim is the one by virtue of which the cryptofoundational one is made. To put it another way, it is the *making* of these related cryptofoundational claims, but a claim-making that exempts itself from whatever strictures it lays down. It is the assertion of linguistic enclosure, the assertion that the life of the intellect consists in language-games, but an assertion excepting itself from the utter relativity to language thus asserted. As we saw, the general cryptofoundational claim takes many forms. But whichever form it takes, it exempts itself from whatever relativity it asserts. Each form asserts *what purports to be the status of language as it is.* Even the last, in its willing embrace of linguistic relativity (there *is* nothing else) purports to be undeceived, to be disillusioned at last, to say at last *what is the case about language*—purports to say, so to speak, what is extralinguistically the case about language, as much extralinguistically the case as it is extralinguistically the case that I am now writing with a pen, for all that I express that in language. It neither reports a sociolinguistic consensus about language-games, nor does it precisely urge us to create one (though, alas, it might help create one among professionals for a time); it asserts what it takes to be the case about language.

The repressed claim by virtue of which the cryptofoundational one is made is at odds with the latter. It is our real foundational claim, and as we now try to express it adequately—express it of course in language— we find that we are not in a linguacentric predicament at all; nor, for that matter, are we playing a language-game that, just because there is no alternative to it, is not a predicament. Our real foundation is not even, except indirectly, what is the case about language or anything else, but rather our capacity for (sometimes) *determining what is extralinguistically the case and expressing it in language.* This means that what is the case about language or anything else is not a linguistic matter except in the trivial sense that it is expressed in language. We may fail to notice this, and indeed cohort after cohort have emerged properly indoctrinated from the graduate schools and have thus failed to notice it; but once we *have* noticed it we can no longer discredit it.

The plausibility of all the versions of linguistic enclosure depends upon the fact that we are indeed sometimes enclosed in the only nontrivial sense in which we can be, namely, when we suppose we are rationally aware of a nonlinguistic reality when we are in fact contemplating something that has been mainly generated by the structure of our language—more precisely by some expression or group of expressions of our language$_1$, perhaps even a group that includes some language$_2$ or some part of one. And this defect probably goes back to one of our virtues, which, seen somewhat askew by Descartes, led him to the representative doctrine, and thus gave rise to a mistaken trend in foundational thought. (There are historical reasons why Descartes saw it this way, but they need not detain us.) The virtue I mean is our very fruitful capacity not only to be rationally and articulately aware in a first-order way of the extra-linguistic *as it is* but also to be rationally and articulately aware in a second-order way of linguistic structures as *they are,* when it suits us to turn our attention to them. (By talking of linguistic structures just here I do not mean to concede that every term of what used to be called second intention is *merely* linguistic; but they are *also* linguistic, and that will do for the present context.)

The lesson of all this is that it is the first function of language to express that which is extralinguistically the case—that it is the first function of language not to express what is an appearance in the sense of being a function of its own structure qua language rather than of the structure of what is the case. And surely our obsessiveness about language in this century can have no saner motive than the desire to escape from the distortions imposed upon us by some particular language-grid. To insist that we are sometimes in a linguistic enclosure is to insist that on some level we can escape from the predicament. And, though it is less obvious, to insist that we are always in a linguistic enclosure, or always playing language-games, is also to insist that on some level we escape from the enclosure, leave off playing language-games. Yet this is not to say that we are trying to circumvent language because we suppose there is a thing-in-itself there to be grasped by some more direct method. It is merely to say that the reigning consensus has put the emphasis in the wrong place. Awareness is linguistic only in this trivial sense: even in the most intensely *rational* kind of awareness, it is rationality grasping the nonlinguistic status of *that which is* that gives rise to the language in which the awareness completes itself. Neither representing what it expresses nor substituting for it, the language arises out of an awareness of the extralinguistic that persists in the unfolding of the language—persists both to justify the language and to exact more adequate language. This neglected—and we neglect it when we become obsessed with language—we are left with mere counters, and it is these we then think of ourselves as playing games with. And, to be sure, there are academic language-games and their players; Wittgenstein led a whole bemused generation of dons and professors in an elaborate and, I am sure, demanding one. Its conventions discouraged, among other things, any serious questioning of the metaphor of the language-game.

5

The True Foundational Task and
the Role of Language

The first function of language is to express what is extralinguistic, just as the first function of subjectivity is to be rationally aware of what is extrasubjective. That is the reason why we have been able to express in this century so many things about language—some interesting and true, and some not true but still interesting—for what is the case about language is extralinguistic. More generally, we can (sometimes) attain what is the case about the first intentions of subjectivity and we can (also sometimes) attain what is the case about the second intentions of subjectivity. Our extraordinary success in this century in building theoretic structures and then saying what is the case about them is an example of the second point. The notion that some theoretic structures—those I have called languages$_2$—are languages without qualification obscures the issue for us, for their first function is by no means to express what is extralinguistic, or for that matter to express anything at all, but rather to serve as things whose structures can be understood—things about whose structures one can understand, so to speak, what is extralinguistically the case.

But how could one express what is really the case about language₁— I mean the only one of our languages that is language without qualification, the one in which we must express what is the case about all the other "languages"—without standing outside language and somehow comparing the structure of it with some supposed independent reality? That is to say, how can we really have a foundational resource that not only we but also all language-obsessed cryptofoundationalists must rely upon? The question only reveals in another form the extraordinary power of the representative doctrine. Anyone who insisted on posing the question would be assuming that the only way we could express what is extralinguistically the case about language is by circumventing a difficulty that could only exist if the representative doctrine were true. And apparently one can labor under this assumption even while explicitly repudiating the representative doctrine.

The true foundational task (the one that we have come in sight of but have not yet begun to perform) is, first, noticing that we already have a foundation, and that the foundation is our capacity for knowing and expressing what is extralinguistically the case—even what is extralinguistically the case about what one tends to call, though the expression is surely too clumsy, the "relation" between language and reality; and, second, showing how this can be so by directing that capacity back upon itself. The true foundational task is subtle, but it can be characterized simply enough: we must make reflexive our capacity for knowing and expressing what is the case. Subtle or not, the very way we state it dismisses the representative theory, so that we need not suppose that the doing of it demands the doing of something else that only the truth of the representative theory could require. Language therefore comes into the task in no paradoxical way: we can not carry out the task without saying in language what is the case about the "relation" between language and reality, but to do that we need not stand outside language: we need only express in language what its "relation" to the extralinguistic is, a thing we can do provided that we have an empirical footing in that "relation." As for the basic capacity whose reflexive enhancement now concerns us, we have the cryptofoundational consensus on our side anyway in at least this sense, that it does rely upon the capacity even though it may have repressed the recognition of it.

So far I have been offering an argument designed to turn the lin-

guistic consensus against itself. It is time to move to an example—
time, that is, to begin to bring the capacity itself under reflexive scrutiny. I shall not be concerned immediately with a *prima facie* knowledge rich enough in what it is directed upon to bring us at once to our
ultimate objective—*prima facie* rational action. I want first to suggest
how our language use, as part of that capacity, can also be brought under reflexive scrutiny. Let me express something that is at least part of
what is the case just now as I sit writing. It is mid-June and I am in
Maine, sitting in a lofty studio made out of the upper part of a barn.
The sky is almost cloudless, the air dry and cool—I feel the stir of it up
and out through a window set high in the north peak. Through that
window I can see only the sky and the leaves of a tall oak tree. Through
a bank of south-looking windows—not so high as the north one but
still quite high—it is mostly sky I look at, together with the tops of
more distant trees. The whole character of the occasion is subtly different from what I remember it to have been in January in the same
place, the light, for instance, having then been qualified by the absence
of leaves and by the intensity of the reflection from the snow.

Let us call this kind of empirical and cognitive-linguistic engagement
with the real (or cognitive-linguistic grasp of what is the case) our *primary and simple cognitive engagement*. By this I mean that the engagement is (a) both empirical and rational, i.e., both sensory and expressed
in language; (b) not focused just upon language or upon entities—like
concepts, symbols, propositions, or statements—that could be regarded
as in some sense linguistic; (c) not reflexive. In describing it I was not
precisely exemplifying it, seeing that I had a reflexive point to make
about it, but I could have exemplified it in a nonreflexive way, and it is
that that I call primary and simple. Now, as we talk about that kind of
engagement, we are in what I shall call a *primary and reflexive cognitive engagement*. I retain the term "primary" to mark the continued
presence in the engagement of features (a) and (b). That is to say that
neither the structure of the language nor the function of language considered as an abstract and theoretical problem is the focus of primary-
reflexive cognitive engagement. I am still engaged with precisely what
I was engaged with before—what is the case about myself in the barn
chamber—except that I am not merely expressing myself about it but
also concerning myself reflexively with the nature of that engagement.
My reflection is therefore ultimately empirically rooted in precisely
the same situation as the original primary-simple engagement was.

What we shall now say, in primary-reflexive engagement, about our primary-simple engagement has of course its own interest, because it will purport to speak about what in another setting might gingerly be called the "relation" between language and reality. But because the primary-reflexive engagement shares all the features called primary, the foundational nature of this reflective exercise will be authentic only if the primary features that are now exercised in reflection are such as to warrant our being able to say in reflection what is the case about them. My expectation that this condition will be seen to be fulfilled is no self-confirmatory maneuver. It is really only another form of the re-pressed foundational claim we have already looked at. It is the pre-sumption of being able to know in some circumstances what is the case, which presumption is then applied to our present exercise. It is the presumption that the primary-simple engagement yields what is the case, and so the presumption also that what is the case *about* that pri-mary-simple engagement may be yielded by a reflexive exercise of the same nature with it and having the same ultimate empirical footing.

As we now carry out the primary-reflexive exercise, we find that al-though the words used in the primary-simple one form part of a lan-guage that is learned as to its basic vocabulary, syntax, and occasions of employment—a language in that sense not original to the one who uses it to express what is the case—they nevertheless emerge directly from what the awareness is an awareness of. They cling faithfully to it and are in a sense its product; they are not applied to it from the outside as words that are appropriate to what the awareness is found on other grounds to be. It is true that it would not *be* an awareness of what it *is* an awareness of unless it was thus expressed in language, but the lan-guage only completes and stabilizes what it emerges from. What was present there, but only present-to-be-experienced, becomes an empiri-cal-presence-to-reason, and this does not happen without language; but, on the other hand, the language does not so much effect this transition as does whatever effects the emergence of language as part of that transition. One does not entertain a set of propositions (or, if you pre-fer, statements) and then fit them to a situation in accordance with a set of semantic rules or in accordance with the less explicit rules of some language-game. It is only by primary-simple moments of awareness brought to linguistic completion that one is ever in a position to es-tablish (in secondary, or second-intention, cognitive engagements) dis-ciplines like the semantics of language$_1$ and language$_2$. And even then, the individual insights of these disciplines about what is the case will often be expressed first in primary-simple engagements upon which secondary engagements with linguistic entities are based. (Consider, for instance, the primary-simple engagement with tokens for symbols as someone engages in a secondary way in the business of formalizing semantics.) Language is a creation of rationality, though the contemporary obsession with language leaves so many of us with the notion that it is the other way round. Each rational agent potentially contributes to its growth, each stands for the creativity of reason with respect to language, even though the slow growth and cultural ubiquity of it sometimes makes the metaphor of an environment seem just right for it—a brilliant hit, that metaphor, but, for all that, still itself an instance of linguistic creativity, of a sudden awareness completed in a word. What emerges, at least sometimes, is what is the case, caught and made communicable by language, but no more a function of language than the latter is a function of our rational awareness of what is the case. So, although we may say that language about the weather and the quality of light in the studio completed and stabilized an awareness, making it an awareness of *what* it was an awareness of and thus making that rationally available, we may say with equal authority that the knower originated the particular fragment of language by expressing his awareness of what was the case, that is to say by completing it. And the mark of success is that what is the case—not the linguistic mediator and not some experience interposed as a phenomenal by-product of it—is what the completed awareness is an awareness of.

It is this feature of the primary-simple engagement—the feature in virtue of which language is in intimate union with what is the case, yet at the same time, and under the guidance of rationality, expressive of (revelatory of) what is the case—that makes our primary-reflexive engagement capable of so focusing upon the primary-simple one as to express what is the case about that, including what is the case about the role language plays in it. For the role language plays in the primary-reflexive one will be the same as what reflection has found to be the case in the primary-simple one, because reflection will be of the same nature as the simple case, being nothing more than the primary-simple function turned reflexively upon itself. By the same token, the primary-reflexive engagement will have as its footing in experience precisely the primary-simple engagement; and, being no more (once again) than that engagement reflexively employed, will therefore share all the sensory directness with which the primary-simple one is experientially based. "Sensory directness" does not imply something *experienced by* sensation; it implies only something that, although given by way of sensation, is only given-to-be-experienced-in-rational-awareness, some-thing therefore given-to-be-linguistically-expressed. What is the case about language in the primary-simple engagement will therefore be part of what the primary-reflexive one is engaged with by the same sensory root. And as the primary-simple one was "direct" in the sense that, although a "mental" enough function, its mentality consisted in transcending mentality rather than terminating in mentality, so the primary-reflexive one will be direct also. As we had no "mental content" in one-to-one correspondence with the real in the primary-simple one, so we have no "reflexive mental content" in one-to-one correspondence with *its* real. No more than in the simple case will the reflexive one be in either a subjective predicament or a linguacentric predicament.

But it is only in the reflexive mode that all this emerges; and as the reflexive mode, so exercised, is not habitual and routine in the sense that the simple one often is, the peculiar creativity and autonomy of reason with respect to completing fresh awareness in new-ordered language only becomes apparent in its primary-reflexive engagement. That is to say that the completion in language, by virtue of our primary-reflexive engagement, of our awareness of the primary-simple one is so much more patently an origination than the more habitual primary-simple one that the originative character of the latter is confirmed. This led me in an earlier book to speak of a foundational effort of this kind as *radically originative reflection.*

6

An Interpersonal Reflection on Our Prima Facie
Knowledge of Rational Action

I have made this foundational point in as simple a setting as I could contrive that would still do justice to the peculiar subtlety and simplicity of the *prima facie* rational act I call radically originative reflection. We need now to make essentially the same point in a setting rich enough to warrant our eventually directing our attention to rational action itself. We turn, then, to direct a primary-reflexive look at the *prima facie* knowledge we have of rational action and of the world in which it takes place. To that *prima facie* knowledge we can attribute a structure analogous to the simpler example of primary-simple engagement we have just looked at, for much of what we know in that *prima facie* way will itself be an example of primary-simple engagement.

Since the reflection we direct upon it will be originative in the sense
just described, we shall not suppose that what we are to look at will be
concretely present as the common objects of experience are, or even
our actions are, to *prima facie* knowledge. The presence to us in reflection of *prima facie* knowledge itself will depend upon the presence to
prima facie knowledge of these things it is concerned with in a primary-
simple sense. Our reflexive "looking" will depend upon what we may
cautiously call linguistic creativity—cautiously because the finding of
appropriate language is more truly the outcome of the awareness than
the awareness is the outcome of the appropriate language. In that marvelous autobiographical essay "A Sketch of the Past," completed just
four months before her death, Virginia Woolf speaks of how sometimes words become transparent, ceasing to be words and becoming so
intensified that one seems "to experience them; to foretell them as if
they developed what one is already feeling."[24] To take up and alter
something so delicately and justly said has the air of sacrilege, so I venture only the remark that she is talking about feeling and our awareness
of it, and that the point holds for awareness of other things as well;
what she says elsewhere in that essay about "moments of being" bears
this out. We sometimes do foretell our words as if they developed what
we are already aware of, so that the coming of the words is the completion of the awareness. Linguistic creativity is not merely the happy
falling into place of words in accordance with rules, with a new-
structured experience, or awareness, being created by the new word
order or a preexisting one being transformed by it in subtle ways. Linguistic creativity is not definable by reference to language alone. We
are not already "seeing" something just by virtue of what linguistic
structures happen to be, and so we are not modifying what we "see"
by simply modifying those structures.

The traditional metaphor of sight, which I deliberately chose in the
conviction that it brings with it no necessary commitment to some
theory of either mental or linguistic representation, articulates what is
at least in part an empirical issue. Not, of course, that we already "see"
something with full rational adequacy before we find the appropriate
language; it is merely that the perfecting of the "sight," the achievement of greater faithfulness to what is the case, is also the finding of
the language. For at least the kind of originative effort we are now discussing, linguistic creativity is neither fitting words to what is wholly
seen to be the case before the words are found, nor seeing what is the
case by virtue of using words hit upon in some merely linguistic con-

text. The character of the effort is far from being as merely receptive as the expression "faithfulness to what is the case" suggests. Although we can not do without some traditional empirical categories, neither can we do without some traditional rational ones. Finding the right language is no manipulative ingenuity, not even one carried on in concrete involvement in the direct empirical confrontation I have in mind. Reason in its function as lord of language unfolds a power for which the traditional notion of innateness is at least a partly apposite metaphor—apposite because the standard for the elaboration of the language is not given by what is passively received from what we are trying to be faithful to; partly so because the rearrangement and indeed new making of words is not merely a following of already actual internal rules but also a laying down or at least a discovery of rules.

These rational and empirical aspects are intimately joined in our primary-simple engagement with the real. As to the rational side, linguistic creativity does not have, or at least need not have, a merely rational-linguistic outcome: engaged in it, we do not produce a merely formal inhabitant either of some supposed merely "mental" ontological region or of some contemporary substitute for it, like logical space. So we need not think of ourselves as using such formal structures to cope with an experience that is epistemically more primordial than our grasp of these structures; nor need we suppose, on the other hand, that we have our experience by virtue of formal structures whose constitutive power "makes" it for us. As to the empirical side—that is, the empirical *intent* of our primary-simple engagement—we are not trying to be faithful to something whose status as what is the case can be captured in terms that are only empirical-sensory. What is the case about what our *prima facie* knowledge is directed upon in its (primary-simple) employment is that its presence is a rational-empirical presence yielding a joint rational-empirical satisfaction.

Our present reflexive procedure—our primary-reflexive engagement—purports to be in that same kind of rational-empirical engagement with our primary-simple one. It therefore purports to place us in the rational-empirical presence of the latter, and to yield a like joint satisfaction signalized by the linking of the term "rational" with "empirical" or with "awareness." In due course, having assured ourselves in reflection of the authority of primary-simple engagement and of the creativity in *it* that we are now trying to employ reflexively, we shall be in a position to turn our primary-simple glance upon *prima facie* rational action itself. But our present reflection on our (primary-simple) *prima facie* knowledge must go on for a while with a somewhat more complex example than the one so far used.

Prima facie knowledge is by no means concerned only with action. As it is merely knowledge uncriticized by either science or philosophy, it is what they presuppose to get their enterprises under way. It therefore excludes from its attention nothing whatever that is accessible to direct or indirect experience, and it is defined not so much by its objects as by the way it apprehends them. It is concerned, then, with the world at large and everything in it, and action comes under its scope as just one item in that world like any other. As it is prescientific and prephilosophic, it has serious deficiencies from the points of view of those disciplines; but as both of them have developed out of it, it seems that in an important sense it is basic to them.

In this century a number of names have been proposed for it. We have looked at some of them already in discussing the second of the two attitudes that in their confrontation signalize the need for a foundational effort. We may rehearse them now in terms of the "worlds" they refer to: the world of common sense, the world of the natural standpoint, the life-world, the world of the manifest image, the world of concrete experience, and the world of ordinary language. I am not proposing that we should rely on *prima facie* knowledge just as it is before science, philosophy, and the arts reshape it for us; this reflection is designed to produce a profound change in it. But with that reservation, there is this much to be said for those several labels, that they remind us that there is a cognitive basis rational agents have in common before they undertake any special discipline.

It is defined, first of all, by what we ordinarily experience of what is there to be experienced; and as we all have the same sensory modalities, it is the same for all of us. Our experience is sense-saturated, body-mediated, and even a phenomenalism that insists that the physical world has the epistemic status of a construction does so only to point out what it takes to be the merely *prima facie* status of experience, not to deny that we have it so. But our natural language is also generally supposed to contribute to the definition of it, for although experience need not on some particular occasion find completion in words, it must have been so completed at some time and in principle be completable again if it is to be an experience of a certain thing. More precisely, the experience becomes the experiential feature of *knowledge* only when one can characterize it in this way. In *prima facie* knowledge there is always a union of the particularity of sense and body and the generality of articulated, symbol-mediated rationality; and, in that rational-empirical synthesis, understanding is a way of experiencing and experiencing is a kind of understanding. This we take for granted even if we at once fall into philosophical dispute about just how sensation and the formal carriers of our engagement with it intertwine to contribute to its definition. Here there are difficulties, because our language use—taking "language" in the broadest sense—differs remarkably from individual to individual; it would appear that *prima facie* knowledge must accordingly differ from person to person. Nonetheless the general structure laid down by the way that sensation and the formal carriers of our engagement with it intertwine presumably does not differ.

The reader and I are of course now reflecting on our (primary-simple) *prima facie* knowledge. We are not merely enjoying it or taking it for granted, and so we are not completely subject to its habitual sway. Still, we are presumably exemplifying it in its main lines even as we try to see it clearly for what it is—that is, reflection itself (primary-reflexive engagement) must rely on the same intertwining of bodily sense with the formal carriers of our engagement with it, even though as one reflects upon such subtle matters the focus of sensation on this or that physical object becomes less important than the general background of the world, some region of it, and one's body that it now supplies.

Examples of *prima facie* knowledge of this kind are not hard to find, so long as we do not press the argument far enough to try to settle the ontological significance of what we seem to know. The one we now turn to is of the same order as the one given in the previous section, but this time we shall press on with the example in a way our use of the term "world" calls for. Now, looking through the lower right pane of the window on my left (a different place, a different time) I see a part of an old granite building: across the middle of the region outlined by the pane marches a corbeled course of block that marks the beginning of the second story; in the cold clear February light an intricate tracery of bare ivy covers the stone, fanning out from the low left where, unseen, its roots lie, upwards and to the right, growing more delicate as one's eye moves away from the root; there are two Gothic windows, a larger one below, a smaller above the corbeled course, each fitted with small panes of colored glass; shadows of an oak tree run across the ivy in counterpoint like a heavier ivy; one branch of the oak itself intrudes across the top of the pane I look through.

Though I took the whole complex I have just attended to as an example, any item in the complex would have done as well—say one square of glass in the lower Gothic window. So will the whole scene outside my own window as I now take in what can be seen through all twelve panes. So will my more general awareness of my world—everything that goes out indefinitely from the place in the room where I sit writing. And this more general awareness would have been invoked even if I had been intent on only one of those items just mentioned. This suggests a "background" feature for which "world" may not in the end be the best term. So too, finally (though never forgetting entirely the "background") will my articulate and intelligent awareness of myself in the act of writing—a body-mediated awareness of the physical act, but also an awareness and understanding of what I write as I write it. The chief feature of all these examples—provided always that we concede that it is a *prima facie* feature—is the union, not always actual but at least potential, of experiential presence (not the presence of experience but the presence of something of which we have experience) and rational articulation. What we characterize with the help of language is, or can be, experientially present as we characterize it: just so the granite, ivy-covered wall was present in a *prima facie* sense as the *prima facie* understanding expressed in language completed it. (The possibility of error here is real, but irrelevant: any correction of an error—"That is not a wall outside; it's a reflection in your window of that picture just behind you"—would be in the same mode, would exhibit the same *prima facie* characteristics.) *Prima facie* knowledge of this sort is a primary-simple one, except when directed upon our own action, in which case it is primary-reflexive, as we shall see in the next chapter.

There is also a secondary engagement, which we shall consider in a moment, and so it will be helpful to note here that both the primary-simple and the primary-reflexive one establish a "background" for the secondary one. It is the same "background" already mentioned, and as it is of some importance, let us now see whether we can refine our grasp of the nature of primary engagement so as to make it clear just how important the "background" is. "Primary," the reader will recall, meant (a) both empirical and rational, i.e., both sensory and expressed in language; (b) not focused just upon language or upon entities—like concepts, symbols, propositions, or statements—that could be regarded as in some sense linguistic. We shall now call both kinds of primary engagement *knowledge in the mode of primary rational-empirical presence*, and we shall say that it takes place by virtue of a *rational-empirical synthesis* having a unity that is best defined by noting that even though two poles, a rational and empirical one, may be abstracted from it, neither of them is what the synthesis is directed upon. The experiential pole is not what we have experience of (are aware of). It is rather the sensory-bodily feature by virtue of which there is a here-and-now, particular feature to our experience of whatever we are intent upon (whether a granite block or one of our own acts). The synthesis itself is not directed towards something that might properly be called experience but rather towards what we mean *to have experience of*. The other pole is that of formal-linguistic-conceptual articulation, but it is not what our rationality terminates in; it is not what we are rationally aware of. Bound in intimate union with the experiential pole, it is nothing more than our rationality intent upon what that union holds it to, so that the here-and-now is not grasped in the abstract version of a *mere* here-and-now. To put it another way, by virtue of the rational pole, the particular, present in some here-and-now, is present as one particular of many that may occur in many here-and-nows; and, in being so present, it is present as one of a Many that are all equally rooted in a One. Primary rational-empirical presence is in this sense the presence of the Many in the One and of the One exemplified in the Many. Out of this synthesis there flows the conceptual-linguistic; its ultimate nonpragmatic telos is its completion of an awareness having this One-Many feature to it. Presence, needless to say, is the correlate of awareness.

Exercising as we are now the primary-reflexive counterpart of *prima facie* knowledge (for we have by no means left the world of what was seen out the window as we acted to talk about it), we can see that those two poles are indeed abstract. We do this by noting that if we were to focus upon either one of them, we could do so only by considering it against the "background" of what we are now focused upon. Let us call this a secondary engagement, noting, by way of anticipation, that it includes but is not confined to what used to be called second intentions. If we were to try to isolate, for instance, some prototype of the empirical, some purely particular, purely bodily sensation, something quite without "rational" import, whatever we then focused on (say our awareness, by way of our eyes, of some presented shade of green) would (a) itself then be the object of a rational-empirical syn-

thesis; and (b) be available only against a "background" like the one
we have so far been considering, which "background," though not focused upon, would still be *present as* a "background," demanding by
the very character of its own presence that the other should be regarded as an abstraction. If, on the other hand, we try to isolate the
rational-formal-linguistic pole, we soon find ourselves entertaining (in
second intention) some theoretic structure or other—perhaps the bare
structure of a language$_2$ whose symbols are not yet interpreted, perhaps
some portion of syntactic or semantic theory. That in turn will (a) itself be the object of a rational-empirical synthesis (we shall be looking
at the symbols and giving some rational account of them as we do so);
and (b) be available only against a "background" like the one we have
so far been considering, which will still be *present as* a "background,"
demanding by the very character of its own presence that the other
should be regarded as an abstraction (all this might happen in a room,
with blackboard and chalk to hand).

In other words, the empirical and the rational poles do not have any
independent authority; whatever authority they do have is within
some rational-empirical synthesis in which something is not only rationally-empirically present but also has its presence judged and assessed. The synthesis may be called a rational *experiencing of* something that then purports to be present as such, for it is not directed
towards something that might properly be called experience but rather
towards what we mean *to have experience of.* The notion of presence
is the correlate of this "realistic" reinterpretation of the notion of experience. All this emerges only in the primary-reflexive mode, as now;
but when it does, it is magisterial in its import: (a) supposed presence
is always presence brought about by virtue of a rational-empirical synthesis having a unity that is inviolable in this sense, that one of its
poles can not be merely experienced and the other can not be merely
rationally entertained; (b) this is true of both primary and secondary
rational-empirical presence; (c) the latter is always present against the
"background" of the former.

In reflection, we perform and take note of this foundational task.
Caught up in it, we can no longer see the speculative-empirical cycle
of science, in which we shuttle back and forth between theoretical
structures and some version of experience in which these are brought
to account, as a sensible pragmatic substitute for a foundation. These
two poles of the speculative-empirical enterprise, like the more abstract poles of the synthesis we have just been considering, will from

our present perspective also be rationally-empirically present and thus
available for comparison with the rational-empirical presence of that
towards which our foundational effort has been tending. And they will
demand to be so compared. One obvious result of such a comparison
is that the (secondary) formal-conceptual-linguistic feature of science
here marked by the word "speculative" has a good deal more of construction, of model-*making*, of theory-*building*, indeed, of representa-
tion-*making*, in it than we have thought to find in the rational pole of
our primary engagement with the real.

   The presence of my window, the granite wall, the act of writing,
"the world," was a presence experienced by way of the mediation of
the senses and the body in general, but as I characterized those things
in language it was a presence not to senses and body but to my *rational*
experience, or awareness. From the side of senses and body this means
that their influence permeates both the meanings of our words and
the structure of our language in subtle ways that Kant perhaps first
gave us a hint of; and at the same time supports the appropriateness of
just the ordered words we use about such things as the wall, the ivy,
our own actions, and "the world." But normally we are not even trying
to attend to the sensory-bodily as such. That pole of the synthesis
merely holds the rational one to the task of saying *what* is present to it
(as *rational* awareness) in this here-and-now. The universals problem
is suddenly relevant, in close company, as it always is, with that of the
One we were speaking of awhile ago. But it is not a problem that need
occur to someone who, unreflexively in the grip of *prima facie* knowledge, attends comfortably to a presence qualified by both particularity
and generality without inquiring further as to precisely what that
means.
   Whoever disagrees with all this will probably at least agree that
things like the wall, the ivy, oneself in the act of writing, "the world,"
are simultaneously present to senses and intelligence in a primary way
in which a quark, a proton, an ion passing through a membrane can
not be present to us, even though we might manage to characterize
things of that kind as theoretic structures more sharply than we can
characterize wall, ivy, the act of writing, and "the world." Moreover,
as in the course of the speculative-empirical cycle we bring such theoretical structures to empirical account, it will not be the secondary ra-

tional-empirical presence of theoretic proton or ion we shall appeal to but rather the primary rational-empirical presence of something else that belongs to the world of the wall, ivy, and the act of writing.

The effect of this reflection, carried on now in privacy but in principle something the reader can be a party to, is paradoxical: it is to see *prima facie* knowledge as it is in its innocence before philosophic reflection or theory of any kind has corrupted it or otherwise transformed it; but to see it so and articulately understand it is already to transform it. The innocence we look for is moreover an abstraction, for rational agents are so given to reflection that *prima facie* knowledge quite free of reflexive taint is probably to be found only in those who have not yet reached the use of reason. We had therefore best think of ourselves as trying to strip off any crust of previous reflection or theory that may hide the true status of *prima facie* knowledge from us. Our goal is thus an immodest one: to see *prima facie* knowledge as it really is and, by seeing it so and articulating it so, to transform it.

Knowledge in the mode of primary rational-empirical presence seems at first glance to be knowledge of some entity or group of entities, their properties or qualities being present only in virtue of the presence of the entities themselves. It is a feature of *prima facie* knowledge that Aristotle evidently felt at home with. But the world known in this way is by no means an assemblage of particulars, as the disturbing intrusion of that ancient notion of the One has already suggested. There is a general character to primary rational-empirical presence that is just as salient as the particular character of the entities that are present. It is, however, difficult to come to grips with, because reflection or theory has intervened to hide it from us behind a thicket of reasoning in terms of the universals problem. This expresses a consensus about generality that appears to transcend disagreements about whether there are universals. Let me first state the consensus as it might be stated by someone who believed in the existence of universals. (a) Our rational capacities, which involve, on the one hand, symbolic structures instantiated in physical shapes and sounds and, on the other, entities like ideas and concepts, which are in some sense mental (or, if not that, then linguistic), put us in touch with entities which, while "particular" in the sense that there are many of them, each distinguishable from the others (as justice is distinguishable from courage), have nonetheless a mode of existence that is general or universal; they are not really particulars in the way in which physical things are. (b) Such entities form a realm characterized by relations between them. (c) Any general feature of the concrete world (i.e., of what I am discussing in terms of primary rational-empirical presence) must consist in the relations between particulars and entities of this sort, for the particulars of the concrete world are merely particular—they have no generality or universality inherent in any of them or in their assemblage. Even the generality of a symbol would have to be so interpreted, for any shape or sound we entertain as a symbol is a mere particular like any other, even though taking it qua symbol is also taking it as a member of a family of shapes or sounds any one of which would do as well. Nominalists will of course give a different account of all this, since they will recognize no entities having a mode of existence that is nonparticular, but for them also any "generality" inherent in the concrete world will still have to consist in relations between concrete particulars and such "linguistic" particulars as bound variables. I do not wish to presume to solve the universals problem in passing; all this is merely intended to point out that both Platonists and nominalists overlook a different sort of generality. It is one of our tasks in this reflection to try to draw attention to it.

Our language, taken in the broadest sense of language$_1$ and all the other symbolic systems (including languages$_2$) embedded in it, ramifies in entities that together may be called the formal outcome, or completion, of (primary) rational-empirical presence. The intimate intertwining of linguistic items with sensation and the body has already been noticed. In completing the presence of a world of particulars they also complete the presence of something that is not present precisely as a particular is. I do not mean just that they help make universals present—those things that have been called Forms, Ideas, Essences, Eternal Objects, Archetypes and the like—though there are still formidable reasons for thinking that there are such things. I mean that whatever position we take up on the existence of universals, the formal things that complete presence do more than help make actual the presence of a vast multiplicity of particulars and particular "universal" items. I suggest that any particular entity and any multiplicity of such entities can be present to us in the mode of rational-empirical presence only as an instance of a more general presence whose ontological status is not that of a complex of Platonic Forms or of any other version of universals the reader might prefer. Its status is rather one for which such metaphors as field, ground, or environment are more appropriate.

It is against this field or ground that all particulars—including all particular "universal" entities (if there are any)—are present, and their presence carries with it the intimation that they are detachable from it only by an effort of abstraction that does some violence to what is thus detached.

The oldest name for the field or ground is Being, although it is also known as nature, the nature of things, reality, or even, as we were calling it earlier, "the world." Apprehended at the level of the *prima facie* knowledge we are concerned with, it is taken more vaguely than that. Whether apprehended at that level or at the present reflexive one, it carries with it the further intimation that, whatever it is, it offers some ontological support for all the entities that are instances of it; but surely it is only an intimation. One more intimation qualifies its presence: revealing itself to rationality in some body-mediated here-and-now, it intimates that it can not be wholly present just here and now and in that sense transcends the mediation of the body. Yet it still seems appropriate to speak of its rational-empirical *presence*, because for all its utter generality, for all its transcendence of any here-and-now in which we respond to it, we do nevertheless respond to it through the mediation of sense and body, just as we do to particulars. The truth of its presence is manifest through all our particular errors; we can express it with clarity and certainty even when we are thoroughly confused about what particular things are manifest against its background. If we do choose to express it explicitly, the best formula we can use is an old one. Parmenides, despite all his overstatements about the deceptions of sensation, about the illusory character of multiplicity and becoming, said it once and for all: "It is." Its ancient name is Being, or sometimes the One; we spoke of it under the latter name a little earlier. It is not only the Being, or One, of Parmenides, Plato, and Plotinus—if I may neglect many ancient and subtle disputes to put the matter in this way. It is also Einstein's Old One, and in this guise and many related guises it has been of great importance for science. We can still call it Being or the One, and can still say of it "It is," even when we are quite uncertain about how to interpret some particular that is present in some here-and-now as an instantiation of it; and quite uncertain too about such matters as whether there "really are" universals. As to the latter point, when we do turn in secondary engagement to consider our linguistic instruments, it seems clear that a host of supposed universals press for our attention. The least they can be are refractions of the universality of the Old One itself; and from the present perspective that is as concrete as any particular we attend to.

Prima facie knowledge of this kind is a social achievement, and the level at which we find particular things rationally-empirically present in this way against the background of what is not a particular is an intersubjective one. We inhabit it together, and it is quite impossible to detach either our awareness of it or our assessment of the powers we exercise in being aware of it from our awareness of our fellows and from theirs of us. Language bears the mark of this intercourse, and this means that there is nothing we can come to know that is not qualified by it. This aspect of *prima facie* knowledge is absolutely indefeasible. No reflexive turn can take us out of it, even though other philosophers besides Descartes have thought that it might do so. Even if one should refrain from overt speech and writing and retire into that inner forum that since the time of Augustine has seemed an appropriate alternative—it certainly still seems so to contemporary phenomenologists—one would not really surmount that aspect of it. When, as a subject, one retires into oneself, one finds that the intrasubjective bears the marks of the intersubjective, for in reflection one talks to oneself and hears what one says. It is not entirely wide of the mark to say that the intrasubjective is in some measure the internalization of the intersubjective, although to say so by no means lays bare all the secrets of subjectivity.

As to subjectivity itself, it is almost needless to observe that in our present reflection we have little temptation to think of it in a Cartesian fashion or for that matter in the fashion of phenomenology. Whatever this reflection or some other should decide about the ontological status of the subject, it is correlate with its object or objects—correlate with rational-empirical presence—and not before it. Anything we know about the *I* in the reflexive mode of knowledge bears the mark of the dependence of the self-knowledge of the subject on knowledge of what is rationally-empirically present in its primary-simple engagement. That there is indeed an *I* potentially correlate with any *prima facie* knowledge of an object, of a world, of Being, seems beyond dispute, although the ontological significance of it is, as always, a matter for argument. That one must move towards philosophical reflection and hence away from a merely *prima facie* knowledge to give it explicit attention seems also obvious, but from that reflexive standpoint it seems reasonable to claim that the *I* was there, present but unnoticed, even before the reflexive turn. From the reflexive point of view, the objection that for "I think" one might better substitute "it thinks" or "there is thinking going on" does not touch the fundamental issue, but merely reminds us that, once we leave primary-simple (nonreflexive) *prima facie* knowledge, the significance of what we normally speak of by using the first person singular becomes a difficult question for philosophy.

But for action as known by the agent (as I might now attend to myself in the act of writing) subjectivity takes on an especial importance. Insofar as we attend at all to subjectivity while we are attending to some object other than our own action, there appears to be a distinctness of the knowing subject from the thing known, so much so that if we are to attend faithfully to the granite block or the ivy, we must not allow an interest in subjectivity itself to distract us. When, however, we attend in the course of action to our own rational agency, subjectivity is included in what we are aware of, even though it need not be the focus of our attention. What it is that is thus included, other than that it is indeed the subjectivity (consciousness, awareness) of the agent that takes itself to be acting, remains somewhat vague. To say, "I am aware that I am writing with a pen" and to be right about it is so far to establish nothing very conclusive about what precisely it means to be an *I*. We shall not attempt to turn our reflexive concern in that direction until the next chapter. Meanwhile, it would appear from these considerations that it is only from the point of view of ourselves as agents that we can truly know what it means to act rationally. The interdependence of the agent's subjectivity with the intersubjective world will qualify our self-knowledge, but recognizing another subject or treating some aspect of oneself in inner dialogue as though it were another subject is still not to put oneself, except imaginatively, in the place of some other subject. *Prima facie* knowledge of one's own rational action in reflection includes an awareness of one's own particular subjectivity more than our knowledge of anything else in some sense overt does. It is a misunderstanding of this point that so often leads to the proliferation of items like intentions, volitions, and mental events in philosophical discourse about action and mind. Our ability to do without them is, however, no argument against the existence of subjectivity in the sense defended here.

There is one very obvious thing about *prima facie* knowledge that

has sometimes been used to mount an attack on its authenticity. It is
that some of its most important features are of a certain scale of magnitude, and that their ontological status seems to depend upon that.
The world we live in by way of direct experience contains our fellow
human beings, other animals, trees, houses, and the like. Our own rational actions are not merely macroscopic; indeed, if we include in
them only our peripheral awareness of action, we include already something of subjectivity, and subjectivity is surely more than a merely
macroscopic thing. But if not *merely* macroscopic, they are *also* macroscopic in a sense congruent with the things just mentioned. Our sensory modalities are attuned to that scale, and things like molecules,
atoms, and subatomic entities on the one hand and galaxies on the
other we experience less immediately if at all. Because much of the
success of science has depended upon the analysis of things known in
the mode of rational-empirical presence in terms of the microstructures
upon which they in some sense depend, it is often argued that the
things that can be known in a *prima facie* sense are merely functions of
physical scale: the true operative powers are in the microstructures, it
is said, and the macrostructures of the human scale are merely appearances, inauthentic to the degree that they purport to be anything else.

It will be wise to defer serious discussion of that argument until
chapter 5. But it should be said at once that the notion of magnitude
does not in itself do justice to most of the important features of *prima
facie* knowledge. My awareness of the speech of my friends, for instance, depends upon a feature of things that is available only at a certain level of magnitude—the level at which sound waves exist—but my
awareness is not wholly elucidated by noticing that it can take place
only at a certain level of magnitude and that the physical events at that
level become more intelligible when we understand something about
the molecular structure of air that underlies it. Certainly its ontological status is not discredited just because the physical processes are elucidated in this way. So with the recognition of some person and the
feeling of affection or even of intense love that might go with it. Human recognition and love do indeed take place at a certain level of
magnitude, and we do not even observe them when we observe their
infrastructures; but we do not wholly clarify their natures by making
this point, still less discredit them.

We can not complete a reflection about *prima facie* knowledge without noticing again that the whole enterprise depends upon a series of
prima facie reflexive rational actions. It is acts of that kind that in this

chapter purport to give us a more adequate knowledge of the structure
of *prima facie* knowledge. They themselves therefore purport to be instances of knowing; and so the entire content of the next chapter bears
upon this one: rational action as we shall see it and express it in the
rational-empirical synthesis of that one is the key to any advance we
may have made in this one by acting reflexively to focus upon *prima
facie* knowledge. The present primary-reflexive cognitive acts are not,
of course, instances of *prima facie* knowing as it is before reflection but
transformations of it from within, for they claim both to uncover the
principles that are always at work in *prima facie* knowledge and to exemplify those principles in the very act of uncovering them.

A turn in the labyrinth of reflection has made the source of the improvement of our grasp of *prima facie* knowledge part of the subject
matter of that grasp, for in reflection we are in the presence of heightened and transformed powers that were exercised routinely and without
self-consciousness in *prima facie* knowledge. We shall make the same
turn in the labyrinth in the next chapter, where our most momentous
examples of action will be cognitive ones, and reflexively cognitive
ones at that. Just here we find that reflexive actions of the kind we are
now engaged in provide our best examples of our power to achieve
knowledge in the mode of primary rational-empirical presence—the
mode we attribute to *prima facie* knowledge. Let us not shirk the most
sinuous turn of the labyrinth: radically originative reflection upon
prima facie knowledge puts us in the rational-empirical presence of
our own reflexive cognitive powers.

That reflection itself becomes part of our subject matter, whether
the theme of the reflection is action itself or our knowledge of it, is
one more instance of the involvement of subjectivity with the topic of
action. As the reflection is qualified by the intersubjective situation in
which it takes place, it is no Cartesian subjectivity. But it is nonetheless still subjectivity: the rational pole self-consciously engaged with
the empirical, laboring under the self-imposed task of so determining
and articulating its engagement there as to make the rational experience that emerges from it more adequate to what is the case about itself no less than what it is directed upon.

IV

The Conditions Fulfilled:
A Reflexive Vindication

1

The Primary-Reflexive Nature
of the Enterprise

The reflection of this chapter is directed upon rational action itself, and not, like the last one, on the nature of our *prima facie* knowledge of action and of other things. But it depends upon the findings of that chapter. For one thing, *prima facie* knowledge was there shown to rest on a primary engagement in the mode of rational-empirical presence and to be capable of intensification in that same mode. A primary-reflexive exercise directed upon the primary-simple one purported not only to make clear the grounds of such an intensification, but to exemplify that intensification itself. It will be recalled that the primary-reflexive exercise merely turned the resources of primary-simple engagement to a reflexive purpose. We now try to effect just that intensification as we turn our *prima facie* cognitive glance upon *prima facie* rational action. For another thing, though we are here concerned not so much with the nature of knowledge as with the nature of action, our theme is *rational* action. The *prima facie* cognitive attention directed upon it is thus necessarily reflexive. The effort to intensify our glance upon action will therefore be by way of a primary-reflexive engagement, and the outcome hoped for will be the more adequate rational-empirical presence to itself of the rational agent. The chapter is designed to intensify and authenticate that presence. Our circle, of course, remains ineluctable: our *via media* relies on *prima facie* action; our intended reflection will be a *prima facie* rational action; and whatever transformation we bring about, we shall never stand outside action to know it.

The emphasis on what purports to be concretely present and to be known in that way means that we are very far from imagining, inventing, designing, or otherwise constructing theories about action, theories that would then be used to interpret action and to stand or fall in what would be a kind of empirical confrontation with it. Still, I would not go so far as to characterize the enterprise by way of a sturdy *hypotheses non fingo*. We do not undertake any rational enterprise of a philosophic kind without some burden of theory in the broadest sense. We vary in our grasp of science, of history, of the structure of philosophic arguments, of epistemology, of methodology; and one does not embark on a topic like responsibility without having one's capacity for rational discourse, either with oneself or with someone else, qualified by one's own grasp of such matters. But this reflection is at any rate not based on the assumption that our experience of rational action is something not only obvious and habitual but settled and unalterable as well—something that is a permanent empirical bar to which we can bring for judgment theories about it, in the way in which scientific theories are brought to the bar of common sense even though they themselves may be very far from common sense and may even seem to convict it of inexactitude. That supposition is appropriate to an attempt to explain rational action with the help of theory but not to our present effort to make its empirical presence more adequate by intensifying our rational (formal, linguistic) grasp of it. We wish to see whether seeming to act rationally is what it purports to be, and so we tentatively accept our *prima facie* grasp of it as a not entirely inadequate way of experiencing that feature of the real we now intend to make our experience more adequate to. Some alteration in the experience now called the experience of *prima facie* action is therefore envisioned: at least enough to allay the suspicion that it is a mere seeming.

The possibility that a rational transformation should bring about a transformation in awareness, or experience, should not be implausible in an age in which it is widely taken for granted that the character of our experience is not independent of the formal web in which it is rationally articulated. It is a pity that an age that seems to understand this so well has elected to do so by way of such metaphors as world-making, creation of symbolic forms, and paradigm shift. They are valuable metaphors for calling attention to the constructive power of rationality; but they also distract us from a more important feature of it:

the power to so articulate what is the case that our rational awareness more adequately approximates what is indeed the case. Overstatement of the prerogatives of that power in terms of the traditional notion of a rational (intellectual) intuition is probably to blame for the widespread reluctance to take it seriously.

From the viewpoint that takes science as our cognitive ideal, it may well appear that we are about to embark on a variant of an appeal to common sense, to ordinary language or, to what Husserl called the natural standpoint, at one stage of his career (when he wished to suspend it), and the life-world at a later stage (when he wished to emphasize its importance).[1] That would be so if we were prepared to stay lodged complacently in the ineluctable circle as we have found it, content to accept something less than the rigor and the detailed amplitude of science in exchange for the comfort that goes with the familiarity and the security of supposing ourselves to be autonomous coadjutors of our own and the world's fate. But the possibility that rational action is authentic is also the possibility that an intensified reflexive effort of the agent in the primary rational-empirical mode of our present *prima facie* knowledge might so perfect our articulated experience of rational action that the authenticity of ontic responsibility would be manifest.

If a reflexive effort of that kind is in order, as the investigations of the last chapter suggest, it is unlikely to be successful if it should be directed towards some mute and primordial grasp of ourselves in action, some pretheoretical or preformal assurance that could then be set against the intricacies of theory. We can not usefully intensify our *prima facie* knowledge of ourselves in action except in a rational atmosphere pervaded by the formality of concepts and language. With the reservations expressed in the last chapter, our enterprise is meant to be linguistically and conceptually creative. The alternative to theory about action, though, is not a preoccupation with either the language of action in general or the concept of action in particular. Our reflexive engagement with the rational-empirical presence of action is designed to make that presence more adequate and to bring it to completion in the formality of the language and the concepts we articulate.

Our exploitation of the reflexive circle will therefore be governed by the following working assumptions.

(a) Our *prima facie* knowledge of rational action, which emerges once we make our peripheral awareness of it the focus of our attention, is quite correct, as far as it goes, but nonetheless vague, habitual, routine, and in that sense ungrounded.

(b) The circle of action and knowledge presents us with an opportunity for a series of rational actions that will have a justifying, grounding, and, in that restricted sense, foundational outcome.

(c) Our *prima facie* knowledge of rational action in the mode of rational-empirical presence, which is also a *prima facie* knowledge of the world in which we act, will be relied on in this sense, that it will not be regarded as systematically delusive—as a merely subjective production of mere phenomena or appearances. It will be assumed to be a level of achievement, an epistemic platform for advance—constructed no doubt over aeons of trial and error—rather than something that must be either disregarded in favor of a more exact starting point or replaced by being "explained" by the science of the future.

(d) That same *prima facie* knowledge must however not be relied on in this sense, that we have not the least idea, when we are ordinarily and routinely given over to it, what features may lie there just outside the fringe of awareness, awaiting merely an intensification of our cognitive glance to bring them in and make them fully present as we develop our awareness in words.

In the course of the chapter I will touch directly or indirectly upon all of our nine conditions for ontic responsibility, although I will not give for each condition a separate demonstration of its fulfillment and will not give each condition equal emphasis. As to the first reservation, the conditions are not logically independent: there is considerable overlap, each condition conveying something that is not conveyed by the rest of the conditions, but some, at least, also conveying something that could be conveyed by some other condition or conditions. Our purpose in the next section is to make rational action *as it is* so appear that its rational-empirical presence shall be seen to be consistent with the nine conditions. Despite our emphasis on *prima facie* knowledge in chapter 3, that was part of our purpose there also; for in that reflection we were always at least indirectly concerned with the authenticity of rational action—with the authenticity of those rational actions in which we articulate our knowledge in the mode of rational-empirical presence. It therefore bore in a similar way upon the fulfillment of all the conditions, and so supplements the reflection we are about to begin.

As to the second reservation, the unequal emphasis, three conditions have been especially salient in chapter 3, and they will be discussed in more detail in the later chapters. The fulfillment of the condition of rational obligation was supported by the sense of effort involved in the

intensification of rational-empirical presence, by the correlate demands
made upon us by the rational pole as we tried to "complete fresh
awareness in new-ordered language," and by the relevance (at least) of
the traditional notion of innateness to these demands. The fulfillment
of the condition of ontically significant appearance was in a sense the
theme of the whole chapter, first for the object of knowledge (in primary-simple engagement) and then for the *rational act* of knowing
itself (in primary-reflexive engagement). The fulfillment of the condition of ontic dependence received some preparatory support from our
discussion of Being (the One) as the "background" for particulars
(the Many), although the full significance of this will not be developed until chapter 7, when the condition of ontic dependence is given
ample consideration. Four other conditions that play some role in the
next section—explanatory ultimacy, explanatory opacity, partial determinateness, and positive indeterminateness (ontic potentiality)—will
also receive further attention in chapters 5–7.

2

An Interpersonal Reflection on Prima
Facie *Rational Action*

We consider first the rational action I am now engaged in. As I write
to you, an imagined reader, I act rationally in a *prima facie* sense to
communicate with you, and with myself as well, by way of words. The
communication is however far too indirect to serve as an example for
what I have in mind, seeing that I am in fact quite alone, writing with
a pen in a quiet room, and can not even be sure that what I write will
ever be read by anyone but myself. There is nothing essential to my
example about the act of writing, but the matter of an action that is
also an interpersonal communication is indeed essential; so let us suppose that I am in fact speaking to you rather than writing, and that I
can take account of your replies. For the moment the truth of what I
am saying is not especially important; I believe it to be sound but
sketchy; but it is important to the example that we should be talking
together about rational action.

As I speak these words, which of course concern action and thus
bring it from peripheral awareness to the focus of my attention, I am
conscious of exercising causal power in the world about me. Deliberately attentive to the exercise of that power, not concerned with its in-

frastructure but with the concrete texture of the act as it is available to me through senses and language, I find that it produces, or necessitates, something in the world about me. How it does so does not concern me; and certainly I do not find it any less available just because I can not propound a scientific explanation of how it comes about. I merely act and attend to my own action; I exemplify action and attend to what I exemplify. Just what it produces I might not know if I did not bring some prior experience and indeed some prior linguistic equipment to this occasion. At the very least I take it that I produce sound waves that by way of your eardrums excite your nervous system. If Hume's account of the way we know were true, I could never know whether my action was producing, or necessitating, an effect—could never know, indeed, that I was acting. But my knowledge as I in fact enjoy it does not seem to have that kind of radical defect. My awareness, or experience, of acting is qualified both by the sensory engagement of my body and by my deployment of the rational structures of language; and I find myself in no doubt about this exercise of power that could be usefully contrasted with some more impressive standard of rational certainty. My own action is present both to reason and to my body, and the two factors are inseparable, reason exercising itself in the body and body qualifying each feature of rational awareness—not least the texture of language itself.

Insofar as my words are heard and understood, I also exercise a power of a somewhat different kind on your mind. But I will not explore that difference just now, but simply say that by my act of speaking I exercise causal power of a complex sort on the world about me— a world of which you are a part. To call it causal power, I suppose it to be authentic, and authentic in the sense that though it is sufficient for the complex state of affairs it brings about—sufficient because the exercise of the power being given, and certain conditions about the world in which it is exercised being also given, it produces, or necessitates, a certain state of affairs that includes the vibration of your eardrums—there is no complex of other entities or other events that is sufficient to bring *it* about, nothing distinct from itself that can produce or necessitate *it*. It is true that we can detect what appear to be causal factors within the act, as we consider it on its own level. There is, for instance, my intending to get this matter clear between us and my felt unrest until the thing is done. And there are parallel things outside of the act—for instance, whatever it was in my perception of the contemporary philosophical scene that "moved" me to take up this issue, together with the whole world that environed me as I took it up. On the other hand, we can regard these things as causal factors only by identifying them as factors in or bearing upon an act already in progress. They are what they are—"causal" factors in an act— only because the act arises, originates, comes into being to take them up and incorporate them in its act-temporal sweep to completion. In this sense "causal" factors do not cause an act at all, although there would be no act without them: it is the act as a temporal power-unity that causes them to be "causal" factors. Obviously we take the causal power of the act to be more fundamental than these "causes"; obviously, too, we must eventually go beyond any of the usual senses of "cause" if we are to show how an act can exercise causal power. (There is, to be sure, another plausible account of an act that could be given by abandoning entirely the level of action and descending to the level of the physical events into which, according to some, an act is properly analyzable. But let us set that aside for the moment and return to it later.)

The reason for my taking this power so seriously would remain incomplete if we had not already considered together the structure of the knowledge we rely on to take it so. This having been done, I have not the least idea—nor, I think, have you—how one could set about acquiring any knowledge without exercising this kind to acquire it. We are now turning this mode of cognitive attention upon the acts in which we speak to each other, and we do this with due respect for the rational-empirical presence it can yield. The joint rational-empirical satisfaction that becomes actual as we focus upon our acts makes it seem no longer appropriate to call them *prima facie* ones. The massive experiential presence of my power to speak and yours to respond seems vulnerable to no erosion by any other cognitive standard. It looms rather so powerfully as a standard for experiential presence that I can foresee no empirical standard in the light of which I should be willing to set it aside. In fact, I can imagine no other that would not either exemplify it or rely upon it. As for some purely rational standard for authenticity, this use of words that is meaningful, structured, and yet intimately bound up with that same experiential presence—so much so that by virtue of it reason completes itself in presence—seems just as magisterial in its own way. An epistemic system like the science of the present—or any future system that developed, as this one does, by way of a constant cycle of theory-construction and theory testing—would seem to depend, directly or indirectly, on this primary rational-empirical standard.

But this is only an entering wedge: the impressive ontic presence of our own action as we attend to it with the particularity of body and the generality of language leaves enough still obscure about it to invite us to go on. If we consider again our awareness of the ontic integrity of the causal power we exercise in the world around us—in this case by talking—we find that it calls our attention to another and internal feature of it. "Feature" is perhaps the wrong word; what I mean is the unity of the act of speaking that pervades the entire extensiveness of it. By "extensiveness" I mean its spatial and its temporal extent, but also the multiplicity that goes with that: the many distinct sub-acts (or, if you insist, sub-events) in which it ramifies; the many distinct spatial parts—indeed the many distinct entities like organs and cells—that analysis can find within the total space that the act occupies or dominates. The unity is a power-unity: a power that is the act insinuates itself throughout a bodily multiplicity, or extensiveness. It is the ontic power required by our third condition, and it is intimately associated with the causal power we have been discussing. As I attend to the ontic power—attend to it with my body and my words—I do no more than notice that the causal power I exercised on you is experientially and rationally present to me only in conjunction with the complementary presence of ontic power, permeating, though I do not know how, my brain, my entire nervous system, and indeed my whole body. By "permeating" I mean dominating them as the power-unity of their manifold, so that the manifold so unified exercises also that production, or necessitation, on something else that we have been calling causal power.

Of ontic power we may say, in a commonsense way and subject to later qualification, that I exercise it throughout the act while exercising causal power upon you; that it is no more than the power-unity of my act ramifying throughout the extensive multiplicity of my body so that I can exert causal power on you. If one knows something of neurophysiology, one can give this claim some interpretation in terms of it: if I exercise ontic power, some neuron that fires in the course of the action, or some neural network through which a complex impulse passes, is subject to it. Theory tells me also that, if it is real, the cells and indeed molecules of my body are also subject to it. But it is not theory we are appealing to here, for the character of our rational awareness of ontic power would persist even if we were unable to give it any plausible theoretic interpretation. We appeal rather to a rational-empirical presence: that of a unified power pervading an extensive multiplicity—in more commonsense language, a unified power permeating the body and a segment of its history.

Something else we can say without relying on theory, although it will have repercussions on any theory: since an action like speaking a sentence takes longer than the firing of a neuron, the power-unit of the action will influence an event within the infrastructure that ends before the act itself ends. The temporality proper to the ontic power of an action requires us to look again at the foundations of the concept of causality. As I attend to my own performance of a rational act the notion that it can be parsed into events in which earlier ones produce, or necessitate, later ones—on a Humean account, into a succession of events that displays a lawlike regularity—seems far from the truth. Whether long or short, a rational action is a unit of becoming, and any account of it as a sum of smaller units—whether physical events or sub-acts—will not do it justice. This I see even as I perform the action of making that point in words. The act of speaking a sentence is not the sum of a number of sub-acts of speaking words; the act of speaking a paragraph is not the sum of a number of sub-acts of speaking sentences. Whether we regard the unit of becoming as a power-unit or as a time-unit, we are dealing with a quantum that is not produced by adding together smaller quanta, although it does indeed express itself in smaller quanta. The temporal aspect of the quantum of becoming in which I speak a sentence to you can not be expressed adequately in terms of a linear view of temporality in which point-instant succeeds point-instant in a dense and anisotropic continuum. What appears in a mathematical expression to be just that instant defined by just that point manifests itself concretely as a stretching or reaching beyond itself to all other instants or phases within the same unit. These, in turn, reach out to the one we were considering, so that any "instant" or "phase" contains, in either a retentive or an anticipatory sense, all the other "instants" or "phases" in the unit. The same feature can be expressed equally well in this way: the time-unit enacts itself in a vital present that always comprises aspects of both past and future, each being contained in its own mode in the becoming of that present. Considered qua vital present, any "instant" or "phase" retains what has been partially achieved and reaches forward to its full achievement.

The unity of my act—it seems no more in fact than an expression of
my own unity—binds past and future in a temporal unity.

Drawing on one of the root senses of "*tendere*"—"to stretch," "to
stretch out," "to reach"—we may say that the becoming of an act has
a *tensive* feature: the act expresses itself in a live present, which
reaches into past and future in the august gesture of coming-to-be. In
an earlier book I called this feature *act-temporality*.[2] Views of time
that replace it with a continuum that depends upon a mathematical
Aufbau exaggerate the sheer passage of things, as though an "instant"
or "phase" not yet come were quite without a premonitory presence in
the present; as though an "instant" or "phase" now gone were wholly
and irremediably lost. They fail to notice that no moment of an act
can be fully characterized without characterizing the whole of it.

If we consider the unit of becoming as one of power and causality
the same features appear again. The power-unit resists complete analysis in terms of linear causality, so that no "instant" or "phase" of an
act can be said to cause a later "instant" or "phase" in the $c \rightarrow e$ sense of
"cause."[3] To put it another way, if we are to use the notion of cause at
all in dealing with the internal constitution of acts, we shall have to
use it in a sense that allows us to say with equal force that a later instant or phase of an act causes an earlier one. We are dealing with a
power-quantum, and the full scope of the power is deployed only
within the whole of the quantum.

When I perform an act like speaking I am aware that the power I
exercise during the act's quantum of time is also deployed throughout
a spatial region—the region occupied by the whole of my body as I act.
Although I am not experientially aware in any detail of the various
bodily units spread through this region, I am certainly aware that this
spatial multiplicity *is* my act no less than its temporal history is. We
may say, then, that an act is spatially as well as temporally tensive. And
the power of the act reaches throughout that space, fills it up and
makes use of the items in it in a way that needs no time to knit together the simultaneous elements in it, although the exercise of the
power is, as we have already observed, nothing if not temporal.

Taking into account both the temporal and the spatial tensiveness,
we can thus distinguish two kinds of relations between spatially distinct infrastructure items. Many items in that spatial multiplicity—and
I am of course aware that it is a spatial multiplicity of some kind long
before theory teaches me to think of it in terms of billionfold neurons,

of billionfold cells of other kinds—are in a causal concourse of which
the notion of causal power (or of c→e causality, interpreted in terms
of the working view) gives us a glimpse, but only an imperfect one,
seeing that all these causal transactions take place within the overarch-
ing temporal power of the act. Many others—all those that are in simultaneous spatial array—are in no such concourse but are nonetheless
within the grip of the act's ontic power. An abstract time-slice through
the whole spatial region of the act would reveal a multiplicity of spatial elements bound in one power relation, even though those infrastructure elements can by definition have no relations of *causal* power
between them. It is of course *ontic* power that pervades the simulta-
neity: two cells or two molecules within the time-slice will both be
qualified by and contribute to the ontic power of the whole act to
whose infrastructure they belong. The spatially tensive power is not
radically separate from the tensive feature of time, since any temporal
slice through the spatiality of the act will be only an abstraction from
the tensive time of the ontic power of the act taken as a whole.

But it is simpler—and more consonant with the attitudes of twentieth-century physics—to express all this in terms of a temporospatial
quantum. As I speak this sentence, the ontic power of my act pervades
a temporospatial quantum, and my awareness of this is part of the experience of acting, now reflexively articulated in words. The whole of
the time-unit and the whole of the space through which the act is deployed must be taken into account if we are to do justice to (a) the
relations between two infrastructure items (whether simultaneous or
not); and (b) the relations between macroscopic features of the act
(where "macroscopic" does not exclude subjective features) and elements of the infrastructure. Considered in terms of the relations
between simultaneous elements within the infrastructure there is a
power-relation that does not take up time; but considered from the
point of view of the whole power-unit from which we have singled out
these simultaneous relations, the whole situation is nothing if not temporal. The causal power exercised in the world—in this case my talking
to you—is a function of this temporally tensive feature of ontic power.

Features of rational action thus come to view, are experienced, become present to us, as we attend to them and develop our awareness in
words. But my present speech acts are reflexive ones, so that my use of
words to make the texture of the action appear to me (and to you as
well, in this interpersonal reflection) are in this case part of the action.
The empirical presence of these speech acts to ourselves depends upon

these words I am using, the empirical texture of the act both contribut-
ing to the meaning of the words and only emerging for attention in
virtue of the words. Reflexive cognitive attention is however an intricate
matter, and the very effort to use words—the effort to allow the right
words to articulate what we attend to—is part of the act we are attending to. If we now shift our attention to focus more directly upon this
effort to use words in a certain bodily situation—my bodily here-and-
now, yours as you hear me and perhaps respond to me—we find that it
discloses itself as a general rational-linguistic power held by the particularity of the body to the task of making something present—in this reflexive case, precisely itself qua rational act.

At this reflexive stretch we seem to be exemplifying the fulfillment
of three other conditions. Caught in a relatively determinate bodily
situation, each of us seems capable of determining it further; indeed
the very speaking of certain words is a further determination of the
body, even though in this case we are deploying them reflexively to attend to the nature of action itself. But the burden of the potentiality
we exercise in this determining effort seems anything but particular. I
do not now seek to express what is determinate in me as a particular;
nor, for that matter, if you challenge me will you express only what is
determinate in you as a particular. Being intent on expressing the nature of action and searching for the words to do so, I am not appealing
to what is determinate in me to succeed in the expression; I am rather
trying to allow that which is in some sense other than I to determine
what is determinable in me, so that what is the case about action shall
emerge. I need to give scope in my act of speaking to something distinct from my particularity (however much it is now united with my
particularity) in order that what is in general the case about action shall
find expression. Here, in a particular bodily situation, ontic potentiality
is felt as a nonparticular burden—as a power exceeding what is particular and determinate, struggling to make itself felt in just this rational-
empirical act of cognitive engagement to so determine it that I shall
see-express what is the case. It is, so to speak, the rationality of the act
held by the particular focus of the body to the task of completing itself
in an understanding that is also an awareness of the real.

The power attempting to realize itself, determining me as it does so,
is not something radically distinct from my particularity, for it is I that
feel the burden of that power; and my feeling it so is partly definitive
of the nature of my particularity or of that of any other rational agent
engaged in a like effort: my particularity is what it is in virtue of its

participating in the power that is here felt as a burden. The conditions of partial determinateness and positive indeterminateness (ontic potentiality) seem to be fulfilled, although only within the confines of our circle of action and knowledge. But the burden of the power is also the burden of a rational obligation felt here within the particular situation defined by my senses and more generally by my body. The burden is precisely the felt obligation that "reasons" should prevail over "causes"; that structured meanings should flow out not in accordance with what is determinate in me but in accordance with the demands the "reasons" make upon me. These are demands for accuracy and clarity; for faithfulness to what is the case; for a transcendence of the particular bodily situation in which this reflexive cognitive exercise takes place—a transcendence it must achieve if it is to be in some sense true. Our reflexive exercise seems to have taken a turn as labyrinthine as one we took in the last chapter, for we now appear to be concerned to see what is the case about rational action by way of seeing what is the case about our cognitive capacities. Our choice of our own acts of speaking as examples of rational action in an interpersonal reflexive discussion of rational action made this inevitable.

By way of this turn we have, incidentally, brought in sight a feature of rational action that was not in view when we first considered the causal power of my speaking to you only as a physical agitation of the air that had an effect on your nervous system by way of your eardrums. The causal power exercised by a rational agent, and therefore the ontic power upon which it depends, has a radically different feature from any power that we might want to ascribe to physical entities like atoms and electrons. It is present only in the kind of action we are using as an example—action that issues in rational speech and is characterized by a rationally articulated understanding on the part of the agent. The variety of such actions is considerable. On the theoretical side, it ranges from the speaking or writing of sentences of modest import up to the enunciation of important scientific or philosophical truths; on the practical, it ranges from the involvement of rational speech with the ordinary tasks of daily life up to its involvement with moral decisions of the most momentous kind. If we suppose that this considerable range of acts not only is supported by neuronal activity but also exercises ontic power over it, then it follows that what in the course of the action is understood, what is articulated, what, it may be, is postulated as a standard for the action, all contribute to the power exercised by the action over its supporting neuronal activity. The burden of rational obligation mentioned a while ago is the felt potentiality of power of that kind. It should be clear that what is articulated in rational actions is akin to what is usually dealt with under the rubric of reasons. The mode of power in which an action exercises ontic power on one of its subordinate events may include the power of reasons: there are reasons *in* an act as well as reasons *for* an act; and this power is potential before it is actual. Just here the conditions of ontic potentiality and rational obligation seem to be fulfilled.

Here, in the full spate of philosophical assertion, I am checked by your response. "Surely it is not proper to distinguish an *I* from the body and all the events in it that go on while the *I* lives. Surely we have no right to distinguish something called an action from all the things that are happening in the body as the action goes on. What you call *I* would seem to be identical with the history of the assemblage of cells that includes your neurons; what you call your action would seem to be identical with everything that goes on in your body while, as we say, you perform it."

I concede to your objection: what you say is true, as long as you do not conceive of the identity as a physicalist would conceive of it. If you are only telling me that both of us are attending to one self-identical "thing"—a rational agent-in-act—and that its self-identity can not be fully characterized without including all the other "things"—neurons, macromolecules, and the like as well as whatever they are "doing," or whatever happenings are taking place within their vast multiplicity— then of course I agree. But if what you want to say is that this vast multiplicity is identical with the rational agent-in-act in the sense that a physicalist intends, then I must insist that you are missing the point of that self-identity. In terms of our aim to attend to the concrete presence of rational action and to bring our experience (awareness) of it to rational completeness in language, missing the point means failing to have an adequately articulated experience of the presence of the self-identity.

What the physicalist intends is a long story, one in which the business of naming and the business of understanding are hopelessly confused. One might agree, for instance, that "Evening Star" and "Morning Star" are equally good names for the one thing, or referent, that we now call the planet Venus; and that the terms "Evening Star" and "Morning Star" are in that sense identical, though different in meaning. But suppose, on this analogy, that a physicalist philosopher were to put forward two terms, one of them "RA" (for "rational agent-in-act") and the other "*PB*" (for "physiological basis," as we might now say, though we should, strictly speaking, take "*PB*" as an arbitrary symbol for the successor to the concept of rational agent-in-act in some ideal science of the future).[4] Would the physicalist really intend to say that they are identical in the way "Evening Star" and "Morning Star" are? I do not think so, for those terms are interchangeable without loss; indeed, that is the point of claiming that they are identical: they are equally good, considered as names, and though different, considered as descriptions, they are equally good descriptions. Yet the physicalist, in claiming the identity of the two terms "RA" and "PB," does not intend to say that they are interchangeable and that it is a matter of indifference which one we use, but rather that although they are used to refer to the one self-identical "thing," they function in quite different ways, the first in a way that amounts to an obscure and inappropriate naming of that "thing," the second in a way that explains, clarifies, illuminates it.

But all that, as you know as well as I, is a long story. All I ask you to notice now is that when I speak of myself as acting rationally and then go on to develop that point as I have been doing, I am calling attention to a self-identical "thing" whose self-identity is complex and subtle; and that operative and powerful features of it are overlooked in your reply, if you intended your reply in a physicalist sense. They are features that, if the self-identity is best characterized in the way summarized by the term "*PB*," are negligible, obscure, deceptive—a mere appearance of power and operative force. But they are precisely the features my words are intended to make us aware of, to make us experience. We miss them if we attend to *prima facie* rational action only with the help of *PB* language.

If we focus instead on action as the supposed reality we intend to be more adequately aware of and then labor to express what is there, our language may at last issue out of the experiential presence of what was indeed there—not there in the sense of being experientially given, but *there to be experienced*—all the while. The matter is the difficult and subtle one of our earlier reflection upon *prima facie* knowledge. I am in effect claiming that the fit of language and reality (in either the primary-simple or the primary-reflexive case) is such that they can never be independently isolated and compared; and that nonetheless questions about the rightness of any particular fit can always be raised. Our primary cognitive engagement is by way of a rational-empirical synthesis that is not directed upon the poles by which the synthesis is

defined. In the past, the poles were thought of as two separate ontological realms—reason and experience—to which we could attend sepa-
rately, finding in the one items defined as mental or conceptual, and in
the other some version of sensation. Here we think of the two poles as
the formal-conceptual-linguistic (universal) and the sensory-bodily (particular) but regard them not so much as objects or realms to be attended to as factors in a union that mediates something other than
itself and something other than those distinguishable factors. In its primary role subjectivity is concerned with neither pole, and certainly with
neither regarded as "within" subjectivity itself. Subjectivity rather exists
as their active fusion directed upon something whose presence they
mediate. We attend with the help of a particular body and its sensory
apparatus, operating in a particular situation; and we attend by articulating in the formality and generality of language what we attend to.
But *what* we attend to we attend to by virtue of the synthesis: we are
intent on having rational experience, or awareness, of *it*. The fit, then,
involves the union of both poles of the synthesis directed upon something other than those poles; and both of the poles, together with that
"something other," play a role in the fit. The best we can do in determining rightness of fit is to move from one such synthesis into another.

The present one, now, as we reflect upon these matters together,
purports to make us rationally aware of features of rational action we
miss if we attend to it only with the help of a *PB* language. They purport to be features of the ontic level of the rational agent-in-act, something whose self-identity requires that we distinguish that level as a
unity from the level of the *PB* multiplicity of which it is the unity.
The presence of the *RA* as distinct from the *PB* is no longer persuasive
in just the commonsense way that makes it a *prima facie* rational agent
but rather in virtue of the new rational-empirical synthesis that has replaced the earlier one; and the new words we have found both satisfy
our demand for a more adequate understanding and mediate the more
adequate presence of what we wanted to be rationally aware of. It is the
shift in experiential level, seen now as a function of the linguistic outcome of the achievement of reason in its primary-reflexive engagement,
that is persuasive. It persuades us, among other things, of the explanatory ultimacy of the ontic level we have been distinguishing, and of its
opacity to explanations couched only in terms of its infrastructure.

When we remember that the present exercise consists of a series of
rational acts, the originative nature of our present reflexive cognitive
engagement reveals itself in another light. It exemplifies rational ac-

tion in general, so everything we have said about *that* applies to *it* as well. But developing, as it does, what purports to be a rational account of action in general, it manifests itself as a set of "reasons" making headway within a bodily situation that is at least partly illuminated by "causes"—that is, by a causal ($c \rightarrow E$) account in terms of physiology. The originative epistemic factor—the one we have been using to justify what purports to be an authenticating account of rational action—in the present reflection therefore also exemplifies reasons overmastering causes, and therefore exemplifies ontic power making use of subordinate causal powers. When we remember that the present exercise consists of a series of *reflexive* rational acts, its exemplification of ontic power becomes even more vivid. It purports to reveal the ontic power inherent in all rational action, and it purports to do so by making its primary-reflexive engagement with that more adequate—that is to say, by bringing about a heightened awareness of rational action and bringing that awareness to completion in new-ordered words, by bringing about a more adequate rational-empirical presence of rational action to itself. But in doing so it becomes our clearest and most persuasive example of ontic power at work. Thus, although the authenticity of ontic power stands or falls according as we do or do not find action rationally-empirically present as a distinct ontic level, reflexive rational action becomes its own best example of that level. Since we do not think of reflection in terms of an image duplicating something else, we need not think of our present reflection as one of a potentially endless series of such images. We take our reflection to be as "realistic" (as primary) as any primary-simple engagement. So, although we are clearly still within the circle of action and knowledge, it is no deprivation to be there. By being there we are not in the least cut off from our own reality as agents.

Although there may be no physicalist identity between the ontic level of my rational act of speaking and the ontic level of its physiological basis, the thought that there is in any case some kind of identity between them is a persistent one. What kind of identity would be consistent with what purports, on the basis of the new rational-empirical synthesis we have been attempting to bring about, to be an ontic distinction between them?

I think we may find an appropriate sense by considering what the self-identity of a complex temporal thing would have to be if it did in fact exercise ontic power. At least from the time of Plato's *Parmenides* self-identity has been felt to be inseparable from unity. It seems reasonable to suppose that a rational agent-in-act has a self-identity only if it is a unity: it is *this* agent, performing *this* act, because it has a unity appropriate to that. But it seems equally clear that we can not make sense out of that unity without noticing that it is the unity of a multiplicity. The multiplicity, moreover, is a ramified one: the act of speaking a certain paragraph ramifies in the sub-acts of speaking certain sentences; these in turn in the sub-acts of speaking certain words. And if we attend to the physiological features of the act we get another multiplicity—or rather a multiplicity of multiplicities—for instance, of entities hierarchically arranged or of events hierarchically arranged. If the self-identity of the agent-in-act is a unity of multiplicities, it is a power-unity rather than a stolid Parmenidean one: it is the unity of the power that unifies just that multiplicity—unifies it as an act. Unity and multiplicity are not in general flatly identical—no one, I think, would claim that the symmetrical relation of identity between two terms holds between the terms "unity" and "multiplicity." In the case of the self-identity of the supposed power-unit of a rational act, unity and multiplicity are nevertheless in an intimate union upon which that self-identity depends. We can not distinguish one act from another in virtue of its unity alone, for even though we can not specify in complete detail the multiplicity internal to an act, we can say of any particular act that it is just that self-identical act in virtue of being the unity of just that multiplicity. The one act *is* its unity—it is the power-unity of just that self-identical act; but it *is* also its multiplicity—it is the speaking of just those several words; it is all those sub-acts subordinated to it; it is just that ramified multiplicity of physiological entities and physiological events.

The unity and the multiplicity are then identical in the sense that self-identity includes both; but as they are not functionally interchangeable, the identity is not the symmetrical one we take for granted in the relation between two identical terms like A and B in the case $A = B$, but rather an asymmetrical one. To be precise, we should not call it a *relation* of identity, because we can not separate the ontic status of the two items clearly enough to distinguish them as pure relata. We do indeed distinguish them, but the distinction is sufficiently *sui generis* as to make it inappropriate to characterize their union in a single self-identity with the help of an expression—(symmetrical) identity—that was devised for terms in the formalized language of logic and mathematics. The agent-in-act is self-identical in its exercise of a unifying power, but the power is not operative, actual, identifiable except as the unifying of a multiplicity. We shall say, then, that the two features thus singled out are asymmetrically identical within that self-identity. The language appears paradoxical, but it is not so if it finds justification in the nature of the rational-empirical presence it mediates for us. The self-identity of a rational agent-in-act—authentically an agent, authentically an act—means that the agent is asymmetrically identical with its body and the body's history; and that the act is asymmetrically identical with everything that happens in its body as the act is performed. In terms of power, the agent's power is dependent upon the nervous system in that it is performed in and with it and only in and with it; on the other hand, that power is exerted over the nervous system and indeed over any particular neuron that fires or is constrained from firing in the course of it.

Although the nature of the power that is operative if the condition of ontic power holds is an unusual one, it appears more plausible if we focus upon just what adjustments it calls for in our habitual beliefs, for the adjustments are not in conflict with the assumptions of science about transactions in which physical energy is lost or acquired. If we compare the power I exercise by way of sound waves upon your ear (causal power) with the power that I, in action, exercise upon some neuron that fires or is inhibited from firing during the action (ontic power), we see a marked difference. The first is an ordinary physical transaction; it takes up time, and I, distinct from you, expend energy (in the ordinary physical sense) to agitate your tympanums. The second is not a physical transaction in that sense. Under the rubric of asymmetrical identity, the agent is not considered to be an entity radically distinct from its body, nor is its act considered to be a function radically distinct from the physiological processes that go on in the course of the act. If the agent exercises power over some neuron or neuronal complex, if these things are subject to the power of the act, the power is not of the kind that is exercised by way of a physical transaction that takes up time and in which physical energy is expended in the production of an "effect." It is not a $c \rightarrow e$ transaction. By the same token, the firing of the neuron or the coursing of impulses through a neural complex does not support the agent's thought and speech by expending physical energy in a $c \rightarrow e$ sense on them, although of course it does expend physical energy on other neurons or neuronal complexes and hence does exercise causal power on them. It follows that there are two modes of ontic power. The agent's power over a neuron or a neuronal complex we may call *supervening*, or *governing*, ontic power; the contributions of a single neuron or a neuronal complex to the act we may then call *conditioning* ontic power.

The whole-part relation of act to single neuron makes vivid the temporal distinction between this mode of interdependence and c→e dependence. Thus it is possible that the repeated firing of a single neuron might be interdependent in the mode of ontic power with a macroscopic feature of action (e.g., conscious understanding) simultaneous with it, while each of the firings also exercised causal power on later neural occurrences in other parts of the brain.

But obviously the theme of ontic power is not so radically separated from that of causal power as the distinction might suggest. Indeed, if we return to my earliest example for a moment, if I am making any sense on the topic of action, then the causal power I exercised in vibrating your eardrums was a function of the ontic power deployed in my act. The insinuation of the unity of my ontic power throughout the multiplicity of my body was what gave that body as a whole the causal power of affecting you by speech. If this should be so, supervening ontic power deserves to be dealt with under some causal rubric of its own. On the basis of what has been said so far, we can not give a satisfactory account of it by analyzing it into the various c→e transactions that can be discerned within that which is asymmetrically identical with it. Nor do we give an adequate account of supervening ontic power by listing the various conditioning ontic powers that contribute to it. It will manifest explanatory opacity in the face of such explanatory techniques. The rubric "ontic cause" suggests itself. The Platonic phrase "real cause," of whose Greek form "ontic cause" is in some ways an echo, or the alternative Platonic phrase "true cause," may also serve, for Plato does use these expressions in a *locus classicus* where the power of the rational agent is at issue.[5] We must however use them with caution, because in the same context Plato also intends to make a difficult and debatable point about the role of the Forms that we do not need or want here. If we call the rational agent an ontic, a real, or a true cause we do not mean just that it was the cause of what happens in the world as a result of its actions, although in the mode of causal power it is just that. We mean rather that it is the unifying power of the total act and thus of the complexity of non-acts into which analysis seeks to resolve the act. The concept of ontic, real, or true cause, then, is simply another way of expressing the concept of supervening ontic power. It is by virtue of being a real cause that a supervening ontic power will be an explanatory ultimate for the totality upon which it supervenes; for the same reason it will be opaque to explanations expressed in terms of that totality. It will be obvious that I have tried to absorb and transform in the concept of ontic cause, or ontic power, aspects of causality that have long since disappeared from the concept of $c \rightarrow E$ causality that does service in modern philosophy of science. It should also be obvious that the concept of ontic power is intended to help renew the old close association between the category of being and that of causality.

We shall return to several of the conditions somewhat later. Chapter 5 is concerned, in a setting of argument rather than reflection, with the conditions of ontically significant appearance, explanatory ultimacy, and explanatory opacity. Some of the arguments, however, are about the reflexive nature of at least some rational actions. Chapter 6 also deals extensively with those conditions, as well as with some of those that have figured in this section. There again the setting is one of argument, but reflexive rational actions are taken as the basis for the whole argument. The setting of chapter 7 is mainly, like this one, that of a reflection; there, as noted earlier, the condition of ontic dependence is dealt with at some length; but the conditions of partial determinateness, positive indeterminateness (ontic potentiality , and rational obligation also reappear there in a way that reinforces what has been said about them here.

3

The Circle Transformed: The Radical Autonomy
of the Reflexive Rational Agent

We must now remind ourselves of what we have been doing in the reflexive exercises of this and the preceding chapter. We have by no means broken out of the circle of action and knowledge, but our reflection should have transformed the merely *prima facie* status of it. If it is a predicament for us to remain within the circle in this way, it is a universal one, for all persuasiveness whatsoever—all that is deceptive no less than all that is authentic—is contained by it. There is indeed a logical predicament for someone who propounds a philosophic argument designed to discredit the authenticity of rational action, for all the concreteness of action as it is known within the circle enframes and sustains all such doctrines and all arguments for them. If the very texture of the circle is a deceptive one—if it is not an ontically significant appearance—the persuasiveness even of arguments to that effect will be infected by it, as we shall see in some detail in the next chapter. There is no escape from that self-made predicament by any strategem that physicalism or any other form of scientism can provide: there is no scientific theory, no philosophic doctrine, no paradigm, no technique— there is indeed no bald single statement—that does not owe its status to some cognitive act that enframes it. It is a point grasped, though (to this observer) not clearly articulated, by existentialists; and it is also grasped, though (again to this observer) articulated in ways too deeply in debt to the Cartesian tradition, by phenomenologists. The plausibility of scientism depends upon either ignoring the point or pretending that the full concreteness of rational action as known by the agent is somehow irrelevant to the doctrine propounded or entertained (in secondary engagement) in the course of it. From the present perspective the possibility for reflexive illumination within the circle looks like an opportunity rather than a predicament.

If all persuasiveness takes place within the circle, what about the persuasiveness of our account of what one sees within it? What is the evidence for our account of rational-empirical presence, for instance? Alternatively what are our arguments for it? As to evidence, if one regards our account as a theory, clearly there is none that we can confront the theory with as one might confront a scientific theory with the evidence. On the other hand, there is indeed the evidence one intends to call attention to by the very language one uses: that is, using the language in just that way is in fact also calling attention to certain evidence, although the evidence would go unnoticed in the absence of the insight articulated in the language. The evidence does not lie *in* the language, for the mediation of senses and body plays a major role in it; but on the other hand we can not juxtapose evidence and language as though they were somehow external to each other. The persuasiveness of the language and the presence of the evidence march together. The linguistic (rational) part of the account is inseparable from the empirical side, and though the language is by no means self-justifying, if it should fail to persuade it would be because the dissatisfaction of someone who rejected it was both empirical and rational-linguistic. The proper response of the critic (setting aside logical inconsistencies in the original account) would be, "no, you do not have it quite right. Don't you see? It's like this. . . ." Whereupon there would follow an alternative account, itself having the same rational-empirical status as the rejected one.

There is the additional complication that the relation between knower and known has been part of our subject matter. We are always engaged with the real, laboring, as rational language-users tied to particularity by our bodies, to bring it into view, to experience it in the mode of rationality. But in this chapter and the last one the very nature of our engagement with it, including the role of language and body just mentioned, is part of the real we are reflexively engaged with. That engagement is not there given-in-experience, no more than something we are engaged with in a primary-simple way is given-in-experience; it is, however, given-to-be-experienced in the same way that things are given-to-be-experienced to our primary-simple power of engagement. According to our new foundational reflection, we must deal with rational-empirical presence in its own terms. The additional complication is that the "foundation" itself is available to us only in the (reflexive) mode of rational-empirical presence.

Whether we are concerned to know in the mode of rational-empirical presence a person, an action, or (in reflection) our own cognitive power itself, what is decisive is the power of reason to articulate, in terms of the formal-linguistic pole in its undivided synthesis with the sensory-bodily pole, a rational awareness of something whose presence is not the presence of either of those poles. We do not (in primary engagement) first experience something and then devise a theory about it. We can do that only when we already have a mode of experience sufficiently formulated in language that for the purpose of theory-testing it can be regarded as a (primary-simple) constant that is not called in question. Engagement with the theory tested against this is then a *secondary* rational-empirical engagement. *Prima facie* knowledge accepted in that spirit by a scientist—and surely it is so accepted as theories are tested against it—is not questioned about its structure in the way we have been questioning it.

As for arguments for the reality of rational-empirical presence, there are none that can be evaluated purely as linguistic-formal structures. The reflexive argument itself—even this present one—succeeds or fails as a *language use* that is also an *experiencing*. What we are in touch with by way of the rational-empirical synthesis is whatever is the case about our *prima facie* knowledge. And it is this, not either the bodily-sensory pole or the formal-linguistic one or both in turn, that we intend to have a more adequate rational experience of. Those who like the metaphor of worldmaking may perhaps see the point of my claim here; but the metaphor may also make them fail to see that part of the point which has to do with the role of the component of awareness, or experience, in knowledge in the mode of rational-empirical presence. When our rational awareness is inadequate to what is the case, it resonates with an "empirical" dissatisfaction that is precisely the dissatisfaction of knowing oneself to be so caught in the artifice of language as to be prevented from adequately being aware of, or experiencing, what is there to be aware of, there to be experienced. There is unfortunately a dangerous parallel satisfaction: the world is full of people who, as they think, express in language the way things are and take much satisfaction in having done so, but who in fact express only the particularity of their selves. So, no doubt the continued importance of conversation in philosophy: think of it as a trying to see together—see, I mean, what reason may happily disclose with words, rather than see just the formal structure of some argument or linguistic usage—and it looks both more complex and more concrete than the Platonic definition of dialectic allowed for.

Our reflexive exercises, whether focused upon *prima facie* rational action itself or upon our *prima facie* knowledge of it, have in any case been nontheoretic in intent. We have been so willingly confined within the circle that we have been trying to intensify our awareness-cum-understanding of what it is to be so confined. We all carry so much theory around with us that it is hard to adhere faithfully to such an ideal nontheoretic program, but that at least has been my negative intent. Our linguistic creativity (such as it was) in this chapter and the preceding one was intended to serve as a transparency whose refractive power intensified the presence of something already concretely before us to be attended to, rather than as a mediator of the presence of some theoretic structure whose presence, qua theoretic structure, might then become the focus of our attention. That is to claim that the (secondary) presence of a theory is less fundamental than the (primary) presence of the background against which we construct it and upon which it depends for *its* presence—less fundamental, indeed, than the (primary) presence of any item in ordinary experience that we might use to confirm or disconfirm it. From within our circle we find the entire cycle of theory-construction and theory-testing to be itself enframed by the rational action we have been attending to, and our reflection therefore suggests that the cycle is by no means the only way in which rationality is engaged in experience and finds satisfaction in it.

Our reflection upon prima facie rational action found it at least peripherally present as the thing done or the thing known was the object of attention, and always potentially present to reflection. The language we used about it—especially the discussion of the two modes of power—was designed to make more vivid what we were aware of and at the same time to make it more intelligible; that is to say it was designed to intensify its rational-empirical presence. Our earlier reflection upon the prima facie knowledge in which we carry this out had the same end in view with respect to that knowledge; and in this case our use of language was designed to bring out the "presence" of that knowledge just as it is—a background knowledge now reflexively aware of its own structure and prerogatives. To the degree the language was successful, prima facie knowledge manifests itself as a certain level of epistemic achievement. When, in the primary-simple mode prior to reflection, it had appeared to disclose the granite wall, the ivy, ourselves unreflexively engaged in action—so we said in effect—it had in fact done so; and had not instead hindered a deeper and more "scientific" effort by placing in its way a distorting veil of appearance. At the same time we attributed a certain structure to it, for we claimed that the particularity of sensation and the rest of the body's mediation of the here-and-now intertwined with the generality of the formal carriers of rational articulation to yield us presence. And now, in thinking about what we have reflexively done, we also attribute to our primary-reflexive mode a certain level of achievement (distinct from the prima facie knowledge it attends to) and a certain structure as well (precisely the same structure as the prima facie knowledge we have been attending to, except that as the reflexive task itself becomes more self-conscious, the autonomy of our linguistic creativity is intensified).

We need not pretend to have carried out this reflexive task as well as it can be done in order to presume to say that it is something that demands to be done—something distinct from the cut and thrust of philosophic dialectic on the one hand and from the pursuit of science on the other. Both those activities have something constructive about them in the sense that they produce carefully crafted arguments, formal systems, theories, and models. But much of the time, either before philosophy or while engaged in it, our linguistic creativity is more directly and immediately enmeshed by way of the particularity of the body with what it is laboring to experience. It labors at the task of making present—making more truly and completely present—what is already present to a degree in *prima facie* knowledge. It is against the background of rational-empirical presence that science makes formal-theoretic constructs, deals with them in secondary rational-empirical engagement, and brings them to an empirical reckoning; and it is against this background that philosophers contrive arguments and examine them.

Within the circle defined by the agent's knowledge of itself in action, rational action now appears as radically autonomous. It is reflexive rational action that has brought this about; indeed, the first exercise of that radical autonomy was in reflection itself. Confined within the circle, the agent did not rest content with its merely habitual self-knowledge, and what was *prima facie* does not remain so after our reflexive exercise. The reliance upon the concrete texture of one's own rational action within the world it reveals does indeed remain; so much so that from one opposed perspective, what was *prima facie* has now become self-confirmatory and viciously so. But it is not perceived from that perspective that convicting rational action of inauthenticity on the basis of theoretic moves that purport to explain it (in the sense of any of the going accounts of scientific explanation) depends, no less than our own, upon a reflexive exercise. If we convict action of being an appearance that lacks ontic significance we must rely on reflexive acts having the same *prima facie* structure to do so. There would then be this odd result: (a) a reflexive assessment pent within our circle characterizes the *prima facie* things that happen there as mere appearance; (b) an assessment of the methodological procedures of science that contrasts it with the *prima facie* knowledge proper to the circle is part of this reflexive exercise; (c) this assessment, which is to be distinguished from the finding or contriving of scientific explanations, rests upon a contrast that not only takes place within the circle but is besides only realizable when the *prima facie* texture of it is taken as seriously as we took it when we began our reflexive exercises. A simpler way of saying all this is that the authenticity of the seemingly responsible rational agent must be assumed by anyone who sets out to convict it of inauthenticity. These matters will be considered further in the next two chapters, and just here I am only concerned to point out that radical autonomy within the circle is something that all parties must assume. In reflection we have done no more than take that autonomy seriously in order to display its "structure."

A number of principles have emerged from our reflections. They do not appear to be postulates about rational action on the one hand or empirical-descriptive conclusions on the other. They are perhaps best regarded as principles manifest in the rational-empirical presence of rational action—principles awaiting modification and criticism by subsequent efforts having the same rational-empirical footing.

1. The full concreteness of rational action enframes every doctrine, every theory, indeed every particular statement. Both before and after a reflexive exercise of the kind undertaken here, one relies on the act to entertain (in secondary engagement) the doctrine, theory, or statement. We need not suppose things of that kind to be mental entities; indeed, the whole tenor of these reflections militates against the existence of (purely) mental entities and events. But we must still suppose that physical shapes or sounds can express doctrines, theories, or statements only in an interpersonal environment of rational acts.

2. An awareness of acting enframes every rational act (enframes all doings, sayings, makings). Most of the time it is peripheral, but it can be focused in explicit but nonphilosophical reflection (as when I might say "I am now writing a sentence"); and it can be still more intensely focused in reflexive exercises of the kind we have carried out. *Rational action is always potentially reflexive.* Reflection of the last kind is by way of a rational-empirical synthesis whose poles are the particularity of body and the generality of discourse, but which yields a more adequate rational awareness (experience) not of those poles but of what it is directed upon by virtue of them. In this case what it was directed upon was not just the particularity of some act, but some act whose presence was also the presence (as an instance) of rational action in general.

3. Reflection about rational action can be adequate only if it is also directed upon what purports to be our knowledge of our world and ourselves acting in it. In characterizing that knowledge as primary-simple knowledge in the mode of rational-empirical presence, reflection also purports to exemplify it in the primary-reflexive mode.

4. Whether we have rightly or wrongly characterized it in our exercises, the self-knowledge of the agent-in-act must be part of the assessment of the relative worth of cognitive enterprises of all sorts—not least the one we call science. The judgment of the relative worth and the interrelations of science, common sense, and philosophy—of religion and art as well, for that matter—is in the hands of a presumptive rational agent exercising radical autonomy in such matters from within the confines of our ineluctable circle. The autonomy consists in coming

to terms with the circle: it can be transformed, but we can not escape from it; and if we claim that confinement in it is to be subject to mere appearance, we can not legitimately make any claim from within it that purports to discriminate between its mere appearance and some hidden reality.

Our reflection appears to be foundational in a different sense from those efforts to find an epistemological foundation that have been made again and again since Descartes. Cognitive enterprises of all sorts require that we act rationally; they have always required it; they always will. Noticing in reflection the rational-empirical roots of all *prima facie* rational action, of all *prima facie* knowledge of it, of all reflection upon it, gives us no foundation that is set beyond further scrutiny of the same sort; and it therefore gives us no basis for deductive system-building. Neither does it envision a thoroughly reliable method that shall be a *strenge Wissenschaft* superior to science and applicable to subject matters of all sorts—as the founder of phenomenology intended that discipline to be. It gives us a "foundation" only in the continued exercise—in morals, in the arts, in the sciences, and in philosophic reflection itself—of our autonomy as responsible rational agents. It gives us a "foundation" in our own status as the ontic ground of the production of all doctrines and all theories—therefore of all scientific explanations. This closes no investigation whatever to us, but it warns us that ingenuities that represent that ground as wholly explicable by one of its own artifacts are self-subverting.

4

The Epistemology of Reflexive Rational Action:
A Practical Postulate

The only "foundation" we have found is that of rational action reflecting upon its own status. It is a foundation we can scarcely do without, but as it is always in process, always subject to supersession by some later and more searching effort at self-knowledge, it is not a foundation in the traditional sense of epistemological foundationalism. There is, however, an epistemology that goes with it. Its chief doctrines are these: (1) rational-empirical presence lies at the basis of all systematic knowledge; (2) it is something achieved by rational action in its cognitive engagement with some here-and-now; (3) all system-building or theory-construction takes place against the background of primary rational-empirical presence, the systems or theories then being rationally-empirically present qua systems or theories (i.e., in a secondary way) against it; (4) when theories are tested against experience the experience is always of some item that is itself rationally-empirically present in the primary mode.

It is plain that this epistemology is a realist one in a well-defined sense of that chameleon word. But as it is justified by a reflexive appeal to rational-empirical presence, it will commend itself only to someone who finds our reflection persuasive or who has already accepted realism on quite independent grounds. The reflection itself is of course non-demonstrative. Many who recognize—though perhaps without adopting our metaphor of a circle—the pervasive importance of *prima facie* action and our *prima facie* knowledge of it may still reject entirely our reflexive exploitation of that situation. Most physicalists, I suppose, would take this line; no doubt others would as well. To all of them I would say that their own practice supports our conclusions by exemplifying what I shall call *the practical postulate of the authenticity of rational action*. There are two parts to it, one of which expresses the central point of our realist epistemology. (a) Rational action is what it purports to be to the agent who performs it: though conditioned by an infrastructure in which there are many powers that the agent need know nothing of, its *prima facie* status as the irreducible exercise of power is not an appearance in the sense of being a deception. Everything that a rational agent appears to do in the full concreteness of *prima facie* action—articulating a position, seeing a point, accepting or rejecting evidence, noting that such and such is the case (that there is snow on the ground, that the monitor reads 9.2835)—is essential to the outcome, must be taken seriously, must be relied on. Only a rational agent in its full concreteness can see and affirm what is the case. (b) The rational agent, articulating its sensory engagement in a bodily here-and-now, transcends its own subjectivity to know something distinct from subjectivity—the root sense of "know" here being rational-empirical presence. It would seem, though we need not press the point any further than we have already pressed it, that it is only as a consequence of its engagement with something else that subjectivity becomes available to its own reflexive scrutiny: presence to itself in reflection is always conditioned by the presence of something else to subjectivity.

The postulate therefore claims the authenticity of the rational-empirical presence one takes for granted in *prima facie* knowledge, and it

claims the authenticity of the rational actions—both primary and reflexive—in which that presence is articulated. Exemplification of the
postulate does not require explicit adherence to it. One exemplifies it
as long as one's practice would be pointless, one's conclusions ground-
less, if the postulate were not at some unnoticed level being affirmed. It
might be thought that (b)—the "realist" part of the postulate—is not
really being affirmed at any level by someone who should explicitly defend some antithetical epistemology, say some extreme form of phenomenalism. But the very language of rational-empirical presence must
be called upon in such a defense: yes, it is the case, transcending all
the potential self-deceptions of subjectivity, that green is empirically
present just now; and yes, the predicate "green" is just right for it; and
yes, it is indeed the case that it is a phenomenon that is present; yes,
that is, what is present is rationally-empirically present, and I, the de-
fender of phenomenalism, can say on the basis of this and other considerations that the commonsense world is present only as a construction out of such items.

The postulate contains a provision for self-correction that is implicitly
relied on. It is assumed that errors can in principle be corrected, and
corrected by a more attentive appeal to what is truly present in a
rational-empirical sense. That is to say that rational-empirical presence
is not in principle deceptive, although it is, of course, sometimes deceptive. Though in principle rational awareness is awareness of something that is distinct from consciousness; though the first mission of
subjectivity is to transcend itself to entertain something else; the very
texture of what we intend by such terms as "awareness," "consciousness," "subjectivity," "experience," and so on, will sometimes intervene
and represent itself deceptively as something that is independently the
case when in fact it is not. Something that purports to be what is the
case—purports to be an entity, event, state of affairs, or even some
formal-theoretic structure—will be nothing more than a by-product of
subjectivity. A supposed rational-empirical presence may not be so.
But our power to extricate ourselves from error of that kind is the
power to see what is in fact rationally-empirically present, what in fact
transcends the texture of our own subjectivity. The postulate alone is
beyond correction in the sense that all corrective efforts must rely on
it. There would appear to be no use of reason that does not purport to
be realistic in that minimal sense.

V

Manifest Image vs. Ontically
Significant Appearance

1

The Physicalist Manifest Image
(PMI) Doctrine Defined

The distinction Wilfrid Sellars made in 1960 between the manifest and the scientific images of man has become well known. In its first appearance[1] the notion of the manifest image is presented in so complex a way that it comes as a surprise to be told, in due course, that it is something we are reasonably familiar with—"the framework of sophisticated common sense." It should not really surprise us, for although it is easy enough to live on the plane of common sense and to be quite aware that one is doing so, it is far from easy to characterize it with any exactness. Some of the complication in Sellars's exposition, however, may come not just from the difficulty of this task but from his apparent wish to come to terms with some of the insights of existentialism as he characterizes the manifest image. "It is, first," he says, "the framework of terms in which man came to be aware of himself as man-in-the-world. It is the framework in terms of which, to use an existentialist turn of phrase, man first encountered himself—which is, of course, when he came to be man." The manifest image, however, is not merely a prescientific, uncritical, naive conception; for behind it there lies an "original" image which it supersedes. In this original image all objects whatsoever were understood to be persons, or rather, to put the matter into the formula Sellars seizes upon to qualify that rather unimaginative one, were understood to be "ways of being persons." The manifest image is a refinement of this original image, and in the refined version much of nature is understood in a different way, leaving only the primary objects—that is, ourselves—as persons. The rest of nature is then understood with the help of a categoreal scheme that has some scientific elements in it but is largely dominated by philosophy. In fact, much of the conceptual refinement of the original image comes from philosophizing; and indeed Sellars speaks of a "perennial philosophy of man-in-the-world" as an ideal philosophical construct around which philosophies in the Platonic tradition cluster, and which "is simply the manifest image endorsed as real, and its outline taken to be the large scale map of reality to which science brings a needle-point of detail and an elaborate technique of map-making." This perennial tradition, however, includes not only "the Platonic tradition in its broadest sense" but also philosophies of "common sense" and "ordinary usage." What is common to all of them "is an acceptance of the manifest image as the *real*."[2]

There are many details about the manifest image that need not concern us here. It is important for our purpose that, according to Sellars's account, when we are dominated by the manifest image we take ourselves to be persons and as such intractable to the same kind of causal account of our careers—especially our careers as knowers—that the "perennial" philosophy applied to things other than persons in ways that anticipate the scientific approach. At any rate, when we characterize ourselves in accordance with the manifest image, there is a conflict with the image of ourselves that science provides. Sellars's distinction between the manifest and the scientific images of man has, then, certain parallels with the distinction I have been making between *prima facie* rational action and the account a perfected science would give of it. There is, however, a difference between the two distinctions, and it is a radical one. His is made in the setting of a recognizable physicalist program—that of scientific realism, which in the sixties was perhaps the most influential form of physicalism; and the ontic status he attributed to the manifest image is accordingly less weighty than the one I attributed to rational agency at the outset by calling it *prima facie*, and certainly far less weighty than the status our later reflections laid claim to for it. Indeed, the term "image" already implies this lesser ontic status. As Sellars developed the doctrine in the course of the decade, the negative overtones of "image" were gradually reinforced; and at length it became clear that he regarded the manifest image as an appearance in a sense of "appearance" that, for all its ancestry in Sellars's study of Kant, is even more depreciatory than the sense Kant had in mind.

The manifest image, in Sellars's developed treatment of it, is at any rate an appearance in a far more negative sense than the one specified in chapter 2 under the rubric of ontically significant appearance and developed further in chapter 4. The difference is so radical that in this chapter I will use a modified version of Sellars's doctrine as a paradigm for a group of views that are opposed to the one I am developing here. But my purpose is anything but polemical. Sellars has modified his views in some ways. But even if he had not, I do not plan to address myself to his views just as they were in the sixties, but rather to a view about the appearance-status of the manifest image that, although it has important features in common with his doctrine, is broad enough to include other physicalist doctrines less influenced by Kant than his own. My target is, then, an ideal one, which I will call the physicalist manifest image doctrine. I intend that term to denote an appearance doctrine so habitual to physicalists that it pervades even identity theory, which should, to deserve its name, be free of it. That issue will not concern us directly until chapter 6. But before stating the ideal doctrine it will be convenient to say something more about the development of Sellars's doctrine.

His purpose in the essay "Philosophy and the Scientific Image of Man," in which the distinction first appeared in print, was to unite the manifest and the scientific images of man in "one field of intellectual vision";[3] in a later book he calls this "the attempt to take both man and science seriously."[4] The original essay told us that the task required "a point of view outside the manifest image from which the latter can be evaluated."[5] That is quite a different matter from our acceptance of the limitations of the circle of action and knowledge. But Sellars nevertheless treats the manifest image with considerable respect in this essay, and the stubbornly persistent character of it is plain to the very end, where he notes the communal nature of the image and goes on to say that it provides "the ambience of principles and standards (above all, those which make meaningful discourse and rationality itself possible) within which we live our own individual lives." Except for the difference just noted, this remark is not so far from what I have been saying about *prima facie* rational agency. But he immediately proceeds to make it clear that his goal is to "complete the scientific image" by joining to it the language of community, so that the "world as conceived by scientific theory" should at length become "our world and no longer an alien appendage to the world in which we do our living."[6] As we shall see, he interprets this task in a way that diminishes the stature of the manifest image.

The subtitle of the later book in which the theme of the manifest image appears, *Science and Metaphysics*, is *Variations on Kantian Themes*, and the notion of representation is accordingly more prominent in it than that of image. The notions however belong to the same family, and they are enough to tell the reader that our reflexive exploitation of the circle of *prima facie* action and our *prima facie* knowledge of it (in which metaphors for knowledge like representation, image, and mirror were repudiated in favor of the notion of presence) can not count as a defense of the manifest image in the sense Sellars intends it. In any event, the manifest image suffers in the course of *Science and Metaphysics* a considerable erosion of whatever authority it still had in the earlier book and still merited, it would seem, in the later book, in view of Sellars's apparent wish to do some justice to Kant's ethical insights. In all this he is guided by Peirce's conception of truth as the "ideal outcome of scientific inquiry," and hopes with its help to bridge the gulf between appearance and things-in-themselves. In due course he argues that "scientific objects, rather than metaphysical unknowables . . . are the things in themselves." As for the "objects of the manifest image"—including, presumably, whatever image of rational action belongs among them—they "do *really* exist," but only in the sense that "the individual concepts of the manifest image have counterparts in the scientific image which . . . can legitimately be regarded as their 'successors.' "[7] It will be clear that the authoritative ontological account, then, is the one to be given by a perfected science.

Sellars's effort throughout the book is exploratory, and surely his concern with Kantian ethics should restrain us from saying that he was without qualification a scientific realist at that time with respect to persons and their actions; evidently, as his preface suggests, he regarded scientific realism as a radically unfinished business.[8] But just as evidently, he regarded it as a program worth working at, and the distinction between appearance and things-in-themselves as he states it suggests that he thought the business could be finished.

Contemporary philosophers who make science their cognitive ideal and shape, in accordance with what they suppose to be its demands,

whatever metaphysical positions they either take or refuse to take are
seldom so much influenced by Kant as Sellars appears to have been. He
is of course no complete Kantian, for his views about what lies behind
appearance (behind the manifest) are very different from Kant's, and
indeed much closer to physicalists who have no such Kantian roots.
For this reason it is not really so odd as it might first appear to take his
manifest image doctrine as a paradigm for a class of related physicalist
doctrines that in effect claim the rational agent-in-act to be an appearance that lacks ontic significance. But in any case we shall now leave
off our examination of what Sellars says about the distinction and concern ourselves instead with the ideal version of his doctrine mentioned
earlier—the physicalist manifest image (PMI) doctrine.

The two main theses of the ideal PMI doctrine are these. (1) What
we experience as *such* is not truly the case but merely the way something appears to us, or the way we represent something to ourselves or
hold a supposed image of it before us. (2) What is truly the case and
stands to appearances (representations, images) as their ontic foundation can only be expressed in the theoretic language of science and can
not be experienced as such. These theses are I think shared by a great
many philosophers whose cognitive ideal is set by the proceedings of
science; who take it for granted that there is no first-order *philosophic*
engagement with the real that can be called cognitive; and who may or
may not describe themselves as holding a metaphysical position called
physicalism. They define a position latitudinarian enough to encompass
both scientific realists and at least some of those who prefer to work
with the metaphor of worldmaking;[9] both physicalists who are not phenomenalists in epistemology and some (and there are some) who are.
Things are moving fast among analytic philosophers, and I do not
know how much longer we shall be able to find analytic writers who
own that they accept these two theses, or indeed any theses with epistemological content. Wittgenstein twice told us that philosophy of
that kind was all over,[10] and now Richard Rorty, much influenced by
Wittgenstein, assures us that this is indeed so;[11] and certainly there is
enough despair about the future of philosophy to make epistemological and metaphysical disputes seem unreal. But if there are still a substantial number of philosophers who hold something like the PMI
doctrine, I hope to show in this chapter that such an appearance doctrine is untenable.

2

Rational Action as the Ground of Explanation

The most serious failing of the PMI doctrine is that it provides us with no ontological ground for the existence of explanations. The doctrine is not alone in this; so much attention has been given to the scientific explanation of action of late that it has been overlooked that the coming into being of a scientific explanation in our world itself requires explanation. When we contemplate *prima facie* rational action with our *prima facie* way of knowing it we have no trouble finding an explanation for the existence of an explanation: some rational agent produced it. It is one thesis of this chapter that this is the proper account of the matter: that the rational agent, just as we know it first in a *prima facie* way and afterwards in a reflection that does not leave our ineluctable circle, is the sufficient reason for the emergence of an explanation—indeed that the expression "sufficient reason" is there used in a way appropriate to the power of agents and can not and should not be interpreted in a way demanded by C→E causality. That is tantamount to claiming that the appearance of a rational act in its full concreteness is not an appearance in the sense in which a manifest image is understood by the PMI doctrine to be an appearance, but is in fact an ontically significant one. What appears in all its body-rooted, body-transcending, goal-directed, language-using, language-expanding, subjectivity-qualified *seeing of what is the case* is precisely what it appears to be—alternatively appears as it is and not as something else.

If one listens to what physicalists say about the achievements of scientists, one might suppose that they would agree with this, for there is nothing that commands more respect in such circles than the creative work of scientists. But for one who defends the PMI doctrine, the manifest image, though in the present state of science still possessed of some authority, will one day be displaced by the authority of what it *really is*; for what reality it has now is only an unclear version of what will be expressed in the successor concept for it that will one day exist in a scientific language. The PMI doctrine is therefore bound to reject any claim that there is something unique about the act of discovering an explanation that leaves it underexplained when the scientific explanations it discovers are applied to itself.

The account of the origin of a scientific explanation appropriate to an ideal PMI doctrine would presumably have to run something like this. There is something unsatisfactory, something not really explanatory, about the claim that Planck discovered the quantum principle—a principle that at the very least goes very far towards explaining a whole range of radiation happenings. We can scarcely call him the ontological ground of the emergence in our civilization of that principle, with its extraordinary explanatory power—not, at least, if we mean by "Planck" something more or less congruent with what we might take him to be in the context of the last chapter. What appears in our prescientific attitude as the enunciation of a principle in the course of a rational act performed by, and ontically dependent upon, an entity called Planck must be understood with the help of successor concepts in a perfected physics. Presumably what we are talking about *is really* a complex physical event of an unusual kind that takes place in and in the near neighborhood of a complex physical structure ("Planck"), and what emerges from it may be understood as a distinct physical structure (the explanation as written down) or a distinct and repeatable physical event (the entertaining or propounding of the explanation). All the structures and events will be highly complex, so much so that it may take some ingenuity on the part of the defenders of the PMI doctrine to persuade us that they are indeed concepts that appropriately belong in even a perfected physics. But however that may be, such a "successor" account of a *prima facie* act of scientific discovery would be no more amplified by talk of it as a "doing," as a "creative act," as a "scientific accomplishment" than would the account of any other physical event that was not a *prima facie* rational act. That is to say in effect that the emergence of explanations does not require that special kind of explanation I called for by introducing that ominous word "ground."

The replacement of the explanation of the origin of explanation by successor concepts may be summed up in this way. We begin with "Planck is sufficient for the origin of the (explanatory) quantum principle," which we abbreviate as "*P* suf *QE*." We want, however, a general statement about the relation between entities like Planck and scientific explanations, and so we reexpress the statement about Planck as "rational agents are sufficient for the origin of scientific explanations," which we abbreviate "*RA* suf *SE*." The successor concepts for *RA* and *SE* will involve both physical structures and physical events; but because of the possibility that one or the other of these notions might one day suffice, we simplify the issue by using instead the notion of physical configuration (*PC*). The successor concepts, then, we shall assume to be concepts of extraordinarily complex and unusual physical configurations. The expression

$$(1) \quad RA \text{ suf } SE$$

will then in principle be succeeded by some such expression as the following, in which CL stands for appropriate covering (predictive) laws set in an epistemic complex that lends them appropriate support and "→" stands for the causal relation understood in terms of what I have called c→E causality.

$$(II) \quad \frac{\overbrace{CL}}{PC_1 \rightarrow PC_2}$$

Two forms of one fundamental difficulty emerge at once. In the first place, the distinction between (1) and (II) in accordance with which the former is an *apparent* "explanation of explanation" and the latter a *real* one can only be made by some rational agent in every respect analogous to P, which is to say that the context in which (1) is taken (falsely, as is alleged) for a real explanation is also the one that furnishes the authority for the claim that (II) is the real explanation. In the second place, (II) is after all ex *hypothesi* an *explanation*, and it can be so only to a rational agent, whose authority is once again restored. If we try to do the same trick with (II) as was done with SE in the transition from (1) to (II)—that is, if we try to explain the existence of the explanation called (II)—we begin an ascent through a series of type levels that is without end. The explanation of explanations by (1) no doubt holds residual obscurities, but not that kind of obscurity.

This is a simple enough difficulty, but it is not to be thought that it can be removed by pointing out that if some intellectual community of the future should accept (II) as the proper form of an explanation of the origin of an explanation, then (II) would *be* the proper form, seeing that the only authority in such matters is, finally, the intellectual community. The intellectual community, having then failed to notice the appeal to its own authority in the sense of (1), would simply be in error. It is a state in which intellectual communities have been before—a consideration, incidentally, that undermines the more extreme interpretations of the position of Thomas Kuhn.[12] We shall look at other examples of this fundamental difficulty in the course of this chapter.

Does any philosopher seriously advocate a program for the production of explanations that should explain (in some way analogous to the way physics explains) the production of scientific explanations? Though I have in effect identified advocates only in such philosophers as might explicitly hold an ideal PMI doctrine, I think that any philosopher who regards *prima facie* rational action as an appearance the corresponding reality of which is to be found in physical structures and physical events, or as an *explicandum* whose *explicans* is to be provided by a perfected physics, will upon careful examination be found to hold that ideal doctrine. There are plenty of philosophers who answer that description, although some of them prefer to express their views in terms of an identity doctrine. Confronted with the demand for a ground for explanations, they would surely have to respond in some such way as the one I have sketched.

From the point of view established by the reflections of the last chapter it is more plausible that rational action is the ground of all explanation. By this I mean that rational action is the sufficient reason for the presence in our world of explanations of all sorts—good, bad, and indifferent. Whatever rational order may characterize reality in general (more accurately, perhaps, whatever mixture of order and disorder may characterize it), it is for rational action to find it out; and to say so is not to say something approximate, commonsensical, prescientific—something that in principle might be replaced by some more profound account of the coming into being of explanations—but something precise, exact, and satisfactory. A good deal has already been said in this book about language—about how the successful articulation of fresh linguistic structures in our sensory and bodily engagement with the world is tantamount to an intensification of rational-empirical presence for us; how against this background linguistic structures (formal structures in the broadest sense) can be elaborated in a cyclic interplay with experience either for their own sakes or for their explanatory value. In that broad sense of "language," rational action is the ground of explanation by being the ground of language.

If rational action should be the ground of explanation and of language we do not set it either quite beyond explanation or quite beyond the power of language to illuminate it, except in the well-defined sense of the conditions of explanatory ultimacy and of explanatory opacity. In the language of our anticipatory supposition of chapter 1, section 4, explanations directed to an infrastructure do indeed explain features of action. In the language of many metaphysical systems, a necessary Being is regarded as the ground of existence of all contingent beings—including those that devise explanations—and if there should be such a necessary Being, the discovery of Its existence by a contingent being would explain the latter's power to make that and other explanatory discoveries. But any explanation, scientific or theological, that purports to demonstrate that its own *prima facie* discoverer need not be entertained as a ground of explanation in any ontologically significant sense is in a *prima facie* logical predicament.

From the reflective point of view that purports to have transformed our ineluctable circle of rational action as the agent experiences it and knows it—that is, as the agent experiences it as such—the rational agent is indeed the ontological ground of explanation. But behind this lies its status as the ontological ground of philosophical doctrines. Our argument against the adequacy of an explanation of the origin of scientific explanation by·way of the "successor" concepts of some physics of the future was an argument against a philosophical doctrine—the PMI doctrine; and if we take "PD" as an abbreviation for "philosophical doctrine," we can easily construct an argument against the supersession of

(III)   *RA* suf *PD*

by some analogue of (II). It would, to be sure, move within the same transformed circle, and would have only whatever authority we have found there. But that does not raise any special difficulty, because any argument between ourselves and advocates of the PMI doctrine will be conducted in an arena appropriate to the authenticated rational agent and will be defined by practical adherence to some version of "*RA* suf *PD*." In this chapter I shall be concerned with the confusions and perplexities that always arise when philosophers who advocate some ancestor of the PMI doctrine or the PMI doctrine itself either fail to notice this point or suppose that it can be circumvented. When in the next chapter we turn to an ideal theory of the identity of rational action with its physiological basis, at least some of our criticism of it will turn upon the point that it includes, though at a different and unnoticed level, the thesis that a *prima facie* rational act is an appearance in the PMI sense. Neither in the present chapter nor in the next will any attack be made on the explanatory value of scientific explanations. If I am right about the status of rational action as the ontological ground of the coming into being of explanations, this does not question the value of scientific explanations but only the value of certain philosophical arguments about, interpretations of, and attitudes towards them.

3

An Ancestor of the Physicalist Manifest
Image Doctrine: Ancient Atomism

There are good reasons for beginning with ancient atomism. Physicalism has no monopoly on the ancient distinction between appearance
and reality, and indeed in the past the distinction occurred more often
in the setting of this or that idealist metaphysics of either the Western
or the Eastern tradition. But in those traditions it is usually not rational
agency whose ontological status is depreciated so much as *individual*
rational agency; and in any event the challenge to the authenticity of
rational agency experienced as such comes these days chiefly from
physicalism. The form that distinction first takes in ancient atomism
could serve, with some few adjustments, as a primitive expression of
the PMI doctrine. There is the further attraction that this earliest form
of the PMI doctrine appears, as we shall see, to express some concern
about its own self-subverting character.

The structure of atomism as a metaphysical doctrine remained relatively unchanged from the fifth century B.C. until quite recent times—
setting aside the introduction by Epicurus of the possibility of an inexplicable swerve, or *clinamen*, in the path of any particular atom in
motion.[13] The original doctrine of Leucippus and Democritus apparently held that an atom's path was a necessary one and could undergo
modification only from the impact of other atoms moving with equal
necessity. The main lines of the atomists' doctrine are familiar enough.[14]
(1) There are many atoms—perhaps an infinite number of them. Each
is a metaphysical ultimate having characteristics like those Parmenides'
(one) Being would have if his poem were given a materialist interpretation.[15] Being is defined by the multiplicity of atoms and by the characteristics each of them possesses "in itself." (2) The being-features of
each atom are absolute solidity, which means that atoms are of uniform
density; size, in which they differ; and shape, in which they also differ.
These characteristics do not come into being but simply constitute being; and they do not change, for that would be to pass out of being.
(3) Although atoms move, translation of that kind does not affect their
being; indeed it is the source of becoming, not of course of the atoms
themselves but of the aggregates (or macrostructures) in which they
combine and recombine in accordance with their shapes, sizes, and

varying positions relative to one another. (4) All this takes place in the void, or not-being. (5) Human beings perceive only these macrostructures, which are in a constant state of becoming, and not the atoms, each of which reposes in its own Parmenidean being. They perceive these macrostructures as characterized by qualities, not just those (like solidity) that go back to the being-features of the atoms, but others, such as warmth, color, and odor, that consist merely in the relation between the perceived and perceiving macrostructures, relations that are only possible because of the streams of atoms moving between them. (6) The account contained in the preceding five points is not propounded by the senses, which give us a bastard (obscure) "knowledge," opinion, or conventional usage, but rather by the intellect, or mind.

Point (6) was seen to offer a difficulty by Democritus himself; and he expresses it in the little dialogue between the intellect and senses that is so often quoted. The intellect, or mind, maintains that color, sweetness, and bitterness (which come to us by way of the senses) are merely conventional; the senses reply that all the evidence the intellect has comes from sensation, and that the overthrow of the senses will be the downfall of the intellect as well. That Democritus was quite clear about the difficulty we can not be sure from the short fragment in Diels,[16] but it is real enough, and we may set it out in this way. The truth of the atomist doctrine depends upon our taking (6) seriously: it must indeed be intellect, mind, or reason that sees the state of affairs described in the first five points, for if they contained just the findings of the senses they would be as relative as the senses themselves are— aggregates of atoms in motion responding to other atoms in motion— and all the pronouncements about being would themselves be patterns of becoming, as evanescent, as much a matter of opinion, or convention—later times would say as secondary, as subjective—as the qualities of color, warmth, and odor. But intellect, or reason, depends on the senses, and though the fragments of Democritus do not say so, intellect itself can be nothing but a pattern of atoms in motion—a conclusion affirmed by accounts of the doctrine, such as Aristotle's,[17] more detailed than the surviving fragments of Democritus provide. The truth of the rest of the doctrine then depends upon (6), yet once the significance of (6) is spun out in terms of (1)–(5), it subverts the doctrine. For either (a) intellect, or reason, has the authority assigned to it, in which case it is an exception to the doctrine, so that the doctrine fails; or (b) it accords with the doctrine, in which case it suffers from all the relativity (the appearance-status) assigned to macrostructures and can not attain truth, so that the doctrine again collapses. In terms of the contemporary approach to such matters, we should have to say that if the *prima facie* act of reasoning that led to the first five points is only *prima facie*—only an appearance of the underlying movements of groups of atoms—then the doctrine that emerges from it, that is indeed enframed by it, can not be sound. And of course it is not.

These remarks do not affect what remains of the doctrine after we excise the far-reaching metaphysical argument. It can then be reinterpreted as a scientific hypothesis, and as such it has great value and indeed is in some sense true. The role of the resuscitated ancient atomism in the development of modern science from the Renaissance until the revolution in atomic theory that took place about the beginning of this century is extraordinarily complex. It could not usefully function as a scientific hypothesis until metaphysical generalities about solidity, shape, and size could be replaced by exact quantitative concepts that were amenable to generalization in laws; and the relations in quantitative laws of such concepts as velocity, mass, and acceleration were worked out for macroscopic objects long before anything of the kind could be done for microstructures like molecules and atoms. Indeed the confirmation of the existence of such entities developed at equal pace with techniques for quantifying their nature. In much of this development some of the metaphysical claims of the original doctrine were often fruitfully set aside. Chief of these were the unqualified identification of the nature of the atoms with being and the application of the doctrine without qualification to the rational agent who propounded it. Materialist metaphysics based on atomism continued to be important, and it had periods of great influence, as in the eighteenth century. But some of the most far-reaching advances in scientific understanding were achieved on the premises that science dealt only with physical being and that scientists themselves were not merely physical beings. That a dualist metaphysics of that kind was itself full of difficulties does not alter the case, for that doctrine was not at any rate self-subverting in the uncompromising sense we have noted in the atomism of Democritus. In a dualist setting of a roughly Cartesian kind—Descartes himself being no atomist—the conviction that macroscopic objects were in some sense composed of atoms and that these in due course would be seen to behave lawfully could be usefully held as a scientific hypothesis without making the objective findings of reason a logical impossibility.

4

Macrostructures as Appearances in an
Ideal PMI Doctrine

The view that something called consciousness, awareness, subjectivity, intentionality, mind, or the mental is epiphenomenal—an appearance in some sense generated by a microstructure—was in its time an influential one in philosophy. It is still influential in certain scientific quarters—sufficiently so that a distinguished neurophysiologist like Sperry can still suppose, in arguing against it, that it represents scientific orthodoxy.[18] Certainly it is common enough in popularized neurophysiology.[19] But there are few philosophers today who hold it. That is perhaps because epiphenomenalism in its usual form assumes that the epiphenomenon is in some sense *caused* by the underlying microstructure[20]—an assumption that would be hard to fit both to the facts and to the c→e view of causality that usually dominates such discussions. Those who hold an utterly physicalist view of mind today are more likely to defend some form of the identity theory. For similar reasons, philosophers who hold some version of a PMI doctrine about rational action are unlikely to claim that it is epiphenomenal upon a microstructure, being content enough to regard it as merely a macroscopic *explicandum* of which the corresponding *explicans* is to be found in the microstructure. By this device some kind of ontic dependence of the one on the other is assumed, but it is not asserted to be one of effect on cause. But there are nonetheless some obvious resemblances between the doctrine that mind is an epiphenomenon upon microstructures and the ideal PMI doctrine about rational agency. Certainly the reasons given to support the claim that mind is epiphenomenal have something in common with the reasons sometimes given for the claim that the ontological status of rational action is that of an appearance in the PMI sense.

Although we shall concern ourselves in this section with the form of the PMI doctrine that lays great stress upon microstructures and microevents, it should be said in advance that a stress of that kind is not absolutely essential to the doctrine. Many writers who are disposed to regard *prima facie* action as something phenomenal, and therefore not really what it purports to be, are nonetheless quite comfortable with the view that the phenomenon is properly to be understood as a macroevent that (a) corresponds exactly in size with what we as *prima facie* rational agents entertain when we are aware of ourselves or someone else in action; and (b) has nonetheless only those properties that physics deals with. In other words, what on this interpretation *appears* is not precisely just a function of size, but rather of our way of taking in, or experiencing, something of any size. Let us say, then, that philosophers who hold this version of the PMI doctrine distinguish between two types of macroscopic things. The first type includes *phenomenal*, or *manifest image*, macroscopic properties, structures, and events— properties like color, odor, taste; structures like people and animals; and events like their overt actions. They are, all these things, experienced as such, and we will say that for this version of the PMI doctrine they are PMI-macroscopic. The second type includes *theoretic* macrostructures and macroevents: they are what physical theory postulates as the physically real counterparts of the PMI-macroscopic things— counterparts that can not be experienced as such, and we will say that they are T-macroscopic. According to this version of the PMI doctrine, some kind of analysis of PMI-macroscopic things in terms of T-microscopic things is indeed possible, but such an analysis must remain incomplete in the sense that when the T-things are ordered in terms of size-levels, the laws operative at any given level are not deducible from, although they are consistent with, the laws operative at the next smaller level. If we wish to understand how a PMI-macroscopic thing really operates, we must have recourse to T-macroscopic things appropriate to that level—that is to say, we must have recourse to the irreducible laws of nature of the macroscopic level in question.

Some influential scientists hold this view, for instance Roger Sperry[21] and Paul Weiss[22] among biologists; and at least one philosopher-scientist, Michael Polanyi, argued for it tenaciously in writings extending over the later part of his career.[23] I have elsewhere called this view the hierarchic view of the laws of nature.[24] It does not envision the replacement of such sciences as psychology and biology—and such present branches of the latter as embryology and neurophysiology—by some physics of the future. Clearly none of the writers mentioned holds an explicit PMI doctrine. Whether antireductionists of this kind hold or do not hold an *implicit* PMI doctrine with respect to the rational agent depends on what attitude they take up towards the macroscopic things that a true proponent of the PMI doctrine naturally regards as PMI-macroscopic; and this in turn, I suggest, depends upon how much they think can be explained by the hierarchic laws they think scientists should seek. Certainly the writers just mentioned hold that the writ of hierarchic science runs through a very extensive country; indeed, it sometimes seems that they suppose that some hierarchic science of the future will make philosophy superfluous. At least one recent writer who apparently holds a hierarchic view of the laws of nature, Edgar Wilson, clearly hovers somewhere between a PMI doctrine and the ideal identity doctrine I take up in the next chapter.[25]

In what follows I shall be dealing, however, with the form of the PMI doctrine that not only makes a distinction between PMI-macroscopic things and T-things but also holds that the true *explicans* is to be found in T-*microscopic* things. The usual scientific claim is that, given initial and boundary conditions of a physical system, causal interactions within it are predictable and thus explicable by an appeal to the laws of nature. In the present case this is supplemented by the further claim that as one moves down through the fine structure, guided by the regulative idea of an ultimate fine structure understood entirely in terms of T-things, the laws discovered are more pervasive, their explanatory-predictive value more powerful. PMI-macrostructures and macroevents are therefore in principle exhaustively analyzable as aggregates of T-microstructures and microevents. We may conveniently call this form of the PMI doctrine T-microscopic reductionism, having in mind a sense of "reductionism" for which Nagel's treatment of the subject can serve as at least a general guide.[26]

Before turning to that, however, it is worth noting that macrostructures of the largest kind—those of the order cosmologists deal in—play an important role in today's science and may become even more important in the future. The continuing effort to bring about some sort of theoretical union of general relativity and quantum theory is based on the assumption that the most pervasive physical laws—including those that prevail at the microlevel—will be found in the T-macrostructures of some unified field theory of the future and not in the T-microstructures considered in themselves. Cosmology may turn out to be as important in the long run for microphysics as microphysics for cosmology. If this should be so, the macroscopic-microscopic distinction would have to be given a somewhat different twist: it could then be argued that subjectivity is not so much prone to creating manifest images that are in effect self-deceptions as it is the victim of sensory modalities that work within a certain size range—the range of what Reichenbach calls our "medium-sized dimensions."[27] It would then have the task of overcoming those size-based limitations by speculative flights.

To return, however, to the form of the PMI doctrine we are to consider: I want to show that it is self-subverting in a way reminiscent of the self-subverting feature of the ancient atomism we have glanced at. The self-subverting feature of T-microstructure reductionism will then be seen to carry over to the hierarchic form of the doctrine that is content to regard macroscopic things as PMI-macroscopic and to suppose that there is a reality behind them that is best understood in terms of T-macrostructures. In the first stage of this argument I will point to two profound difficulties that have to do with the role subjectivity is assumed to play relative to PMI-macroscopic things. I will then interrupt that line of thought to show that the notion of PMI-macroscopic things (properties, structures, events) must be modified in a significant way before it has any application at all to *prima facie* rational action. We will then return to our two profound difficulties to notice how our modification has compounded them.

The earliest successes in explaining (alleged) PMI-macroscopic things in terms of T-microscopic things were achieved with things other than ourselves, although a more speculative metaphysical application of the doctrine to human beings in eighteenth-century materialism preceded these scientific successes.[28] The (alleged) PMI-macroscopic structures that are chemical compounds, which are experienced in (alleged) PMI-macroevents like seeing, tasting, hearing, and so on, are understood to be functions of the T-microstructures we call molecules. These in turn are functions of atomic structures, and these in turn of the still finer T-structures it has been the task of this century to discover. The macroscopic properties are assumed to be relative to ourselves (in a PMI sense), and because that relativity has always been more striking in the case of the so-called secondary qualities, we will use them as examples, although without any thought that any ultimate contrast of them with primary qualities can be sustained. Color, warmth, odor can be regarded as appearances in the sense that T-microevents can be used to give a satisfactory explanatory account of them, an account that depends upon their macroscopic availability to a normal observer whenever the corresponding T-microevents can be shown to be taking place.

Supposed PMI-macroscopic appearances of this kind created no serious problems for the ontological self-confidence of the observer, for no such far-reaching explanatory claims of the kind traditionally made for agency were ever made for such things as colors. But the status of macroscopic things becomes more pressing in the case of organisms in general, still more in the case of the higher animals, and very pressing

indeed in the case of human beings. The logic of the PMI doctrine we
are concerned with has developed at equal pace with the progress science has made in studying the finest grain of the physical world in
terms of T-microstructures; and although the trick of making available
to an observer the macroscopic *explicandum* by contriving certain physical events that are then given interpretation in T-microscopic terms
can seldom be performed unambiguously, an elaborate train of reasoning nonetheless seems to make it plausible that such an explanatory
move has in fact been satisfactorily made. At any rate, the PMI doctrine
of the T-microscopic reductionist sort we are now considering requires
us to take the tree I see outside my window now, or the Monarch
butterfly I saw light on a milkweed blossom last summer, as PMI-
macroscopic in much the sense in which colors and the like are presumed to be so.[29] Their T-microstructures—their coded DNA, their other
macromolecules, and the still finer structures upon which they depend—explain them, and whenever the appropriate pattern of such
things can be shown to be present the normal observer will have PMI-
experiences like the one I am having now when I look out the window
or the one I had last summer. The macroscopic properties, structures,
events—the full concreteness of tree, butterfly, or blossom before some
philosophy tells us otherwise—are therefore PMI-macroscopic: they are
appearances that are brought about by the authentic microstructures
and microevents that do not appear but are understood in terms of
T-microscopic things. They are, these authentic things, understood by
scientific reason to exist, much as intellect assured Democritus that
the swarm of Parmenidean atoms was real.

Once this line of reasoning is embarked upon, there is no reason for
the PMI doctrine to stop with plants and insects. The disconsolate
puppy tied by his thoughtless mistress to the tree below my window
and left to shiver in the cold as she attends class must have the same
PMI-macroscopic status, even though, as he tugs at his collar and howls
dismally, he seems to give the lie to this sense of quasi-epiphenomenal
inefficacy we might take for granted in other things—seems to lay
claim to an authenticity for his macroscopic self more insistently than
tree, butterfly, or blossom do. So with that marvelous combination of
macroscopic properties, structures, and events we call the rational
agent-in-act: it too is to be understood as a PMI-macroscopic thing,
although the case is so much more complicated that we shall defer consideration of it until the next section.

If we ask why those inauthentic appearances—those PMI-macroscopic

properties, structures, events—should be there, the PMI doctrine traces
it all back to the subjectivity of the knower to whom it appears. The
term "subjectivity" may or may not be used, and I myself do not use
it here in the guarded and non-Cartesian sense I introduced in the last
chapter. Indeed I do not use it just here in any very fixed sense, for I
mean it to do service for a variety of related views in which one might
find in its place such other expressions as "consciousness," "awareness," "experience," "the mental," "intentionality," "the mind," and
so on. With these reservations, we may say that, according to the PMI
doctrine, that is where the fault lies; that is where PMI-macroscopic
things (appearances) are generated, in the subject's response to something that does not appear: it is the texture of subjectivity itself that
supports the PMI-macroscopic thing it entertains and, in entertaining,
supposes itself to be in the authentic presence of. The subject supposes
that its rational awareness of the concrete macroscopic features of tree
or dog is an awareness of something that has a real status independent
of that awareness, that it is in the presence of something authentic. But
in point of fact it is the deceptive texture of subjectivity itself that the
subject is encountering rather than the tree as it is or the dog as it is.
The true realities are the real microstructures, understood by virtue of
T-microstructures, that manifest themselves to a deficient subjectivity
in this PMI-macroscopic way.

The PMI doctrine can scarcely maintain that subjectivity itself is to
be understood as a PMI-macroscopic thing, for such things are defined
in this doctrine by their being entertained by subjectivity. We have
come upon the first of the two profound difficulties I mentioned earlier. It can be summed up as follows. (a) According to the PMI doctrine, the distinction between (inauthentic) PMI-macroscopic properties, structures, and events and (authentic) T-microstructures and
microevents depends upon the former's being available to subjectivity
whenever the appropriate instances of the latter are known to be present or taking place. (b) Although subjectivity may be said to be reflexively available to itself whenever anything else is available to it, it
can not be available to itself in the sense intended in (a)—that is, can
not be available to itself in the sense in which the tree, butterfly,
or puppy is alleged to be available to it. (c) Even if subjectivity
should be inauthentic, it can not therefore be inauthentic in the sense
the holder of the PMI doctrine intends to apply to so-called PMI-
macroscopic things.

The second difficulty is already laid down in the first, although it is easy to overlook it. It is that the very assessment of the ontological distinction between PMI-macroscopic things and the class of T-microscopic things that serve to explain them—that is, the assessment of the distinction between appearance and reality—is made within the (allegedly) PMI-arena of the same subjectivity the logic of the PMI doctrine would convict of inauthenticity. Perhaps no advocate of the PMI view would want to claim that the *distinction* is a PMI-macroscopic thing, but on the other hand it is subjectivity that affirms it, just as it is subjectivity that affirms a color, a butterfly, or a howling puppy tied to a tree. The full concreteness of subjectivity can therefore not in principle be a generator only of PMI-macroscopic things—it can not, that is, be a mere appearance breeding mere appearances—if within it there emerges an allegedly sound ontological distinction between (inauthentic) PMI-macroscopic things and (authentic) T-microscopic things.

5

*The Role of Subjectivity in the Full
Concreteness of Rational Action*

When the PMI doctrine is applied to the *prima facie* rational agent-in-act, it must hold in effect that the latter is a PMI-macroscopic structure or event having PMI-macroscopic properties (for short, "PMI-macroscopic thing"). But the full concreteness of a *prima facie* rational act to the agent that takes itself to be performing it includes subjectivity, so that the two difficulties just noticed are compounded. Because I have given an account of subjectivity in the last chapter that is realist and non-Cartesian—it was said to be self-transcendent with respect to rational-empirical presence and therefore to have no special problem about affirming the presence of a physical world in some sense distinct from itself—I want to remind the reader that that account of subjectivity need not be accepted for the argument of the present section to hold. It will be enough if "subjectivity" (or one of the alternative terms that are used in discussions like this) has only whatever meaning an advocate of the PMI doctrine wishes to give it. For the central point is simply that a *prima facie* rational act, whatever else it may be, is also a *prima facie* way of attending, being aware, being conscious, understanding, and (sometimes) articulating in words. It is sometimes more than one of these things, and it is potentially any of them.

The importance of subjectivity to the PMI doctrine is conceded by

anyone who defends it, because PMI-macroscopic things are said to have
their appearance-status in relation to subjectivity, which is in that sense
a deficient, deceptive, or delusive thing. It is, in that doctrine, a way
of attending to something that assigns it a status it does not really
deserve and fails to notice that it is properly characterizable in
T-microscopic terms. To put it another way: subjectivity takes the PMI-
macroscopic thing for what it purports to be—takes it for something
authentic—whereas it is in fact merely a PMI-macroscopic thing. In our
present argument, however, it is important to note that subjectivity is
not just what attends to something, but rather an essential aspect of
what we are now trying to attend to, namely, *prima facie* rational action. Whether subjectivity is or is not authentic, it qualifies rational
action and does not merely attend to it. What the rational agent is reflexively attending to when it is attending to itself-in-act has subjectivity as a prominent, indeed an essential, feature of it.

To make that point secure, it will be enough to review some of the
conclusions about subjectivity obtained in the interpersonal reflection
on it in section 3 of the preceding chapter. We excise from the conclusions only whatever is in conflict with the attitude towards subjectivity held in the PMI doctrine, for throughout this chapter it is our intent to show that doctrine to be self-subverting, so that we must rest
content with whatever sense of subjectivity it employs.

There is, in the first place, a peripheral awareness of acting that accompanies all rational action—all doings, makings, sayings, and know-
ings. It is by no means an observer's awareness, but is a concrete and
essential feature of the *rational* aspect, of the *rational* side, of acting
rationally. It comes to the fore and is seen to be integral with the full
concreteness of the action when in reflection upon itself a rational action becomes, what it always is potentially, a reflexive rational action:
one attends to one's action, and also in doing so attends to one's attending, as we did in the last two chapters. The example is perhaps ex-
cessively complicated, but we were there drawing attention *to* our subjectivity as an aspect of action—i.e., drawing the attention *of* subjectivity
to itself. These remarks, too reminiscent perhaps of the tortuous dealings with these matters at the frontier where phenomenology and
existentialism meet, may be supplemented by a more obvious and
less tendentious point.

Advocates of the PMI doctrine will surely agree that the writing of a
sentence, paragraph, or chapter can be called (in the PMI sense) a rational act or series of rational acts. They will presumably extend that

courtesy even to writing they disagree with, as long as it meets certain
minimum standards of intelligibility. I will therefore assume that the
preceding chapter, which purports to be a reflexive vindication of ontic responsibility, was written by virtue of a series of rational acts.
From the point of view of the PMI-doctrine, that series of acts will be
qualified by subjectivity in the sense of being trapped in the condition
of what *they* regard as the manifest image. From the point of view I
am defending in this chapter, the notion of manifest image distorts
the true status of *prima facie* rational action, and the notion of subjectivity that goes with it distorts the sense in which (I would concede)
all rational acts are qualified by subjectivity. But all we need for the
present argument is that advocates of the PMI argument should say
that speech-acts can be qualified by subjectivity in *their* sense of
"subjectivity."

6

The Self-Subverting Character of the Assessment
of Prima Facie *Rational Action as Mere Appearance*
(as PMI-Macroscopic*)*

We may now review the argument that lies behind the PMI-doctrine's
assessment of the ontological status of rational action; we will then
gather together the threads of the last two sections and show that the
argument is self-subverting. The argument, in which we will take the
liberty of supposing its advocates to be aware of and to be rejecting
our own terminology, runs as follows.

(a) When the *prima facie* rational agent attends to its own action
and supposes itself to be cognitively aware of it, the cognitive awareness is *only* a *prima facie* one: it has no authentic ontic significance. In
that sense, the rational agent, taken not as an ideal neurophysiologist
or even ideal physicist would take it, but in the ordinary way in which
the rational agent "experiences it as such," is *only* a *prima facie* agent.

(b) The gradual improvement in such sciences as neurophysiology
suggests that the *prima facie* rational agent is a PMI-macroscopic thing,
available to be experienced and "rationally" affirmed only at a certain
level of magnitude—that of the *prima facie* agent itself. The *explicans*
of this *explicandum* is to be found in the microstructures and microevents that science expresses, with more and more adequacy as time
goes on, in terms of T-microstructures and microevents. To say that the

agent is a PMI-macroscopic thing is to say that, in attributing to itself
the power and efficacy it finds there in its *prima facie* self-knowledge,
it is concerned with an appearance, with something phenomenal or
phenomenological, rather than with something that, just as it is experienced and "rationally" affirmed, is ontically significant.

(c) The reason for this is that the experiential self-awareness of the
prima facie rational agent as it is expressed in nontechnical, nonquanti-
tative language is subjective; and that the ontological level, state,
or function designated by such terms as "subjectivity," "consciousness," "awareness," "mentality" is deficient whenever it "rationally"
affirms things that are experienced as such. It is theory, dealing in
terms of T-microstructures and microevents and invoking the predic-
tive-explanatory ideal, that tells us what things experienced as such
really are. Since PMI-macroscopic things like the rational agent-in-act
are in fact *appearances of* something else, the outstanding and most
prestigious feature of *prima facie* rational agency, its ontic responsibility, is not what it purports to be but is a PMI-macroscopic *appearance*
feature.

So much for the argument itself. Its self-subverting character may
now be brought out in this way.

(A) In a *prima facie* set of rational acts the advocate of the PMI doctrine maintains that all such acts are PMI-macroscopic; that is to say,
that they are appearances to a (deficient) subjectivity of a reality that
is quite different.

(B) The most plausible reason for assigning something PMI-macroscopic status is the availability to an observer (a subjectivity) of an experience of a certain kind when the appropriate microstructures and
microevents, understood in terms of T-microstructures and microevents,
are present or occur.

(c) But, as was shown in section 4, subjectivity (however understood) can not itself be a PMI-macroscopic thing; furthermore, as was
shown in section 5, subjectivity is an essential qualification of *prima facie* rational acts of the kind the proponent of the PMI-doctrine is engaged in, so that they too can not be PMI-macroscopic in the sense
intended. Indeed, such acts would appear to be the ground of PMI-
macroscopic things in somewhat the sense we have seen subjectivity itself to be.

(D) But in any case the *prima facie* rational acts making up the
argument of the proponent of the PMI doctrine affirm their competence to distinguish appearance from reality, PMI-macroscopic things

from the т-microscopic things that really explain them. These *prima facie* acts, moreover, do not purport to propound explanations, but rather to compare their own (PMI-macroscopic) self-assessment with an explanation of them in т-microscopic terms and to assess the comparative ontic worth of the two approaches. They therefore maintain they are *not* PMI-macroscopic, for part of what "appears" to them— "appears" within their PMI appearance-texture—is an authentic ontic distinction.

It is difficult to display this self-subverting argument without seeming to propound some more familiar argument—that of twentieth-century phenomenalism, that of Berkeley himself, or that of contemporary phenomenology. The epistemological point I am trying to make is more simple, more realistic, even more naive than that. It is that there is a realistic thrust in all subjectivity (no longer in the PMI sense of "subjectivity") that expresses itself in language, theory, and action. While enjoying and indeed relying on its own full concreteness (which includes but is by no means limited to its own "interior" texture), the subjectivity of the agent-in-act takes itself to be dealing with something that transcends it. It is incapable of giving up this claim. If it says (in the person of someone who would make a mere *explicandum* of a cognitive act), "What 'I' am now expressing is inauthentic in the sense that it is the work of neural nets and their laws; this 'I-in-act' *does* nothing," it both relies upon the full concrete texture of the I-in-act to make the point and insists also that the I-in-act transcends its (supposedly deceptive) subjectivity to see the point to be (presumptively) sound.

7

Rational Action as the Ground
of Ontic Assessment

It is reasonable to suppose, seeing that it is only what we have shown our ideal PMI opponent also to suppose, that *prima facie* rational action, just as we experience it and articulate it as such—being aware, formulating what we are aware of in language, understanding, taking a point, propounding a scientific theory, testing a theory, deliberating and making a decision, and so on—that *prima facie* rational action is capable of ontic assessment of both other things and itself. This is not to question the role its infrastructure plays; it is merely to suppose that an exhaustive analysis of what each item or group of items in that bil-

lionfold complexity "does" is not an analysis of what we do with the
help of their contributions. That without that infrastructure we could
not be aware of things and articulate our awareness in language means
only that rational action could not be what it is if the items in the infrastructure were not what they are. Bishop Butler's famous maxim is
perhaps too often quoted, but sometimes nothing else will do: everything is what it is, and not another thing; to which we may add that
many things that are indeed other things—as synaptic vesicles, ion
gates, and neurons are each of them severally and all of them together
another thing than rational action—may contribute intimately to a
thing that nonetheless remains precisely what it is.

Just here it may help to turn again to the epistemology summarized
towards the end of the last chapter, for it suggests why our being able
to see rational action for what it is—our being able to make it appear
as it is rather than as a distortion of something else—is consistent with
our finding a profound explanatory value in what science can tell us of
the infrastructure of an act.

Our interpersonal reflection on *prima facie* knowledge purported to
confirm its capacity for ontic assessment. Confronted with its world,
it brings each thing it attends to, as well as the unity of the whole, to
rational-empirical presence, responding within the limitations of its
sensory modalities and completing that response in a rational articulation that both makes use of and is limited by those modalities. (This
last point echoes Kant, insofar as he can be echoed within an epistemological framework in which the notion of representation is replaced by
the notion of presence.) In the present context this means that human
knowledge, functioning in the mode of rational-empirical presence, is
in principle capable of discriminating ontological levels in any complex
entity. This capacity, though colored by the limitations of our sensory
capacities, does not in principle miss what is the case about any level
whose presence it discloses in its primary function. When the primary
function is intensified by reflection upon itself, it also discloses at least
the possibility of making what it focuses upon more fully present. It
may also change its focus, and when it does, more than one level, together with the interdependence of the levels, may be in view.

The achievements of the community of rational agents in dealing
with the infrastructures of their own actions in the mode of science are
profoundly illuminating. They provide an explanation of the conditions of action that really does explain: the relentless search for the
microstructure underlying anything (however small) casts at least a

partial illumination on what it purports to explain. But the rational agent's instinct for the ontic presence of an entity at any given level is an instinct for the partial independence of that level. The distinction of an entity at one level is at once the basis of its contribution to another level and a sign of its partial independence from such levels as condition its own ontic status. Just so, each level will be partially opaque to explanations couched entirely in terms of another level. Our own rational action is a case in point. To say that someone acted rationally—perhaps even acted rationally to devise a predictive explanation—is to say something whose significance can be much amplified by physiological explanation, but whose own significance and explanatory value can not be superseded. It is an explanatory ultimate, necessary to any adequate account of the relevant state of affairs, and if the relevant state of affairs includes the existence of a certain body of science that affords predictive explanations, then it is necessary to an adequate account of that state of affairs. Being an explanatory ultimate, it is necessarily in part opaque to any explanatory analysis that does not itself employ the category of action.

VI

Rational Action and Its
Physiological Basis

1

An Ideal Theory of the Identity of Rational Action
with Its Physiological Basis

If one's cultural memory takes in any of the period between the two
great wars, when it was common doctrine in the philosophy of the
English-speaking world that metaphysics is meaningless, it comes as
something of a shock to realize that this latter part of the century is a
very metaphysical time. Not everyone who is committed to a metaphysical doctrine is as yet aware of it, no more than M. Jourdain was
aware until that famous moment that he had been speaking prose all
his life. The reason for this is that the dominant metaphysics of these
times is physicalism, or materialism, and the notion that science justifies that doctrine still seems, to some of those who hold it, to exonerate
them from the charge of propounding a metaphysics. Still, many others, having discovered after much soul-searching that they do indeed
have a philosophical preference that can only be called metaphysical,
have come out of the closet and pronounced themselves metaphysicians.

By far the most influential form of contemporary physicalism in recent years is the identity theory of mind and body. Its attraction presumably lies in its simplicity, for it is a monism that purports to repress
sternly that velleity towards a dualism of the mental and physical that
can be discerned even in epiphenomenalism. It is so powerful a cultural force that there are signs that even B. F. Skinner has embraced
it.[1] It would be a pleasant irony if his commitment should be more explicitly acknowledged and if the rank and file of behaviorists should

then join him and acknowledge—what I think has always been the case—that they are closet metaphysicians.

What concerns me in this chapter, though, is not the identity theory of mind and body but rather an analogous theory of the identity of rational action with the body. I will deal with it in the special form of the theory that a rational action is identical with its physiological basis, and identical in the sense that a physicalist would intend. The chapter will be primarily critical—if not indeed polemical—but the positive doctrine of the authenticity of rational action developed in the earlier chapters will nonetheless be advanced in some important respects. I will, for instance, bring out features of subjectivity and reflexivity that are present in most rational actions. The examples I use should remind us, by their very differences from those that writers like Anthony Kenny and H. L. A. Hart use to discuss legal questions, that the feature called *mens rea*—in the broader root sense of involvement of mind suggested in chapter 2, section 6—can be found in rational actions that are not the concern of the law. The examples are also designed to keep before us the need for a radical change in the conventional view of causality if we are to do justice to rational action.

That a rational act (*RA*) is in some important sense identical with its physiological basis (*PB*) seems to me to be true. The sense in which that identity is properly to be understood is a very subtle one. The *RA* has a self-identity; it is one "thing"—so much so that if the category of event were adequate to characterize it exhaustively, we should be justified in saying that it is one self-identical event, and thus one referent. It is the subtlety of the self-identity of the *RA*—together with the even more subtle self-identity of the rational agent that acts—that concerns us in this book, and it probably demands more ample discussion than terms like Frege's "referent," as modified by the assimilation of referring to naming in recent semantics, make possible. The unity of that self-identity is the unity of a multiplicity, a multiplicity that can be characterized in many ways, among them as a multiplicity of physiological events and entities; and by this line of reasoning we might plausibly say that the rational act was identical with the multiplicity of which it was the unity. It is a sense of identity appropriate to a temporal thing, and it is clearly distinguishable from the symmetrical sense of identity that is usual in discussing relations between logical and mathematical terms. In an earlier book I called it an asymmetrical identity to mark that point;[2] the notion is developed in greater detail in chapters 2 and 4 of this book. But in this chapter we are con-

cerned chiefly with the negative point that the identity is in any case
not properly to be understood in the sense that a physicalist (materialist) would maintain. The physicalist theory of the identity of RA
and PB is analogous to the theory of mind-body identity maintained by
central state materialists, but I will not deal directly with the latter
theory, for reasons that will soon become clear. All the same, if the
present refutation of a physicalist identity of RA and PB is successful,
it will be seen to be a *fortiori* effective against the analogous mind-body
identity.

The theory of RA-PB identity we are concerned with is an ideal one
in the sense that no physicalist that I know of has proposed all its theses.[3] It will be convenient to begin by sketching out the main lines of
the ideal theory by exploiting its analogies with the well-known theory
of the physicalist identity of mind and body. After that, I will point
out a decisive difference between the theory of RA-PB identity and
that of M-B identity.

(1) The identity is construed in the usual terms derived from Frege.
There is a genuine difference in meaning between RA-expressions and
PB-expressions, but nonetheless their referents are in fact contingently
identical. There is not really a duality of entities, RA and PB, nor is
there really even a duality of functions or aspects of a single entity.
The duality is a matter of expressions, meanings, designators; more
generally, it is a duality of languages, the RA-language and the PB-
language.[4] There are not two referents, but only one.

(2) To say that the identity is a contingent one is to say only that
the arguments for its truth are not based on analysis of the meanings
·of "RA" and "PB" but rather upon empirical considerations.[5]

(3) Since the ideal theory is a physicalist one, the single referent is
appropriately to be described, understood, explained, in terms of the
PB-language, or at least in terms of an ideal PB-language towards
which science is tending. There is, therefore, something deficient about
the RA-language, even though it is not in principle reducible to a PB-
language. Some may say that the PB-language expresses the nature of
the single referent while the RA-language does not; others may prefer
to say merely that explanations of the single referent in PB-language
are more adequate than those in RA-language.

(4) Nonetheless, there are in fact two apparent, or *prima facie*,
referents, and indeed if there were not, no one would labor to demonstrate the identity of RA and PB. But to say this is merely to concede
that there is an experiential correlate of the RA-language. When, for

instance, I now say that I am writing a paragraph, there is indeed a sense in which I experience the act of writing a paragraph, or am aware of, or conscious of, myself in the act of writing a paragraph. But this is only to say that the person in the grip of the RA-language experiences the referent as an act. It is by no means to concede that there are two genuine referents, seeing that the person is in fact experiencing the very same thing that the PB-language expresses and expresses more adequately. If there is a deficiency in the RA-language, it therefore can not lie in its failing to express the experience that purports to be an experience of RA, since it does that very well. Its deficiency must lie instead in its failing to express the nature of the single reality in question, a thing which the PB-language does more effectively. It follows that what purports to be an experience of RA is deficient in not being adequate to the nature of the thing of which it purports to be an experience.[6]

(5) The reasons for saying that the PB-language is the appropriate one for expressing the single referent are familiar enough, and it will suffice if I merely repeat the brief summary already given in the first chapter. The PB-language forms part of the epistemic system of science, in which the laws of nature, or if not the laws of nature, then supposed nomic universals that do service for them, play the controlling role. Such RA-language statements as "Hume wrote the *Treatise*," "Planck discovered the quantum principle," "Professor Hylas propounded the theory of the identity of mind and body," and similar statements that seem to express some power, or force, peculiar to the agent must therefore give way to the more complex expression of the same matters in the language of the sciences. Instead of the agent, we talk of events or physical states, and these may be of a very fine-grained sort. A body of laws, meaning postulates, definitions, semantic rules, and so on (for short "body of theory") stands in such a relation to the events or states into which we resolve the agent that certain kinds of statements about those events or states can be regarded as instantiations of the body of theory. In particular, statements about an event or state we call the cause, when joined with this body of theory, entail statements about the event or state we call the effect. The explanatory power thus ascribed to the PB-language has as much determinism in it as is implicit in all this.

If our ideal theory of a physicalist RA-PB identity is in these respects analogous to the theory of M-B identity so exhaustively discussed in the literature of central state materialism, there is one important respect in which it is quite different. The *prima facie* distinction between the RA and its PB is at least in part an overt and public one, in a sense in which the equally *prima facie* distinction between mind and body (or between mental events and physical events) is not. Whether the supposed action is one that is observed by someone else or one that the agent himself is aware of as he performs it, the action is in part a bodily matter and the bodily features are as available to public inspection as the body itself is. Consider the act of writing a paragraph. To an observer who watches the writer, that action is overt and public, in a way in which the supposed mental events of others are not. And to the agent who writes the paragraph, his hand moving the pen is equally public—as public as the hand of someone else moving a pen—even if it is not precisely true to say that he observes himself writing a paragraph. There is a subjective feature as well, of which something was said in the earlier chapters and of which more will be said in this. Its intimate involvement with bodily action in such rational acts as writing, together with the self-transcendence we have already attributed to it, delivers us from the temptation of thinking of it in terms of a realm of mental events.

The authenticity of the *prima facie* RA-referent can not, therefore, legitimately be challenged from the behavioristic point of view so often adopted by central state materialists in arguing for M-B identity. From that point of view, the *prima facie* distinctness of mind depends upon an experience that is deficient, in the sense that it is not an experience of what it purports to be an experience of (the mental, or mental events),[7] and that inauthentic mode of experience is contrasted unfavorably with our commonsense experience of the behavior of the body and our understanding of dispositions to bodily behavior. The subjectivity of the rational acts we are concerned with governs the movements of a body, and it is so little to be conceived of as enclosed in a realm of mental events that one of its chief concerns is to be faithful to the bodily things of which it alone can give us a rational experience.

The bodily involvement of rationality reminds us, furthermore, that a *prima facie* RA, to just the degree that it *is* a macroscopic physical happening, is on exactly the same experiential and ontological footing as the PB is. If the identity theorist should attack the authenticity of rational action on the ground that it is a macroscopic thing and therefore only a *prima facie* referent that is in fact identical with secret powers that do not appear, the attack would undermine the status of the PB as well. If we refuse to assign the RA a distinct empirical status, on the grounds that its macroscopic status is that of a construct out of more primordial empirical data, and a distinct ontological status, on the grounds that its true ontological status is that of a construct out of more fundamental physical entities, events, states, we must also refuse to assign a distinct empirical and ontological status to the PB and to the instruments we use to study the PB, because these too must be constructs in both senses.

2

The Ideal Theory Refined: The Real Single Referent in Such an Identity

This last point suggests that the identity urged on us by the ideal theory of the identity of RA and PB is not precisely what the presence of the term "PB" implies. If there is something inauthentic about the *prima facie* macroscopic referent common sense calls the act of writing a paragraph, then there is something equally inauthentic about the *prima facie* macroscopic referent common sense calls the physiological basis of that act. And since the *prima facie* macroscopic referent that common sense calls the body (B) is on exactly the same footing as the one it calls PB, the inauthenticity of the PB as a referent implies the inauthenticity of the B, as well. All this remains true, even though we have used an important distinction between a physicalist theory of RA-PB identity and one of M-B identity to establish it. We must suspect, then, that even if some sort of physicalist identity theory should be tenable, it can not be a theory of either RA-PB or M-B identity. This suspicion is reinforced by what was said in (5), section 1, about PB-language, for that description was not, strictly speaking, of a PB-language at all, but of the language of science in general.

To establish a more precise sense of physicalist identity, let us look at what sorts of things the physical sciences refer to. Evidently there is some felt connection between the notion of referent and the notion of experience, since (a) such *prima facie* referents as RA and M are held to be inauthentic on the grounds that the experiences that seem to support reference to them are not experiences of what they purport to be experiences of; and (b) the sound empirical basis of science is held to support reference to the authentic referents. But as we shall see, there can be no exact correlation between being a referent and being experienced. The concept of experience is, of course, notoriously obscure, even though it is tolerably clear to the working scientist when experience tends to support his theory and when it does not. Science is well able to make effective use of empirical tests all the while philosophers of science continue to debate the question how precisely theoretic structures make contact with experience and what (if anything) a raw or pure experience, unmediated by theory, symbol, or concept might be. The day-to-day advances of science are secure enough—and empirically secure enough—whether the empiricism of the Vienna Circle, or that of C. I. Lewis, or that of Quine dominate the philosophers. Yet every claim about what is to count as a referent (for science, if not for pure mathematics and logic) seems to require some decision about whether or not experience directly or indirectly supports the reference. Consider some senses of "referent" that are relevant to science.

(1) Science refers constantly to such macroscopic entities as an anatomized brain, an electrode, a particle accelerator, a bubble chamber; or to such ordinary macroscopic events as the movement of blood in an artery, the movement of a needle on a dial or of an inked needle on a revolving drum, the formation of an image on a photographic plate, the moving image on an oscilloscope. Sensory experience plays some role in making these references possible, but precisely what role we need not attempt to say. These *prima facie* referents seem to be things or events of which we have experience, even if the experience is not "pure" but saturated with theory, language, and symbol. But they are surely not the ultimate referents of science, since they belong in general to the class of things science seeks to explain. Evidently in one sense explanation means the relegation of the thing explained to the status of a mere *prima facie* referent in favor of some real referents upon which the explanation somehow rests.

(2) On epistemological grounds it is sometimes argued that science does not, strictly speaking, refer to entities and events at all, but to something or other in experience out of which these *prima facie* referents are constructs. At the extreme of phenomenalism, these real referents are experiences themselves, not items experienced; observations, not things observed; or whatever else tinged with subjectivity one wishes to call them.[8] One remembers that for logical positivism "this green now" was the paradigm of experience and the paradigm of empirical reference as well.

(3) In yet another sense the real referents of science (RRS) are

whatever entities, events, states satisfy the most basic and advanced kind of science. In this case "satisfy" implies that the theory has been somehow brought to the bar of experience, but it is enough if this is done indirectly, by way of the everyday sense of experience correlated with "referent" in sense (1) above. It certainly does not mean that what is a real referent by satisfying the theory has been experienced as such. Indeed, if the real referent were somehow to be experienced as such, it would immediately assume the status of a mere prima facie referent and would then have to be explained. In this sense the RRS are theoretic entities, events, and states. Some might want to say that as theoretic things they are constructs; others might insist that to be a theoretic thing is merely (a) not to be experienced as such (as a quark is not experienced as such), and (b) to play a role in explaining such prima facie referents as are experienced as such. Such theoretic entities clearly change. Quarks are a far cry from the items that were supposed to be ingredients of Rutherford's atom. In that sense, the RRS change with progress in science.

(4) But, in another sense, the RRS are not theoretic entities at all— not atoms, electrons, fields, quarks, not whatever purely mathematical entities are needed to characterize such "concrete" theoretical referents. There is only one real referent, the physical reality—matter, energy, nature, the nature of things, or whatever else we wish to call it—that these theoretical entities help us to characterize properly. It is often supposed that this referent does not change, in the sense that all empirical change exemplifies its abiding lawfulness, and scientists have been known to display a certain Victorian religiosity when they speak of it.

All this awakens the suspicion that any sense of "referent" that implies a name, or designator, in one-to-one correspondence with some item called (referred to in general as) a referent is of limited and, so to speak, merely local interest in science. The notion of referent may indeed be more useful in elucidating particular encounters with the empirical than in elucidating the relation between a theory and what the theory purports to explain. Sense (1) would, therefore, be the most important sense for practical purposes, even though the ontological intent of identity theory logically requires senses (3) and (4). At any rate, the only reason for maintaining a physicalist identity theory (as distinct from some other kind of materialism) is to make the point that experiencing something as such is usually an ontological deception and that true referents are not experienced or indeed experience-able as such, but must in fact be experienced as something else. Although there is no exact correlation between being a referent and being experienced (as such), the notion "referent" always implies (in these controversies) some reliance on experience, as well as a refusal to take it at its face value.

It follows from all this that even if a physicalist identity theory of some sort should be tenable, the identity in question can not be one of RA and PB or of M and B. Any circumspect physicalist theory developed in terms of Frege's distinction can maintain that RA and PB are identical or that M and B are identical only in the trivial sense that all four members of these couples are merely *prima facie* referents that are actually identical with instances of the RRS. And these (or this) will be some concrete reality not experienceable as such but referred to in sense (4) and characterized with the help of current theory, which theory will always include some theoretic entities, events, or states (often all three) that, though perhaps constructs, are nonetheless also referents, in this case in sense (3).

That there is considerable obscurity in all this goes without saying. It is, I protest, not of my making but arises from the identity theorist's wish to use the notion of referent, which is probably most at home when applied to something experienced as such, in a context in which such experience is never taken at its face value. Because of this obscurity, I will assume that the claim that RA is identical in a physicalist sense with RRS means no more than that RA can be explained so adequately in terms of physical theory that there is no unexplained remainder that needs to be dealt with by means of RA-expressions. Since, however, it is unfair to demand that the identity theorist carry out a complete reductive program in order to make that point, we will assume that it is only necessary to show that RA-explanations can be replaced by PB-explanations. That would, at least, be a first step towards showing the ultimately required RA-RRS identity. I will therefore continue to speak of an RA-PB identity.

Interpreting the alleged identity in this way allows us to deal in a relatively simple way with the claim that the identity is a contingent one. That claim will now mean no more than that it is an empirical question whether what is experienced as RA can be so brought under a certain body of physical theory, in this case physiological theory, that there will be no intractable remainder that must be dealt with by means of RA-expressions.

3

Preparing to Refute the Identity Theory:
Self-Referential Rational Acts

Two actions, both of the same kind, will be used as examples. They
are the actions, *RA-I* and *RA-II*, that consist in the writing of the two
paragraphs that follow immediately. But the reader should not be dis-
tracted because what follows are paragraphs. My examples are actions
rather than paragraphs, and I am in fact performing them as I write the
paragraphs both for myself and for the reader. I am therefore calling
attention to their status as *prima facie* referents; more precisely, I am
calling attention to the sense in which they are *prima facie* referents
for me and in which similar actions could be *prima facie* referents for
anyone who performed them.

(*RA-I*) As I write this paragraph, physical events of unimaginable
complexity take place within my body. The act of writing has, in the
first place, gross or macroscopic features—for instance, the movement
of hand and fingers—and in these features alone, the experts tell us,
any number of delicate and subtle neuromuscular loops are brought
into play, even though neither the agent nor someone who observes
him may be aware of them. Complex events taking place in the brain
will form part of these loops, as, of course, they will form part of similar
loops that subserve much simpler activities such as raising a glass to
one's lips. But the act we are considering is an especially subtle one, for
the rapid and complex movement of the fingers springs from the intelligence that informs the act of writing a paragraph, shaping words
and sentences towards an end that is at least vaguely foreseen, and the
events taking place in the brain will be accordingly subtle and complex.
Neurophysiologists tell us that they themselves do not understand the
details of these electrochemical events, let alone the precise part they
play in the growth of consciousness in the intelligent being who writes.
It is nonetheless safe to say that as I try to express something in this
paragraph—not only for the reader but for myself as well—the billionfold particularity of the neural connections in my cerebral cortex is
possessed by orderly electrochemical events of awesome complexity. It
is also tolerably clear that without those events the intelligent act of
writing, including the intelligent consciousness that (as some suppose)
goes with it and alters in the course of it, would not have been possible.

(*RA-II*) Suppose, however, that my act of writing were not directed towards what is expressed in the first paragraph, but towards what I shall now express in this new paragraph. How shall we elucidate the relation between the two acts of expression and the two different sets of physical events upon which they respectively depend? Let us take the dependence upon the physical events for granted for a moment. Is it not true, however, that the neurophysiological events, in turn, depend upon the act of writing? Did not *RA-I* shape or help shape its neurophysiological events, does not what I am now writing shape or help shape the neurophysiological events that will end as I bring the paragraph to a close? And if this should be so, is there not some sense, however elusive and indeed inconceivable it may be when it is approached with presuppositions about causality that are usual in contemporary philosophy of science, some sense in which I, as the agent writing the paragraph, may be said to have caused, brought about—or at least contributed to causing, or bringing about—the very neurophysiological pattern that supported my acts? And must not this sense of "cause" allow for the fact that, although an act ends just now, some parts of the neurophysiological pattern it is said to have "caused" took place some seconds or minutes ago?

These two acts have several important *prima facie* features. They share some of these features with all acts; others they share only with rational acts.

(a) They present themselves as units, and indeed even as power units, and present themselves so even if the features just dealt with in the paragraphs left behind by the acts do not really belong to them.

(b) In a *prima facie* sense, they are macroscopic, physical, experienced directly in a commonsense and immediate way, but in a way that is proper to the agent who performs them rather than to some observer. But their *prima facie* macroscopic, physical, commonsense character is open to no special criticism because of that. They are as "objective" to the agent as an observed act would be.

(c) They are expressive, articulate, and more or less intelligent acts. As such, they purport to involve awareness and understanding, and we may, indeed must, deal with them in a way that makes such terms as "subjectivity," "intentionality," "awareness," and "consciousness" relevant.

(d) The acts, as *prima facie* referents, are also self-referential. By features (a), (b), and (c), any articulate act can be experienced (E_1) as one performs it. But, as *RA-I* and *RA-II* purport to refer to and characterize themselves as members of the class of acts, they lay claim to an experiential component (E_2) that includes E_1 as part of its purported "content." E_2, then, is whatever in experience purports to substantiate the cognitive claims expressed in the act. The act refers, and what it refers to is itself; in doing so, it makes a cognitive claim that purports to be experientially grounded (E_2) upon the experience (E_1) the agent can have in performing any articulate act, even one that does not refer to itself.

In what follows, I will sum up these features in the following convenient formula: as *prima facie* referents *RA-I* and *RA-II* are objective acts-qualified-by-reflexive subjectivity.

The suggestions made about causality in *RA-I* and *RA-II* were not expressed in terms of the mind-body controversy: there was no juxtaposition of mind and body, of mind and brain, or even of mental events and physical events. If a perplexing "relation" is insisted upon, it is not between mind and body but rather between the macroscopic act of writing a paragraph of a certain kind and all the physical events into which a rigorous scientific analysis might seek to resolve it. The efficacity of mind comes into the argument only to the extent that mind qualifies actions of this kind.

The linguistic correlative of these *prima facie* referents *RA-I* and *RA-II* is surprisingly rich. This RA-language includes not just first-person locutions in general, but also all those locutions, both first person and third person, that I used in performing *RA-I* and *RA-II* and that contribute to the reflexive subjectivity of those acts. And it would appear to include as well all the language I used after I performed the acts and was retrospectively discussing the features summed up in the formula "objective act-qualified-by-subjective reflexivity."

4

Refutation (A):
The Problem of Explaining Self-Referential
Rational Acts by Productive Correlations

In the rest of this chapter I will try to show that in the case of acts like *RA-I* and *RA-II*, the *prima facie* RA can not adequately be accounted for in terms of *PB*-theory. If, in this sense, the *RA-PB* identity does not hold, it will follow that the identity of *RA* and *RRS* does not hold either.

The most common way of giving a scientific explanation of such *prima facie*, or sense (1), referents as a colored surface, common salt, the apparent movements of the planets, the functioning of the mammalian heart, a Monarch butterfly poised on a milkweed blossom, is to establish a correlation between the referent experienced as such and some physical reality that is offered as the explanation of the apparent referent. Usually the correlative *explicans* is smaller in scale than the *explicandum*. For instance, the genes that are held to control its development and behavior are smaller than the Monarch butterfly, and the wave-length of orange light is smaller than the colored surface of its wing. Similarly, the formation of a macromolecule is a smaller-scale process than the *prima facie* referent we take to be a cell in the process of division, although now the *prima facie* referent is only available through a microscope that is itself a *prima facie* referent. Again, the movement of ions through the membrane is a smaller scale event than the *prima facie* referent our instruments tell us is the firing of the neuron. A successful correlation of *explicandum* with *explicans* is one in which the experience that purports to be an experience of the *prima facie* referent is always available to an observer, when it can be established that the correlative physical process is taking place. This is a more general statement of a point that is often made in terms of the distinction between secondary and primary qualities: it covers the supposed status of the Monarch butterfly we suppose ourselves to see, no less than the supposed status of the color of its wing.

Consider, now, any attempt to give a complete physiological explanation of acts like *RA-I* and *RA-II* in this familiar way. Making the experience available to an observer is of course out of the question, for although our RAs are objective enough, they are also objective acts-qualified-by-subjective reflexivity, and that qualification does not appear to the subjectivity of an independent observer, although on other grounds it may be inferred. The trick of making subjectivity appear to an observer in the sense in which a macroscopic quality or entity may be made to appear—in which even the distinction between something macroscopic and its infrastructure may be made to appear—can not be done. Appearance *to* someone's subjectivity is needed, so that subjectivity itself must be presupposed. This creates a special difficulty for any attempt to see the *M-B* or the *RA-PB* distinction as a special case of the macrostructure-microstructure one. I used the difficulty in a somewhat different setting in sections 4 and 5 of chapter five.

In the present case we are not dealing with an observer, but are taking the point of view of the rational agent who performs the *RA*. This would appear to make the task more feasible, but as we shall see, there is another formidable logical difficulty. In the first place, it is obvious that any such explanation is so remote and implausible that we can scarcely even call it programmatic. Suppose, however, that all practical difficulties have been overcome. If the physiological processes correlative to the *prima facie* referents *RA-I* and *RA-II* were contrived independently of how they were "contrived" by the performance of *RA-I* and *RA-II*, the experiences that purport to be experiences of referents *RA-I* and *RA-II* would then, it would seem, be available to the agent who "performs" the "actions."

Before the crucial demonstration in which the physiological events were contrived and the *prima facie* referent thus made "available," an enormously detailed investigation of the *PB* would have to have been made and the *prima facie* RAs would have to have been taken at least as seriously as they are in everyday commonsense experience, in order to establish the desired correlation between *prima facie* referent and the alleged real one. There must be an exact correlation of all the details of any supposed RA with all the details of its *PB*. No nuance of *PB* is to be analyzed without an equally detailed analysis of the features of RA that accompany it.

Two contrasting kinds of correlations must have been developed. (a) In one respect, the RA can be considered a macrostate as over against the microstate of the *PB*. The case is roughly analogous to the contrast between the observed lightning and the microstate charges that make it up. (b) In another respect, the RA, considered as qualified by reflexive subjectivity, seems to be a correlate of a quite different kind, one that has some resemblance to what some writers take to be mental events. But if this were so, it would not be sufficient just to offer the two kinds of correlations as complements to each other, because, in the case of *RA-I* and *RA-II*, we do not have two distinct *prima facie* RA-referents: one, the action as a macrostate available to (though not precisely observable by) the person who performs it; and the other, the mentality that accompanies it. The reflexive subjectivity so permeates the act as the agent performs it as to be as much a part of what we have been calling (for the sake of the argument) the macrostate as any of the visible features are. The *PB* correlation provided must do justice to this subtle unity of the *prima facie* referent.

Yet as soon as one states the program in this way, one is struck not so much by the technical difficulties as by its sheer unintelligibility. Any contrivance of a *PB* would produce a set of physical circumstances

different from the set of physical circumstances normally present in the
course of an act, yet according to the identity theory, the RA is identical with precisely the PB that was present when (in *prima facie* terms)
the agent performed the act. The simplicity of this objection must be
grasped at once. I am not saying, for instance, that if a pseudo-perfor-
mance were contrived by contriving the appropriate PB, the agent
would then feel something odd and mechanical about the performance.
I am making the simpler point that the agent must perform the act in
the normal *prima facie* sense in order for the appropriate PB to occur,
because, on the identity theory, the RA is identical with just that PB
and no other. So the contrivance of exactly the experience of acting by
the contrivance of a series of physical states that did not follow one
from another in precisely the way they follow one from another in the
case of, say, RA-I, but instead came about through the medium of
some other set of physical events, those contrived by the experimenter,
would miss the point entirely.

5

Refutation (B):
The Problem of Explaining Self-Referential
Rational Acts by Predictive Correlations

We need not, then, seriously consider a correlation of the kind discussed in the previous section. There is, however, another sense in
which the correlation program might figure in an attempt to explain
acts like RA-I and RA-II in terms of PB-theory alone. It is a sense related to our discussion of the explanatory power of PB-language under
(5) of section 1—especially the predictive aspect of it, which is often
perceived as implying some kind of determinism.

   Suppose that physiologists of the future have come to understand
acts like RA-I and RA-II so thoroughly that for any phase of these
prima facie referents they could supply a physiological counterpart.
We are to conceive of a situation in which, while some sentence or
word was being written, and written with a full burden of reflexive
subjectivity, some physiological monitor of the future were able to
print out in detail exactly what each neuron was doing and in exactly
what sequence of firing with other neurons. We are even to conceive
that this monitor yielded information not just at the neuron level, not
just at the level of each synapse, but at the much more fine-grained

level of each synaptic vesicle. We are also to conceive that, given the details of the *PB* as data, our monitor could supply the phases of *RA* in comparable detail. Monitors naturally interfere with whatever is monitored, but we shall assume that the interference is negligible.

Having come so far, the identity theorist must abandon common-sense reliance on the *prima facie RAs* that have, *ex hypothesi*, made it possible to establish the needed correlation. The argument must now deal entirely in the *PB* and have recourse only to the explanatory power of *PB*-theory as developed in section 1. It must now deal only in *PB*-entities, events, and states and so articulate them that future *PB*-entities, events, and states will be predictable from them on the basis of *PB* laws only. The true explanatory task will have as much determinism in it as was implied in our earlier discussion of the explanatory power of the *PB*-language. In principle, the parameters of the physiological system at time t_1 should permit prediction of its parameters at time t_2 with an adequacy that is related to the measurement techniques available, the state of knowledge of the laws of nature, and the limitations laid down by the indeterminacy principle. Whether the predictions are trivial or ample, there must be no reliance on nonphysical information in making them. Thus, if we take time t_1 as the midpoint of *RA-II*, the words I had already written by then and my intention to go on with what I was trying to say would contribute nothing of value to what an ideal physiologist would know of my physiology at that point, and accordingly would contribute nothing that would help in the prediction of the state of my physiological system at time t_2. On the contrary, if it should be possible to establish correlations between particular physiological states and the writing of particular words, the predictions would have to go the other way in a physicalist setting. That is, predictions of what I should be saying at time t_2 would have to be based only on the physiological state at time t_1. From that *PB* state the *PB* state at time t_2 would be predictable, and only the establishment of prior correlations would make it possible to predict how this *PB* state would be refracted into the *prima facie* speaking or writing of certain words.

In the present case identity theory requires that science should simply monitor and predict in *PB* terms. It should be able to predict in passing everything that in the earlier case it had set out to "produce." This will include all the *prima facie* subjective features that make the referent objective act-qualified-by-reflexive subjectivity. Since determining that all these subjective qualifications are present would in-

volve interference with the actual performance of an act (we should
have to ask the agent to report constantly), we set aside this last requirement. We will expect science to predict only the PB and what
can be observed of what the agent actually does. What the agent actually does, in terms of what can be observed, is speak or write a paragraph. What is at issue, then, is the prediction of a meaningful pattern of words that can be taken in and understood by the observer,
and the prediction of these words on PB grounds alone.

The implausibility of all this is so extreme that we can see nothing
in the present state of the art that promises to produce any evidence
of this kind. But even if the predictions were actually made, there
would still be an important sense in which the RA remained unexplained. For the RA is, whatever else it is, a *prima facie* referent, and
even if RA accounts of it can be dismissed, no PB-explanation of the
totality of its presence as a *prima facie* referent has yet been offered.
The identity theorist has merely shown that one objective feature
(namely, the words spoken) of its *prima facie* phases can be predicted
on the basis of the PB.

6

Refutation (C):
The Self-Refuting Character of a Defense of Identity
Theory that Attacks the Prima Facie Features of
Self-Referential Rational Acts

Even if we neglect this flaw in the predictive program and make instead the implausible assumption that some predictive program has allowed the identity theorist to predict on the basis of the PB and thus
explain, in that sense of "explain," the *totality* of the *prima facie* features of acts like RA-I and RA-II, the program nonetheless turns out
to be self-defeating. That is because the *prima facie* features of acts
like RA-I and RA-II, taken in their own terms, are absolutely central
to the cogency of the identity theory itself.

The totality of *prima facie* features of RA-I and RA-II were discussed as (a)–(d) in section 3. These were acts purporting to give an
account of all RAs of that type, and though all those features were
vital to whatever cogency that account had, we will consider here
only features that are common to other RAs that might give quite a
different account of the nature of action. In the first place, whatever

authority *RA-I* and *RA-II* possessed manifested itself in a macroscopic
setting familiar to common sense. The agent's pen and table, the
agent's companion in argument (if there is one), are macroscopic objects. The action itself is a macroscopic happening—the movement of
the hand to articulate written words, the movement of mouth and
larynx to agitate the air as we articulate spoken words. With this goes
both the experience of articulating words and the awareness and understanding of what is articulated—a constant feature of articulate action even when what is articulated is antithetical to what was articulated in *RA-I* and *RA-II*—together with a sense of purpose and an
appropriate feeling tone, all in a developing and dynamic pattern. In
short, an *RA-awareness-cum*-understanding that transcends what is
articulated is a feature of any articulate *RA*. No matter what is asserted in some *RA*, it is by virtue of features like these that it has the
character of expressing and asserting some supposed truth. The cogency of any articulate *RA*, both for the agent and for someone else
who attends to the *RA*, depends upon these features, and the cogency
vanishes if they are exhaustively understood in a *PB*-language that
deals with them only as physical processes having certain parameters.
Quite apart from the particular content of the assertions made in acts
like *RA-I* and *RA-II*, the physical language can not even characterize
them by such more general expressions as "assertion," "truth," "cognitive," "experiential," "empirical," "about the topic of action and its
physiological basis," and so on. These expressions add nothing whatever to our understanding of the single referent that is exhaustively
understood as a physical process.

It is quite in order, from the point of view of the identity theorist,
that acts *RA-I* and *RA-II* should have their *prima facie* status thus
discredited. But now suppose that the discrediting of them has been
carried out in another act, *RA-III*, which, for simplicity, we will assume to consist in the writing or speaking of a paragraph in which the
paragraphs of *RA-I* and *RA-II* are refuted in condensed form. It will
have all the *prima facie* features we have just briefly attributed to
RA-I and *RA-II*, and it will even have the self-referential features discussed earlier in greater detail. Therefore everything it says about *RA-I*
and *RA-II* will apply to itself as well. Its *PB* description will adequately
express the only referent that is there, and even the abbreviated designator "*RA-III*" will be superfluous. The three real referents of which
RA-I, *RA-II*, and *RA-III* are the corresponding *prima facie* referents
are now fully characterized by the *PB*-descriptions or explanations in

which they are expressed as physical configurations, and no fresh information about any of them will be added even by the minimal statement that someone asserts something truly or falsely in the acts *RA-I*, *RA-II*, and *RA-III*. The one who performs *RA-III* can not take seriously those *prima facie* features of it by which it purports to say something truly about the identity of RA with PB and ultimately with RRS.

It should be observed that nothing has been said so far about the truth or falsity of the paragraphs left behind by *RA-I*, *RA-II*, and *RA-III*. The argument has concentrated instead on the need for the agent who performs the expressive and cognitive act to take seriously the *prima facie* features of the act of speaking the paragraph. But it is worth mentioning that the status of the paragraph left behind by *RA-III* is full of contradictions. If, for instance, it is true, it is because *RA-III*, in which it is expressed and asserted, can be fully expressed in PB-terms that make no mention of its being an assertion. It is true, then, because there is something spurious about the *prima facie* assertion it makes, and therefore something spurious about the assertion that it asserts truly.

7

Refutation (D):
The Paradox Arising from the Expression of an RA
in a PB-Language; the Persistent Dualism of RA and PB

One apparently promising way of bringing RA under PB-theory without leaving an inexplicable RA-language residue is to introduce into PB-theory expressions that do justice not merely to the clearly physical correlative of the *prima facie* referent RA, but also to the *prima facie* RA-referent itself precisely as it is experienced and understood by the agent that takes itself to be performing it. It bears repeating that if it is RA-I or RA-II that we are dealing with, the experience will not actually be the RA-experience unless it has the character of being a cognitive experience of itself, for those acts purported to express a reflexive awareness and understanding of the *prima facie* RA-referent itself. We are not obliged to say how this feat can be performed in a PB-language. We may indeed suspect that it can not be done. We need interest ourselves just now only in what will follow from the assumption that it has indeed been done.

It will not have been done unless at least one more complexity is built into our augmented *PB*-language. For the augmentation purports to express what the *RA* really is, and *ex hypothesi* it is merely a *prima facie* referent and not a real one. Though experienced as an *RA*, it is said to be in fact an instance of *PB*, and the *PB*-language must therefore express this feature and at the same time explain it. That is, the augmented *PB*-language must make it clear how the *RA*, which is in fact identical with the *PB*, is nonetheless experienced as an *RA* and why this experience is inadequate to the true facts of the case. Since this means the augmentation of the *PB*-language to include the re-expression in *PB* terms of such words as "authentic," "apparent," "real," the new language will also incorporate the notion of truth. What this would mean, we are once again not obliged to say, although it is clear that it would not be sufficient simply to have the notion of truth part of the language in which a scientist uses or talks about *PB*-theory and about the acts of theory-building and experiment.

Supposing this augmentation of the *PB*-language to have been successfully carried out, we find that our *PB*-language is by now unrecognizable. It will include as part of its own theoretic texture all the things that physical science has decided—and probably with good reason—to exclude over the past three to four centuries: all the macroscopic and holistic experiences and *prima facie* entities that common sense is so familiar with; all the subjective features that qualify them. No matter that, *ex hypothesi*, the formal structure of this new language will include relations between such terms and the more conventional terms of the sciences. Every principle that clearly distinguishes an *RA*-language from a *PB*-language will nonetheless have been violated, and the *PB*-language will have embraced the *RA* only by becoming something other than what it purports to be.

Setting aside what is self-contradictory in this feat of combining in one theoretical structure two antithetical modes of expression while retaining the absolute dominance of one of them, we turn now to a difficulty that militates against our calling the outcome an identity theory. Suppose, then, whether the notion is intelligible or not, that in a *PB*-language that has retained its purity the *prima facie* referent objective act-qualified-by-reflexive subjectivity has been both expressed and shown to be identical with what the *PB*-language expresses.

This means, at the least, that the *prima facie* duality of *RA* and *PB* has been found to be spurious and that any claim *RA* has to a distinct reality must be dismissed. But what a curious dismissal this is. Clearly the feat we assume to have been performed with some *PB*-language of

the future does not mean that our *prima facie* duality has been removed root and branch and replaced by an overwhelming Parmenidean physical unity. Even if (as some suppose) the old RA-language
were to disappear completely, the identity theory does not require that
the "agent's" curious objective/subjective awareness-*cum*-understanding
of performing its actions should disappear, but rather that it should be
recognized as spurious or deficient. The source of the spuriousness is
understood to be the "agent's" (deficient) subjectivity, which supposes itself to be attending to an RA when in fact it is attending to
a PB.

It is precisely this spurious RA, engendered by a deceptive and deficient subjectivity, that the identity theory takes to be identical with
the PB. Let us say, therefore, that we are dealing with RA-identical-
with-PB; better, because this might look like an attempt to restore the
status of RA by a notational device, let us say that we are dealing with
an entity properly called "false RA-identical-with-PB." But within
this unity there is now lodged an inner duality—the spurious "agent's"
(deficient) subjectivity, manifested in an awareness of its own supposed objective act-qualified-by-reflexive subjectivity, contrasted with
the authentic PB it is said to be identical with. However Parmenidean
a PB-unity we assign to false RA-identical-with-PB, it gives rise to a
spurious, a deficient, *Doppelgänger*—a feature radically separated by its
very falsity from what the identity theory claims it to be truly.

                                          8

Refutation (E):
The Requirement That the Identity of RA and PB
Be Propounded in the RA-Language; the Persistence within
the PB-Language of a Distinction between RA and PB

Let us, however, assume that the identity theorist has made an adequate reply to this difficulty. Once more, we also assume that acts like
RA-I and RA-II have been wholly expressed in a PB-language, and
one so pure that we need not suspect it of being in fact an RA/PB-
language. In what language will the philosopher persuade us that all
this has indeed been done? Certainly the RA-language will not be
wholly dispensable, because the success of the program envisioned requires that the PB-language and its empirical correlates be distinguished from each and every "RA," including the "RA" or "RAs"

in which our theorist propounds his argument. It is true that I now place the symbols for action in quotation marks to note the fact that the ideal theory requires that the distinction between "RA" and PB be spurious, but this very point can be made only by virtue of a distinction. We have, then, a monolithic PB world distinguished from a (spuriously distinct) "RA" world, and the RA-language is needed to make this distinction.

So that it will be plain that we have already conceded to the identity theorist the achievement of the main lines of the program, let us rehearse the complexities of the PB-world that has now emerged. (1) There is, first of all, the empirical referent of PB-theory or any fragment of it—precisely the physical reality the scientist studies—and this is distinguished from any (spuriously) empirical correlate that is expressed in RA-language. (2) There is, next, the PB-theory that refers to and explains any (empirical) PB. Both the structure of that theory and the holding or propounding of it must itself be expressible in PB-language. This means that the (spuriously distinct) "RA" in which some scientist might hold or propound PB-theory must be distinguished from its authentic PB counterpart. (3) Furthermore, the propounding of the identity theory itself is also expressible in the augmented PB-language, and this, too, is distinguishable from another (spuriously distinct) "RA," namely, the one in which some philosopher actually propounds the identity theory in a language using RA-expressions.

In sum, then, whatever is under discussion is formulated in terms of a monolithic PB-world whose authenticity is then distinguished from a (spuriously distinct) "RA" correlate. Not an identity, but an assertion of identity requires the preservation, in some sense, of the distinction that the assertion designs to make inauthentic, spurious, unreal, or illusory. The prima facie duality we began with therefore persists even in this most implausible display of virtuosity we have envisioned for the PB-language, and it persists because an "RA" must be distinguished if only to deprive it of ontological significance, and because it is not really distinguished if it appears only as just another PB-configuration.

But there is a more profound sense in which the RA-language remains indispensable. Consider, first, item (3) just above, that is, the "RA" in which some philosopher propounds the ideal identity theory, using language congruent with language actually used in RA-I and RA-II. If we replace it with a PB-counterpart, we lose not merely an archaic cultural feature, but precisely *the language in which identity theory must in principle be propounded.* In saying this, one does not fail to notice what we have already implausibly conceded, for even if anything whatever can be reformulated in a PB-language, nonetheless, the assertion that some particular feat of this kind has settled what is in dispute and settled it for such and such reasons can be effectively formulated only in an RA-language. By "effectively formulated" I mean "so formulated as to be effective in a discussion between philosophers." In such discussions the effort to escape from the RA-language yields only a sequence of reformulations, each of which only restores an RA-statement of a higher order. The agent must labor at an infinite sequence of RA-statements of higher and higher type-level if it wishes to disburden itself of its own agency.

9

*Causality and the Authenticity
of the Rational Agent*

Action is no delusive, inauthentic double, only spuriously non-identical with PB. If a rational agent makes happen precisely that pattern in an infrastructure that is asymmetrically identical with its action, then it is up to us to revise our concept of causality to fit that fact. We are back with our examples RA-I and RA-II and the odd approach to causality they suggest. It is worth entertaining the possibility that the macroscopic unity of an action presides over, or dominates, the myriad physical happenings into which analysis would resolve it. If the enactment of thought in speech or writing—or even the enactment of thought not so overtly expressed—should in its development govern energy relationships in a physical infrastructure with which it is asymmetrically identical, the world that science studies will not, just by possessing this interesting feature, betray the faith in the rational order of nature that seems to motivate scientists.

VII

Participant Powers: The Ontology
of the Rational Agent

1

*The Condition of Ontic Dependence and the
Traditional Substance Problem*

In this chapter I will take it for granted that the view of rational action developed in the earlier chapters is essentially sound. I do not mean to make the outrageous claim that I have settled what may well be the central controversy about human nature. I mean only that, with one important exception, the main outlines of the view are now before the reader and can be judged and suitably modified; and that to complete it I must ask you to suppose with me that the interpersonal reflections and arguments of the earlier chapters have made out a substantial part of the case for ontic responsibility.

We must now ask what view of the ontological status of the rational agent all this leads us to. That question has certainly not been totally neglected, and indeed I do not think it could be, where *prima facie* rational action is our theme. It is true that we have often enough focused upon the structure of an action rather than upon the *prima facie* agent, but there is very little one can say about action that isolates it in any way from what purports to be the agent that performs it. Indeed, even when the focus was upon action I have made free use of the expression "rational agent-in-act." But there are many questions about the agent itself that we have not been directly concerned with. In what sense is the rational agent an entity? If it is, what are we to make of its self-identity, seeing that actions seem to modify the self-identity in which in a *prima facie* sense they originate? These are questions that touch upon the condition of ontic dependence, and although I trust something was said in chapter 4 to suggest that that condition is fulfilled, it was probably not enough. There is always the possible suspicion that even in a nonphysicalist setting an act-ontology would be just as plausible as one based upon entities called agents. However unclear we may be about just what an entity properly called a rational agent might be, it does not seem to me that the notion of an unattached act—one that does not arise out of some entity called an agent and does not qualify it in any permanent way—would be any clearer. Yet the possibility of an act-ontology must be faced, if only because it would make the ascription of ontic responsibility exceedingly complicated, if not indeed impossible.

Certainly common sense and common language assign actions to entities called agents or persons; certainly they also assign responsibility (in the ordinary sense, of which ontic responsibility purports to be a more exact version) to them. And if the notion of an agent does not comprehend all of what we mean by "person," both of those terms are at any rate ways of characterizing what is, in a prima facie sense, a being, or an entity. Our reflection purports to have taken us beyond prima facie knowledge of rational action. We must now try to look more intently to see whether the ontological sense in which we assign actions to entities called agents can be made to share in that transformation. Supposing, then, that what has been said so far about rational action is more or less sound, in precisely what sense can we assign it to a continuing entity out of which it springs as from a source and which it then forever qualifies?

Whatever the answer may be, it is unfortunate that the question is usually discussed with the help of the word "substance." It is now widely believed that the self-identity of the rational agent (the human self, the person) can not be that of a substance. When the word "substance" is used in the sense current in modern philosophy, I share that belief. But some reservations are in order. The history of the notion we render by that word is full of difficulties, many but not all of which go back to the way the notion has been reworked in post-Cartesian philosophy. Some of them, however, go back to the word "substance" itself, which carries over very little of the Greek word, "ousia," it purports to translate. Two important things have been lost in the series of moves that have left us with the word "substance": (1) the idea of being that is present in "ousia" because it is a substantive formed from the feminine participle of the verb "to be"; (2) the overtones of a dynamic development to a completion that are present in such Aristotelian phrases as "*ousia energeia*" and "*ousia entelecheia.*"[1] The full account of the human *ousia* in *De Anima* and the *Nichomachean Ethics* represents it as the exercise of a power in which the rationality of the agent shapes, by virtue of its choices and its actions, its own coming-to-be.[2] The self-identity of an entity of that kind is inseparable from its self-integration, which takes a long time, and whose outcome is always in some doubt. Yet Aristotle calls this human self an *ousia*. With certain reservations that will be clear soon enough, I have no hesitation in following him so far; but it is important that we choose the right word to translate "*ousia.*" Translate it as "a being" or "an entity," and although we may still want to quarrel about whether it applies to the rational agent in any sense more searching than that of common language, we shall at least no longer be arguing about whether it is a substance in the sense that most of the great philosophers from Descartes onward would have accepted.

Why "substance" has become the accepted translation for "*ousia*" is at first puzzling. Follow the question step by step through late antiquity and on into the contributions of Neoplatonism to the theological controversies about the Trinity, and it is no longer so puzzling, although that intricate story leaves us with the disturbing thought that there is after all some truth in the saying that the history of philosophy is the history of mistranslation. But this is not a book in the history of philosophy, so I will leave the matter in the decent obscurity of a learned note.[3]

What is important to our present purpose about the development of the notion of substance in post-Cartesian thought is readily summarized. One feature of the Aristotelian *ousia* that was singled out from all the rest by Descartes and the philosophers who followed was that it remained, despite its developmental history, the same entity, whose permanent self-identity could then be contrasted with the qualifications, accidental or not, that could be seen to succeed each other in it. In the modern tradition the one permanent qualifier definitive of its self-identity was often, though not always, called its attribute. It was the characteristic by which we distinguished it from other substances—thus mind, thought, or soul (one substance) might by some such term be distinguished from body, matter, or extension (another substance). It is not an approach that makes it easy to say what the self-identity of any *particular* substance might be. It was not quite forgotten that for Aristotle the self-identity of at least organic *ousiai* consisted in their particular developmental histories, for Leibniz's powerful backward glance kept the developmental theme still alive;[4] but it was seldom remembered. Substance came more and more to be thought of as a permanent and general substratum whose chief ontological job was to lend support to such changing surface characteristics as individual thoughts and feelings (in the case of mind-substance) or individual sensuous qualities (in the case of material substance). A new epistemological bias—Descartes' "New Way of Ideas"—both contributed to this restricted notion of substance and made it inevitable that after a while it came to be thought of as an unknowable whose presence was merely inferred from the modes or qualities that diversified it—was perhaps dubiously inferred at that.

Aristotle's own terminology must bear some of the blame for the view that became more or less standard for a long while after Descartes. When he wished to contrast the permanent self-identity of some particular *ousia* (say Socrates) with its accidental surface changes, he used the term "*hypokeimenon.*" That is usually translated as "substratum," and he applied the term even to developing organic *ousiai* when, in a general analysis of the problem of change, he wanted to make the point that any *ousia* could be regarded as a permanent substratum over against such changes as qualitative ones. Thus Socrates, for all the particular developmental history that belongs to him and no other, might nevertheless be regarded as a persistent and, in that limited sense, permanent *hypokeimenon* for the qualitative change from pale in winter to tan in summer.[5] "*Hypokeimenon*" might well have been translated as "substance," but that was the fate of "*ousia*" instead; and so, by the time of Descartes, "substance" had been standard for centuries where "*ousia*" once stood. We may conveniently sum up a long story by saying that, despite the notable exception of Leibniz, after Descartes the *hypokeimenon*, or substratum, feature prevailed in the idea of a substance's self-identity over the dynamic-developmental feature that was originally basic to Aristotle's doctrine of at least organic *ousiai*.

In this chapter I will consider the ontology of the rational agent and the related condition of ontic dependence in a setting that will make contact with the notion of substance only to the extent that the themes of the exercise of power and of a development through time can be made to predominate in the notion of the agent's self-identity over the theme of a static, permanent, *hypokeimenon* diversified by changing features that are best expressed in predicates. It will, however, be both natural and profitable to abandon the term "substance" altogether in favor of some more suitable term.

2

Rational Agents as Primary Beings

Let me try to put the question in a way that makes its original connection with Being salient. Although no one who reads the unconventional view of causality and temporality set forth in chapter 4 will suspect me of trying to restore Aristotle, the dynamic side of the concept of *ousia* and its resonance with the theme of Being have always seemed important to me. Wishing to preserve the overtones of a developing power that are present in such Aristotelian phrases as "*ousia energeia*" and "*ousia entelecheia,*" I once considered using "actual entity," which is a much better translation than "actual substance," to refer to a rational agent. But since it had already been preempted by Whitehead and put to a different use, that did not seem advisable, the more so because Whitehead's conceptual scheme does not make it possible to call a rational agent an actual entity. Indeed, his standard for the self-identity of an actual entity is so atomistic that nothing we can identify in experience—nothing, that is, that we can experience as such—will fulfill it. He is thus moved to postulate entities that do meet the standard and are therefore proper entities to use as the basis for a rational reconstruction of the things we can experience as such. And so he is quite unwilling to apply to the human person, whose struggle with its own self-integration takes so long, is so vulnerable, is so flawed by multiplicity and what might even appear to be radical interruptions, this honorific term "actual entity." I am not at all reluctant to take this momentous step. But with the term already put to a different use, it seemed wise to choose another expression. And so, in an earlier book, I used the expression "fundamental entity."[6] Later, still wanting the resonance with "*energeia*" and "*entelecheia,*" I tried "actual being" in a context in which I was criticizing the view of human nature that Whiteheadians have been building on the basis of his system. It is not precisely an act-ontology that Whiteheadians propound, but like an act-ontology it would see the human person as less fundamental in an ontological sense than the much smaller items—in Whitehead's view they are minuscule entities that he also calls "actual occasions"—out of which it must be reconstructed. It is, incidentally, a view of human nature that has a considerable and growing influence in philosophical and theological circles that writers about action seldom interact with; we return to it briefly in section 4, and the matter is then pursued further in a note.

Here, though, I will use the expression "primary being." Must an act, understood as we have agreed to understand it, have its source in an agent that is a primary being? A primary being we will understand to be one that has a continuity even though it may be in continuous change; one that, if it is complex, may be analyzed in terms of an infrastructure in which there will be other primary beings of less complexity; one for which we can not give a thoroughgoing explanation. The chief reason for the last point is that explanations of all sorts, from reductive ones based on some version of the covering law model to explanations of more modest intent that might be put forward by a biologist or a psychologist in a nonreductive spirit, would be directed upon the infrastructure of our primary being and not upon the primary being itself as it appears to us in its own terms under the disclosing power of our cognitive glance. But this is tantamount to saying that the reference of something to a primary being is in fact one way, though not the only way, of explaining it. The career of any infrastructure element would in some measure be under the influence of the operant power of the primary being.[7]

It will be perceived that there is very little of what has been said about rational acts and about the rational agent-in-act in the course of this book that could not also be said of a primary being regarded as the source of the acts and as further qualified by having performed them. In both cases we are concerned with a supposed ontological level that on the one hand demands treatment in terms of such categories as cause, power, and explanatory value; and that on the other must be regarded as having an irreducible meaning, as being present to human awareness and understanding, as being an authentic object of human experience. Whether we are dealing with acts or with primary beings, their operant powers are not taken in when we note merely the powers exercised by infrastructure elements either seriatim or in concourse.

In terms of the interpersonal reflections of chapters 3 and 4, the *prima facie* rational-empirical presence of a primary being—and not just the primary beings we call rational agents—is just as impressive as

the presence of that dynamic unit of shorter duration that we call a
rational action but are always prompted to call a rational *agent*-in-act.
Indeed, on the *prima facie* level the rational agent-in-act is in fact
nothing less than a primary being-in-act, though one of relatively short
duration. The *prima facie* status of a primary being-in-act is therefore
open to exactly the same kind of transformation from within our circle that we claimed to have achieved in the course of our interpersonal
reflection. And if we take seriously what our *prima facie* cognitive
power was understood to be at the outset of our reflection and then
again after what we took to be its transformation, it is plain that it suf-
fices to disclose with authority the presence of a primary being no less
easily than that of a rational action. Indeed, when in section 7 of chapter 5 rational action itself was affirmed as the ground of ontic assessment, our cognitive power to disclose the presence of a primary being
was also affirmed. More than that, it appeared itself as an instance of
a primary being at work: the category of being became in effect more
fundamental than that of action.

Turning to the matter of appearance, it would seem that we have no
more reason in the case of a *prima facie* primary being than in that of
a rational action to take it for an appearance in the PMI sense—to take
it to be phenomenal in the ontically deficient sense of being a distortion of what is the case. We have no reason, that is, to suppose that it
is anything but an ontically significant appearance. That is a way of
being an appearance that no knowledge, however authentic, is exempt
from; for with whatever compelling presence something should present itself to someone who is said to know it truly, that presence would
nevertheless be an appearing. We can not arbitrarily excise from the
cognitive relation the duality of knower and known, and that is all the
expression "ontically significant appearance" calls attention to. If it is
an ontological flaw to so appear, it is a universal one, and does not
serve to distinguish knowledge either from opining or from outright
delusion. To put it a different way, it is not just our bodily state and
our sensory modalities that confer an appearance status on what is
known. Even the thing-in-itself, known with the profound assurance
of an intellectual intuition of the kind Kant establishes as an absolute
standard for knowing by the same line of reasoning that leads him to
think we have no such power, would still *appear* to any divine or an-
gelic understanding that should know it thus. It would, of course, be
an ontically significant appearance: what is the case would then have

truly appeared, shown itself as it is, become authentically manifest in a sense that is antithetical to the sense of "manifest" appropriate to the PMI doctrine.

The upshot of all this would appear to be that we have already made out as much of a case for the existence of primary beings as for the existence of authentic rational acts.

We have nevertheless some obligation to answer someone who should still feel that we can make do with an act-ontology, for there are certainly some plausible arguments for that position. For one thing, an authentic rational act—even an insignificant one of very short duration—is already an *explicans* of a powerful sort. Indeed some might think that our supposition attributes to an act everything one might wish to attribute to a primary being, except the greater duration of the latter. Granted the considerable supposition of an act-ontology understood as we have agreed to understand it, we may find an ontology of continuing agents superfluous as well as a vulnerable complication. So-called agents might be more or less continuous infrastructures visited and revisited by acts. We might say that the writing of the E flat major symphony is one act and the writing of the Jupiter Symphony a later act; the continuant that ties them together is merely an infrastructure, and it is only a commonsense convenience that ties the two acts together under the common name of Mozart.

There are, however, some good grounds—grounds arising out of the presence of an act even when it is isolated as much as possible from what appears to be a continuing rational agent—for supposing that we must attribute acts to an agent who is a continuing primary being. In the first place, the relation superordinate-subordinate, although it does not immediately give us an agent that is a primary being, seems to require that each of the subordinates of one superordinate act belong to the same act-source—an agent that endures at least for the life of that superordinate act. In the second place, the relation superordinate-subordinate, which seems to be a very patent feature of action, points to what I might call the transcendability of any particular act. A superordinate act is not inevitably simply ended and then succeeded by another act of the same hierarchical rank. Often it is taken up and incorporated into another act of still higher superordinate rank, as when, for instance, a sentence originally spoken for its own sake (and thus superordinate in relation to the sub-acts of speaking individual words) is incorporated into a paragraph of wider import. We seem to need an agent who is a primary being to account for the new superordinate act that, heretofore merely potential, now embraces and gives a different significance to a superordinate act that had already been actualized. One might suppose that the writing of the Jupiter Symphony began in an act in which some germinal thematic material was first expressed and that the act, until then superordinate, was then subordinated to the act of writing the first movement.

The point about an act being embraced by a superordinate one attributable to the same agent seems sound enough, though there may be some artificiality in supposing that even so intense a labor as the Jupiter consisted of one act. On the other hand, if we take the Jupiter itself to have an internal unity of structure, then this seems to reinforce our need for a primary being—the continuing Mozart who may have interrupted his task with a meal or with sleep. We seem to require an agent that holds latent in it the future that is some half-completed act, as well as the possibility of transforming it by subsuming it under some new superordinate act of still wider import. To put it another way, we appear to need a continuing agent who sustains any act, its sub-acts, its superordinate act, and the possibility of subsuming the superordinate under another superordinate of wider import.

We shall see soon enough that there are problems about the self-identity of this agent we appear to need. But it is no problem that we shall not be able to find an entity whose continuity is such that changes in it are merely incidental—more properly, accidental—to it. As temporality is intrinsic to an act we take to originate in the agent, and intrinsic in the sense that its quantum of power is also a temporal quantum, so with the agent itself. An act requires a time span for our identification of it—a point that is scarcely invalidated by the possibility that an act like the speaking of a paragraph may be cut off in midpassage. Self-identity over a time span is also a characteristic of the entities we call persons, and although we do not hesitate to ascribe identity of some sort to those who are cut off in midpassage, it is clear that a time span of some magnitude is needed for the completeness without which we should hesitate to apply the term "rational agent." Persons are entities that have a development and a history. The problem is not so much how we can continue to ascribe self-identity to someone much changed (perhaps in body or memory) but how we could ever ascribe self-identity *as a person* without that kind of developmental history.

3

Against a Radical Pluralism of Acts: An Ambiguity
in the Particularity of Rational Acts

We must now introduce an important qualification about the ontological self-sufficiency we seem to have attributed to particular acts
and particular primary beings. We will apply the qualification first to
particular acts—that is to say, we will proceed for a while as though an
act-ontology were less vulnerable than I have claimed it to be.

Certainly we did attribute a kind of ontological self-sufficiency to
acts when we said that they were not fully explicable, in the limited
sense that they are themselves explanatory factors. Our supposition rejected in principle the notion that we can formulate nomic universals[8]
of such unlimited scope that they are indefeasible by any possible experience, and that we can then use them in explanatory moves that
show one space-time region of the infrastructure of an act to be totally
calculable from another. If we take this self-sufficiency literally we are
led to a kind of radical pluralism. The question why this particular
act, having just this self-identity, happens just when it does and just
as it does is answered by saying that after all explanatory factors that
might be discovered are in fact discovered—we may tentatively take
them to be factors that concern the infrastructure—there remain others that can only be summed up by saying that in the end the act is
its own reason for being what it is. If we were to insist on this without qualification we should have set aside a long tradition of reasoning
in which the self-sufficiency and necessity of Being is contrasted with
the dependence and contingency of each particular being.

The temptation to think of a particular act as self-creative, or even
to make bold to use the expression *causa sui* about it—an expression
that Spinoza reserved for *Deus sive Natura*—is a strong one in this
century. Our own supposition does not require us to go so far in the
direction of radical pluralism. Indeed the same rational-empirical scrutiny of action that makes the supposition so plausible requires us to
place strict limits on any movement in that direction. The reason for
the restriction we may express tentatively by saying that any particular
act—any act that we no doubt rightly think of as just *this* individual
act—is not wholly intelligible in such terms. The act itself, which is
indeed, a *this*, or *tode ti*, which is indeed this particular act, turns out

nonetheless to include features that prevent such notions as "this," "particular," "*tode ti*," from characterizing it adequately. The act itself eludes us when we try to express it as a mere particular.

Even when we are dealing with things other than acts there are obscurities about the mere particularity we seem to try to point to with the term "this." The source of the difficulty is presumably the flat contrast usually intended between *this* particular thing and the general, the universal, the transcendental. The flat contrast is simply not justified. In another context this point might lead us to see the traditional problem of universals in a somewhat different light. Just here, though, we may well confine ourselves to the odd fact that terms like "this," "*tode ti*," "particular" express a general category no less than they refer to the particular thing in question. Perhaps we shall be in sight of the issue if we conclude that any particular thing is never just a particular thing. It always—and it is no less particular for that—expresses, manifests, is an instantiation of, what we may loosely call the nature of things. If this were not so we should never be able to make the first step towards any general truths. The point was made in terms of presence in section 6 of chapter 3. We shall see in due course that this point brings the present view much closer to what science takes for granted than our present metaphysical language would lead one to expect.

This general problem about particulars is intensified whenever we try to approach an act with the thought that it is self-caused, or self-creative, in the sense that a radical pluralism might intend—try to approach it, that is, with the thought that the act itself causes or creates itself. In the first place, an act is at one time only a potential act, and at another it is an act indeed—"actual act" is an expression one shrinks from. Even if we agree for a moment that an act is the exertion of power over time and that the full time unit is needed to make sense out of the term "power," we should still not want to say that the act *in its completed particularity* initiated the process in which it then actualized itself. That completed particularity is so much the outcome of that actualization that some factor other than the "act itself" seems needed to account for the change from potential act to act indeed. Before the act we have prior acts and we have a physical complex that is a potential act-infrastructure—a highly complex state of affairs that affords opportunities for certain acts and makes certain others impossible. It is only when pervaded by the unity of a particular act that the potential infrastructure becomes the actual infrastructure of an act. And the particular act itself can not account for that movement from its own potentiality to its own actualization.

But the notion of the act itself is equally obscure and ambiguous even after the act has begun and is in the course of realizing itself. Certainly the achieving unity of the act itself is not determined by the completed particularity of the act—a particularity that we should have to invoke if we were to try to consider the act as a "mere" particular. The achieving unity of the act seems instead to be what determines the particularity to be just this rather than that other particular it might have been. The very thisness of the particular, its very status as *tode ti*, seems to be derivative from the achieving unity of the act. It is, in short, difficult to make sense of the act as just *this* act unless we think of it as qualified by a feature that is not a *this*. However indissolubly the achieving unity is bound to the particularity it gives rise to, it presents itself as indistinguishable, qua achieving unity, from that of any other act. The most noncommittal way of expressing this is to say that the nature of things is present in any particular act. To put the matter in this way is not to suggest that the achieving unity is actual "outside" acts; nor is it to suggest that it comes to the act "from outside"; indeed, if the achieving unity were truly "outside," there would be no act, for the unity is intrinsic to the nature of all acts—this one and all the others as well.

We can call the act itself ontologically self-sufficient only if we modify the expression "the act itself" to include (a) whatever it is that makes an act that is potential at one time into an act indeed at another; (b) an "achieving" unity that is not flatly identical with the thisness that is achieved. We could then say without offense that an act is *causa sui*, that it creates itself, for we should have considerably modified the radically pluralistic overtones those expressions otherwise have when they are applied to particulars. All this amounts to recognizing in the act itself something that transcends it. To put it another way, the act is seen as an instantiation of something that has a general aspect. We could then say with some justification that the act was a particular power by being a participant power. It would be no less particular for that, if there are in fact no powers that are not participant powers.

It now becomes important to note that the terms "general," "universal," "transcendental," "participant power" do not signalize some mysterious and probably inauthentic feature of things that is only apparent to those who are trapped in metaphysical discourse. The point I have been laboring to make about particular acts is a commonplace in science. Indeed, little separates us from the philosopher of science here but our insistence that this feature of things need not be expressed only in terms of the explanatory categories of science. To see this, let us consider again for a moment the physical complex or situation that I described earlier as the potential infrastructure of an act. For simplicity let us say that it is a person's body together with everything that is the case there immediately prior to an act. The actual infrastructure of a speech act will then be everything that takes place in that body in the course of the act. So understood, the infrastructure is clearly what used to be called a principle of individuation in the sense that the full identification of a certain act as just this act requires some reference to it. Indeed, according to one theory that many writers find persuasive, what I have called the infrastructure is flatly identical with the act, so that identifying the act as just this one is in fact identifying just this period of just this body's history.

Our earlier reflections and arguments, however, require us to say that it is in fact the infrastructure of an act. As a physical complex it has just this history because it is pervaded by the unity of just this speech-act. In that sense the infrastructure is a principle of individuation, but not a principle of being. Before the act it was only a potential act-infrastructure: it was, that is, a physical multiplicity—a highly complex state of affairs that afforded the possibility of certain acts and made others impossible. When the act takes place, however, the infrastructure is possessed by something that transcends its own status as just this physical complex, and that transcends as well whatever allows us to identify the act as just this act.

Despite its preference for the language of physical events and states and for nomic universals fitted for the explanation of them, physical science takes much of this for granted. When in some strained physical situation some evanescent particle appears, whatever it is about the particle's appearance that is not expressed by just this set of parameters is expressed by lawlike expressions of the utmost generality.[9] The assumption is that the unity of things—"the nature of things"—has so to speak leaned into that particular physical situation and instantiated itself in the appearance of just that particular evanescent particle. The particle is no less particular for that. Just so, when the unity of things leans into the particular physical situation here called a potential infrastructure, the act that then takes place is no less particular for that.

Though the analogy with the assumptions of the sciences is an important one, we do part company with the prevalent philosophy of
science from here on. On our supposition, something that we have to
characterize as general is present as a constitutive feature of the particularity of any act. The oldest name for it is Being. In the light of
that presence, an act is self-sufficient only in the limited sense that
adequate explanation of it as a function of a multiplicity of other particulars is not possible. It will be helpful to think of the self-sufficiency
of an act as a "received" one, so long as we remember that what is
thus received does not come from outside to an act that would have
some ontological status without it. What is received is received in the
peculiar sense that it is intrinsic to all particularity whatever without
itself being particular. Although incompatible with scientific determinism as that is usually construed, the present view is compatible
with other explanatory categories in which the demands of what the
participant power participates in blur its own "freedom," "spontaneity,"
and "independence." They are demands probably best expressed in
moral and aesthetic categories: goodness, obligation, fitness, beauty,
appropriateness—categories often enough intertwined, at least in the
arts, with themes of fate and necessity no less than with those of freedom, chance, and grace. But it would appear that the fulfillment of
the conditions of partial determinateness, positive indeterminateness
(ontic potentiality), and rational obligation is not in conflict with
these demands.

4

The Self-Identity of Rational Agents
Regarded as Primary Beings

In view of everything that has been said so far, I will assume that there
are primary beings and that each is characterized by an order that includes a temporospatial one. Some, we will suppose, are minuscule in
both their temporal and their spatial aspects. Some are very extensive,
perhaps as extensive in both aspects as rational agents are. All display a
unity of temporal and spatial aspects that makes it fruitless to wonder
how something can remain the same primary being while undergoing
very fundamental changes.

We interpret "primary" to mean "not completely explicable because
itself a fundamental ground of explanation." It is obvious that the rela-

tions between entities all of which were primary but which existed at many levels of magnitude and complexity would themselves be very complex, and it would not be in the least surprising if not all of them could be expressed in terms of nomic universals of the kind the physical sciences look for. If rational action itself is primary in this sense and if there are beings capable of it over an extended period, then these beings would be primary beings. All of the qualifications about particularity developed in the previous section would not alter that status. The thesis of the remainder of this book is that the *prima facie* rational agents recognized by common sense and by the law are indeed authentic primary beings, and that they have an ontic responsibility appropriate to that status.

That acts really do originate, in some sense, in the being we call a rational agent will not be further argued. The least sense in which they originate there is that a rational act takes place in a physical body in which other such acts have taken place. The category "rational act" and the category "rational agent" are inseparable. But when we try to show that the rational agent has authentically the ontological status of primary being, there are still difficulties. If it has that status authentically then it must be a continuing entity that before the act is capable of the act, that in action is the source of the act, and that after the act is capable of other acts. It is no help that common sense concedes this at once, for common sense deals, after all, with the *prima facie* rational agent. The difficulty exists only for metaphysics: it is the one we met before, when we entertained the possibility of an act-ontology in which the *prima facie* agent is "really" only a more or less continuous body (perhaps just an aggregate of more fundamental things) visited and revisited by acts. Defining what we are after in contrast with that ontology, we may say that we are attempting to show that the *prima facie* agent is really a being with a continuous self-identity and that it really is the source of acts that forever qualify it—in short, a primary being that is ontically responsible for its acts.

We have, I trust, long since lifted the rational agent out of its original *prima facie* status; but there are still difficulties, and the matter needs more development. There are two powerful criteria for the continuous self-identity of a primary being that complicate our task unnecessarily. Both are associated with atomism. One of them is the criterion of the impassible, unchanging self-identity of a Parmenidean particle. It is a criterion that a rational agent must necessarily fall short of. One might suppose that in the present state of physics one could

dismiss it out of hand, but I suspect it has a profound if unacknowledged influence still. Physical models of molecules, for instance, have
a way of persuading their users that what they model really are wholly
intelligible as aggregates of such particulars. There is a more prudent
way of putting this: in these models the importance of stable structure is exaggerated to such a degree that the patterned activity that
underlies it is lost sight of.

The other extreme criterion for continuous self-identity is the self-
identity of a spatiotemporal event of indivisible unity and minimal
spatiotemporal extent. The fruitfulness of this notion in quantum theory needs no argument. Preoccupation with it led Whitehead to gen-
eralize it (adding features that do not concern us here) to his concept
of the actual entity (actual occasion). He was then able to reinterpret
the apparent Parmenidean stability of a "particle" as a succession of
these minuscule, active, patterned entities. This in itself seems to me
to be a happy outcome. But to require that kind of self-identity for the
proper use of the term "actual entity" was to deprive of that status
other *prima facie* entities of greater extent. Like the "particle," they
too had to be regarded as "really" a succession—or rather a complexity
of a vast multiplicity of successions—of such atoms of activity. The
criterion is so exacting that it is not only rational agents that fall short
of it: even their actions become inauthentic in the sense that they too
are seen as "really" complexities of vast multiplicities of successions of
events of minimal spatiotemporal extent.[10]

Both of these criteria for continuous self-identity are excessive when
viewed from the perspective developed in this book. Against the first
and in partial accord with the second, I have held that continuous
self-identity and profound change are indeed compatible; against the
second, that continuous self-identity is compatible with hierarchical
complexity in which primary beings of lesser spatiotemporal extent contribute to and condition those of greater extent without relegating the
latter to a merely aggregative status.

5

Self-Identity as a Problem for
the Rational Agent

Despite all this by way of preliminary defense of the ontological status
of the rational agent, there are other problems about self-identity that

we must come to terms with if we are to show that the agent is in fact
a primary being. Seen from one perspective, the continuity of the self-
identity seems so massive that it threatens the "primary" feature our
supposition attributes to acts. These acts spring from the past of the
agent and would seem to be entirely functions of it: far from being
inexplicable grounds of explanation, they seem to be, at least in principle, explicable in terms of the physical situation from which they
spring. Indeed, their being acts of an entity called an agent seems from
this perspective to mean no more than that they do indeed have their
locus in a certain physical situation. Seen from another perspective,
the continuity of the self-identity of the agent seems not so much a
massive *donnée* as a matter awaiting resolution by the agent itself.
Whatever self-identity we attributed to that agent would have to be
consistent with its capacity to alter it in fundamental respects. Self-
identity from this perspective is not so much a given feature of an
agent as a task for it.

Both perspectives make powerful demands on us. As to the first, it
would appear that rational agents do not cause or create their own self-
identity even in the limited sense we have established for the acts that
originate in them. Whatever the true ontological status of agents may
be, the received character of their self-identity is even more salient
than it is for acts. Far from being entirely shaped by their actions,
agents seem to be at the mercy of a received self-identity that defines
the possibility of action. From this self-identity there appears to be no
escape: it affords certain opportunities for action and also sets certain
limits upon it. Action sometimes seems from this perspective to have
only a little to do with what the agent has become at some moment.
Whatever the sources of it may be, the radical but gradual changes to
oneself over the years often give one the feeling that they have simply
befallen one. Hugo von Hofmannsthal expresses this very precisely in
a moving poem on the transitoriness of things. How strange it is, he
says, that my own ego glided unhindered over to me from a little child,
as dumb and alien to me as a dog—

> Dass mein eignes Ich durch nichts gehemmt
> Herüberglitt aus einem kleinen Kind,
> Mir wie ein Hund unheimlich stumm und fremd.

And of course that earlier being might well have said the same thing
about the self-identity it received from its own past—received in the
first instance at the very moment it began its *genesis eis ousian*. What-

ever freedom the rational agent possesses, it is never free from the lot
of being just that self-identical particular that at a given time and place
is capable of certain acts and not of others. What any of us is to do
next may not in principle be completely predictable on the basis of
the infrastructure parameters and covering laws, but there is another
predictability that is almost as daunting. It is a predictability not of an
appearance, or macrostructure, on the basis of secret powers, or microstructures, but rather of one phase of a macrostructure (it is not, I have
been maintaining, *only* a macrostructure) from an earlier phase. Great
things in music in his maturity were legitimately, though not deter-
ministically, predictable from the childhood career of Mozart, and
analogous if more modest predictions can be made about others by
someone familiar with the developmental patterns of children.

From all this we can see that if there are primary beings that are
agents, they have much in common with other complex primary beings that are not. If complex primary beings exist, they are free, are
operant powers, have authentic ontological status, to just the extent
that they are more than the outcome of the secret powers of their infrastructures. And they are not free in the sense that their infrastructures will afford certain opportunities and foreclose certain others.
Even though it should be true that the image of logical necessity or of
any other kind of necessity misses much of the point of the career of
any primary being, one must still concede that once the self-identity
of being just *that* particular primary being is received, it is then necessary that the entity operate within the constraints of being just that
particular.

But as we turn back to agents we see that all this contains an overstatement. One thing that sets an uncanny distance between a certain
child and me, between another child and you, is the sum of the past
acts that have contributed to our gradual coming-into-being as what
we are today. Our self-identities are in part intermittently wrought by
our acts. One is what one is in part because one has acted in certain
ways. And what I have called "what one is" includes the potentiality
for being able to act in certain ways in the future and not in others.
Self-identity, which one is inclined to take as paradigmatic for primary
beings, appears to be a problem for rational agents.

It is of course not the kind of self-identity that some philosophers
have in mind when they talk about the criteria for identifying a self.
One might well concede that the well-worn criteria of memory and

bodily continuity settle the question of identifying someone—perhaps for legal purposes—and still consider that other self-identity a problem for the agent, who must, after all, always decide what to do next. A person capable of rational action must decide what promises to make, what tasks to undertake, what attitudes to take up, what relations to cultivate or undo, what habits to cultivate or break—the list is very long and very various, and it includes both the momentous and the trivial. In that sense the agent must decide what its self-identity—or at least important features of it—is to be. One thing one does know is that five or ten years' time may make a good deal of difference in the self-identity one had in that time formed as distinct from the several others one supposes one might have formed instead.

We all know the source of the anomaly: it is the rationality that qualifies some of our actions and the consciousness, the awareness, the capacity for attention, that is one feature of our rational lives. It is in some ways the fruit of action, but in other ways it is something that, qua individuals, we receive at least in the limited sense in which we receive our identities. Much of the potentiality of the agent seems to lie in the purely receptive feature of it, which should warn us that although it is much in fashion, the category of action will not illuminate the whole of the human condition. With respect to self-identity as it is at any moment, rational consciousness, in both its receptive and its active aspects, is a principle of potential disunity and discontinuity. If it does nothing else, it sets up an inner discourse between different aspects of the self that some take to be of the very essence of consciousness. At any rate, it drives a wedge into the kind of unity that one takes for granted in other primary beings, opening up a great space within which then play all the possibilities of both self-integration and self-dissolution. The inner diversity of rational consciousness makes possible the discontinuities in our history that are the necessary preludes to any change in self-identity, whether for good or for ill. Sometimes one's present self is precisely what one must be discontinuous with if some years hence one is to be able to say, in a spirit related to but somewhat different from Hoffmansthal's—that is what I was, but now I am somebody else, and how good it is that I did not continue in those ways. And the obverse of this is that some must look back with a sense of profound regret to a vanished self that from the standpoint of the present seems like a soul in bliss, with all sorts of happy possibilities stretching before it that are now lost.

6

Against a Radical Pluralism of Agents: An Ambiguity in the
Particularity of the Ontically Responsible Rational Agent

Consider now some agent just before an action that will be momentous
for its future. We wish to say that the agent is capable of that action.
It has, as it prepares to act, a self-identity we will suppose to be in part
received and in part achieved by its past actions. Let us for simplicity
call that self-identity its achieved self-identity. Where in it shall we
find a sufficient reason for this next act? What do we mean, that is to
say, when we say that *it* is capable of this next action? The question
of course applies also to its past acts in their time. The achieved self
will be describable in detail in terms of its infrastructure, and we may
perhaps take the risk of thinking of the infrastructure of the primary
being as containing among other things a range of possibilities that
constitute potential infrastructures for new acts. But where are we to
find the actualizer of those potentialities? Where is the achiever; where,
that is to say, is the agent? Where is the new act to come from if it is
not to be just a function of the achieved self-identity? The whole
course of our argument so far forbids that: for better or worse, it holds
that the act itself, not an earlier one of which it is an effect, not a set
of conditions including earlier ones, is itself an irreducible factor in
explanation.

The problem is a real one only if we suppose that a new act fulfill-
ing all the conditions of ontic responsibility can not belong to the
agent unless it springs only out of the achieved self-identity of the
agent. From that point of view, an achieving act—one that is not
merely a function of the achieved self-identity, one moreover that
brings about alterations, trivial or momentous as the case may be, in
the achieved nature—seems to be an intrusion "from the outside" into
the being we call the agent. The problem vanishes, however, if we remember that the achieving act—the act indeed—is a particular, a this,
a *tode ti*, only by virtue of being an instantiation of something general. As the participant nature of the power of the act was not an intrusion into the act from outside but was intrinsic to it, so that same
act is not an intrusion into the nature of the agent from outside but is
intrinsic to it. The possibility of such an act arising just *there* in an
entity with an achieved and settled nature is precisely what we mean
or should mean by speaking of a primary being capable of rational ac-

tion; and, indeed, that is precisely what the condition of partial indeterminateness (ontic potentiality) requires.

To make this point is only to call attention to an easily missed feature of the particularity of primary beings. It is a feature that does not make the particularity of the agent any less fundamental than we usually take it to be. The *this*, the *tode ti*, whether it is just this wave front, just this subatomic particle, just this cell, just this organelle, just this macromolecule, just this agent, is still taken to be a fundamental fact of nature. This argument does not try to diminish its importance. It claims only that no particular is radically self-sufficient: however active and dynamic it may be, however much it may be a factor to be reckoned with, we can not use it to account fully for its own character as just that particular. Compresent with it is a factor not particular yet contributory to its particularity, not identical with its self-identity but the source of its self-identity, not a unity in the sense in which it is a unity but essential to its unity, not exercising power in the sense in which it may exercise power yet nonetheless the source of its power. It is precisely what confers upon any particular primary being the character of not being fully determined by the other members of a context of particular primary beings, however wide. It is what makes a rational agent capable of acts that are not fully explicable by explanatory procedures that dismiss the categories of agent and act. It is what confers upon any particular the character that tempts philosophers to establish theories of a radically pluralistic kind. Yet it is what makes radical pluralisms ultimately unacceptable, because it is what all these primary beings share.

Since we are talking of primary beings, we may appropriately think of it as Being. Whatever it is, one is not aware of it "in itself," but one is indeed aware of it to the extent that when a primary being is empirically present as such, this is also present as a feature of its presence. The same point can be made by saying that if there are particular primary beings that exercise power in action, then they do so by virtue of their status as participant powers; and that this feature is part of their rational-empirical presence.

If the agent is understood in this light, the multiplicity that is particularized as the infrastructure of some new act does not determine that act in all its details but rather lays down limitations within which the particularizing power—within which, if you prefer, the nature of things—must work. Our agent is a particular self because the multiplicity of particulars that make up its infrastructure is possessed by a power-unity that can not be completely understood as the achieved and completed particular that the agent will be at the end of its career. Its failure to be captured in the notion of the achieved particular is the obverse of its being a real factor in the agent regarded as either a potential achiever, or as an achiever-in-act. In this sense we preserve in our ontology of agents regarded as primary beings whatever was worthwhile in our earlier notion of "agent" as a commonsense term for an infrastructure visited and revisited by acts. We are incidentally in a better position now to interpret that feeling, so common in human experience of the more heightened kind, that it is as true to say about acts that they take hold of or possess one as that one performs them.

When a particle appears in an experimental situation in accordance with the necessities the lawlike statements of science purport to express, it does so because "the nature of things" possesses the region of its appearance. As the particle is the bearer of what transcends it, giving it the identity of being just *this* particle, so the primary being or one of its acts is the bearer of a Being that transcends it. Articulate understanding, continuous with experience, completing sensory awareness, is quite familiar with that transcendence—familiar with it in the sense that, following with its gaze the very lineaments of particularity, it finds particularity exhibiting its own received status as an aspect of its status as primary being.

Conditioned by an infrastructure of peculiar amplitude—conditioned by the human cerebral cortex among other things—the rational agent is extraordinarily receptive to the general (ideal, universal, transcendental) feature that informs all particular primary beings whatever. What is common to all of them is so magnified by the refractive power of the rational agent that attends to its own rationality that it becomes the appropriate governor of action. Not the least result of this is that the particular agent then tries to make clear to itself the very status of its own particularity. So it is that language, with all its exuberant generality, is concerned not just with elaborating theoretic structures to deal with experience, but with fastening upon the nature of the particular as well. It is at this point that the agent discovers in various ways, of which my present exercise purports to be one instance, the status of rational particularity and the various demands it makes. These demands are familiar to us: the demand for universalizability in ethics, the demand for the utmost generality in scientific laws, the demand that the artist should express something more universal than the particular circumstances in which the work of art begins.

Notes

I

The Question of the Authenticity of Responsibility

1. The expression "causal power" rightly suggests the attitude towards causality against which Hume directed his criticism. Hume's view has until recently been the orthodox one in English-speaking philosophy, and although many attempts have been made to overturn it, they have not been given a serious hearing until quite recently. In 1975 two books were published that made extensive use of the notion of causal power. See R. Harré and E. H. Madden, *Causal Powers* (Oxford: Blackwell, 1975) and E. Pols, *Meditation on a Prisoner: Towards Understanding Action and Mind* (Carbondale and Edwardsville: Southern Illinois University Press, 1975). Although I share with Harré and Madden the expression "causal power," I disagree with their position in a number of ways, some of which are discussed later on. I first used the expression "causal power," in a sense close to the one developed in the present book, in *The Recognition of Reason* (Carbondale: Southern Illinois University Press, 1963). See esp. pp. 107–201, 208–19, 236, 249.

2. The first monument in this sequence of Max Planck's rational acts is his doctoral dissertation, *Über den Zweiten Hauptsatz der Mechanischen Wärmetheorie* (Munich: Ackermann, 1879); the last, his epoch-making paper "Zur Theorie des Gesetzes der Energie Verteilung im Normalspektrum," *Verh. Deutsch. Phys. Gesell.* (Leipzig, 1900).

3. The literature on reasons and causes is too extensive for adequate treatment here. Many of the more influential writers appear in one or more of the following collections: R. Binkley, R. Bronaugh, A. Marras, eds., *Agent, Action, and Reason* (Toronto: University of Toronto Press, 1971); N. S. Care and C. Landesman, eds., *Readings in the Theory of Action* (Bloomington and London: Indiana University Press, 1968); T. Honderich, ed., *Essays on Freedom of Action* (London: Routledge & Kegan Paul, 1973). The first two contain extensive bibliographies; of books published too late to be included in them, J. R. Lucas, *The Freedom of the Will* (Oxford: Clarendon Press, 1970) and A. Kenny, *Freewill and Responsibility*

(London, Henley and Boston: Routledge & Kegan Paul, 1978) seem to me to be of especial interest.

4. For instance at *Phaedo* 99B, in the famous distinction between the "real cause" and "that without which the cause could not be a cause." It is certainly a *locus classicus* for the distinction between reasons and causes—one, however, in which reasons are distinguished from conditioning causes in virtue of being called real causes.

5. It perhaps needs no argument that until relatively modern times agency was assumed to be the clearest example of causation. Among the several recent advocates of agent-causation, von Wright stands out as the one most clearly committed to the position that the concept of the agent is prior to that of causation. G. H. von Wright, *Explanation and Understanding* (London: Routledge & Kegan Paul, 1971). I made a related but somewhat more general point in 1963 when I argued for the priority of the category of an entity that exercises power over that of causation. *The Recognition of Reason*, pp. 196–201.

6. The account of the voluntary nature of virtue and vice in the *Nichomachean Ethics*, III, 5 makes it plain enough that for Aristotle the agent could, in some circumstances, have acted differently from the way it did. Even a character trait that now makes it impossible for one to do otherwise, in circumstances relevant to the trait, would not have been there if one had refrained, as one could have done, from performing the acts that gradually led to the development of the trait.

7. It is not easy to decide what the proper criteria for a nomic universal are, let alone find some particular lawlike statement that meets the criteria. Any philosophy of science that accepts Hume's claim that experience consists of sequences of events that exhibit a regularity in which event C is typically followed by event E, but exhibit nothing that supports (1) the claim that C exercises a power on the later event E, (2) the claim that C produces E, or (3) the claim that C and E are in necessary connection, so that the occurrence of C necessitates the occurrence of E, must also accept the consequences of that position. Hume himself developed the consequences in arguments more persuasive than the premises about impressions and ideas he asks us to accept in order to follow him. Of these arguments the chief one is that no generalization based on such a sequence can be accepted as an absolutely necessary and universal law of nature, from which it follows in turn that no generalization to the effect that nature is absolutely regular or absolutely uniform can be accepted as absolutely necessary and universal. The circle this creates for a philosophy of science so grounded is a familiar one. Science is concerned to establish laws of nature. It is a feature of a genuine law, a feature we can not hide entirely by circumventing the troublesome issue of necessity by employing a term like "nomic universal," that it should be indefeasible. It is this feature that makes the conjunction of a statement about a state of affairs called the cause and a body of laws, meaning postulates, rules, and so on, entail a statement about a state of affairs called the effect. Indeed it is this feature that should make this latter statement as indefeasible as the law itself. Yet these laws, however indefeasible they might seem when we characterize them as nomic universals, must rest in the long run upon generalizations of empirical sequences that by definition can provide no such indefeasibility.

We must concede at once that there is no serious practical issue here. The humility of science before nature, the very principle upon which it advances, consists in recognizing that any generalization put forward at a given time as a law is tentative because in principle defeasible, defeasible (at least in highly special circumstances) because it can only be an approximation to the laws of nature. It is this point that has made the arguments of Popper so widely influential. Since the assumption that there are laws of nature forming some systematic order, if only we could formulate them, is a version of the Regularity of Nature Principle, the latter is as defeasible on Humean premises as any tentatively advanced nomic universal. But regarded merely as a methodological assumption it has exhibited such heuristic power that its in-principle defeasibility can safely be set aside in practical affairs.

Although this refuge in practice is the core of Hume's philosophy of science and the core of such sophisticated Humean doctrines as the one Ayer defended for the greater part of his career, it has troubled most contemporary followers of Hume sufficiently to move them to devise elaborately guarded schemes in which the ideal form of the ultimate generalizations of science is represented as that of nomic universals—generalization of such unlimited scope that they are in principle indefeasible. Perhaps we should regard them as saying, by this enterprise, only that this is indeed an ideal form, and that if causality is defined in terms of an entailment relation to such generalizations then there are no causality statements properly so called, because there are no actual nomic universals that conform to this ideal. But at any rate they have been trying to establish criteria for nomic universality against which any supposed nomic universal might be tested.

Controversy within Humean philosophy of science and between Humeans and those who accept only some of Hume's doctrine has centered around the question whether mere factual universality, even of unlimited empirical scope, is sufficient to qualify a generalization as a nomic universal or whether the modal notion of necessity is indispensable among the criteria. In this controversy Hume's atomic theory of knowledge has not loomed large, even though one might well feel that without it no such controversy would have arisen. But William Kneale is surely correct in observing ("Universality and Necessity," *BJPS* 12 [August 1961]: 89–90) that nonetheless "there are a great many modern philosophers who think that Hume was right in principle" in that "he freed the notion of natural law from a confusion with logical necessity in which it had been involved by previous philosophers." So that the controversy within the Humean camp about whether factual universality must be supplemented by some sort of necessity to establish a generalization as lawlike has never called in question the assumption that at any rate it can not be logical necessity that is at issue. Logical necessity, it has been taken for granted, plays a different role: it is seen in the fact that certain contingently true universals stand in logical connection with elements of an epistemic system of some complexity, and that by way of entailments certain empirical situations can be seen as instantiations of these lawlike universals. The lawlike universals themselves, whether merely universal or universal and in some sense necessary, are never logically necessary (a priori) truths.

For Kneale, nomic universals have that lawlike status not because they express a generalization upon the actual, however unlimited in scope, but because they are true for a group of possible worlds having certain common features. It is because they range beyond the actual that they have a modal force that supports counterfactuals in a way in which merely universal "laws" can never do. Though Kneale distinguishes the natural necessity inherent in nomic universals from logical necessity, on the grounds that the former characterizes possible worlds of a determinate kind while the latter is unlimited in scope, he sees at the least a family resemblance between the two: in both cases the term "necessity" carries the meaning "a situation without alternatives." Kneale's concern here is not, of course, merely for natural necessity, for he wishes to show that the a priori character of logic itself can not be accounted for in terms of universality, and that it has a modal component that material implication in its usual interpretation can not provide. Natural necessity then becomes a special case of the unlimited necessity of logic.

If we suppose that Kneale is right in requiring the modal notion of necessity in nomic universals, it would still seem that the Humean circle I mentioned earlier can be invoked to assure us that nomic universals of that sort can not be extracted from a nature regarded as not exhibiting particular necessities and not exhibiting in experience the completeness over which the predicates purport to range. As I observed earlier, the best one can do is treat the supposed law as though it were a nomic universal having the required intrinsic marks, from which it would follow that we could treat the entailed statements as though they were true in the same (contingent) sense in which the premises were true.

Harré and Madden also distinguish between logical necessity and natural necessity, although they use the expression "conceptual necessity" where Kneale uses "natural necessity." They themselves reserve the expression "natural necessity" (sometimes "physical necessity") for what follows from the particular exercise of particular powers in nature, as befits their attack on Hume. They claim, that is, that what they call natural necessity is encountered a posteriori in our dealings with particular powers in nature. About nomic universals it is their claim that no intrinsic formal marks are sufficient to enable us to distinguish them from accidental ones, and that even when these formal criteria are augmented by either simple or ramified epistemic criteria, it is still possible to provide counterexamples that show that the required distinction can not be made. These moves to epistemic criteria, they argue plausibly, either turn out to be reducible to formal criteria or else covertly introduce explanatory models that are not in fact Humean. For a more extended account of their position, see my review of Causal Powers in International Philosophical Quarterly 16, no. 3 (Sept. 1976): 369–77, from which I have taken this note.

8. It is no accident that except for that contemporary and rather unpleasant interloper, "raw feels," this catalogue bears some resemblance to the familiar one Descartes uses in the Meditations to define a thinking being (Second Meditation).

9. For instance, Eugene Wigner and Arturo Rosenblueth; see chap. 6, n. 8.

10. Meditation on a Prisoner, as indexed under Causality, c→e.

11. Harré and Madden seem to incline to a view of the relation between what they call the one Great Field and particular causal powers that would lead to a deterministic consequence of this kind. See my review of Causal Powers, cited in n. 7.

12. *Meditation on a Prisoner*, pp. 17–20 and elsewhere, as indexed.

13. R. M. Chisholm, "Freedom and Action," in *Freedom and Determinism*, ed. K. Lehrer (New York: Random House, 1966), and *Person and Object* (London: Allen & Unwin, 1976), esp. chap. 2. G. H. von Wright, *Explanation and Understanding*, and *Causality and Determinism* (New York: Columbia University Press, 1974). R. Taylor, *Action and Purpose* (Englewood Cliffs, N.J.: Prentice-Hall, 1966). Chisholm first used the expression "immanent causation," in contradistinction to "transeunt causation," in the article cited first. What he means by "transeunt" is in radical conflict with the traditional sense. See chap. 2, n. 3.

14. For instance, to A. Danto, in *Analytical Philosophy of Action* (Cambridge: At the University Press, 1973), pp. 51–63, 72–73, 205, n. 1; and to J. Hornsby in *Actions* (London, Boston and Henley: Routledge & Kegan Paul, 1980), chap. 7.

15. An introduction to the literature of the identity theory is available in J. O'Connor, ed., *Modern Materialism: Readings in Mind-Body Identity* (New York: Harcourt, Brace & World, 1969) and in C. V. Borst, ed., *Mind-Brain Identity Theory* (London: Macmillan, 1970). Both books have bibliographies. See next note for a book with an extensive bibliography on the subject.

16. E. Wilson, *The Mental as Physical* (London, Boston and Henley: Routledge & Kegan Paul, 1979).

17. The best account of epiphenomenalism, to my mind, is still William James's in *The Principles of Psychology* (New York: Henry Holt, 1890). See vol. 1, chap. 5, "The Automaton-Theory." In a recent article M. Hodges and J. Lachs, without claiming that epiphenomenalism is true, try to dispose of some well-regarded arguments against it; see "Meaning and the Impotence Hypothesis," in the *Review of Metaphysics* 32, no. 3 (March 1979): 515–29. They note that the most recent defense is probably Keith Campbell's *Body and Mind* (London: Macmillan, 1972); I know of no other recent one.

18. See, for instance, D. E. Wooldridge, *The Machinery of the Brain* (New York: McGraw-Hill, 1963), esp. chap. 11.

19. Danto, *Analytical Philosophy of Action*. Contrast his definition of the identity of an action with a brain event on p. 63 with the discussion of representation towards the end of the book, esp. pp. 188–96.

20. T. S. Kuhn, *The Structure of Scientific Revolutions* (1962), 2d. ed., enlarged (Chicago: Chicago University Press, 1970).

21. A. Kenny, *Will, Freedom and Power* (Oxford: Blackwell, 1975), and *Freewill and Responsibility*; S. Hampshire, *Freedom of the Individual* (New York: Harper & Row, 1965); and P. F. Strawson, *Individuals* (London: Methuen, 1959). Both Strawson and Hampshire take part in the discussions in D. F. Pears, ed., *Freedom and the Will* (London: Macmillan, 1965), pp. 48–68, 80–104.

22. *Die Krisis der europäischen Wissenschaften und die transzendentale Phänomenologie*. Parts 1 and 2 were first published in *Philosophia* (Belgrade, 1936). The whole work, including part 3, was not published until 1954, as vol. 4 of *Husserliana* (The Hague: Nijhoff, 1954). There is now an English translation, E. Husserl, *The Crisis of European Sciences and Transcendental Phenomenology*, trans. with an introduction by David Carr (Evanston: Northwestern University Press, 1970).

II

The Metaphysical Conditions of Ontic Responsibility

1. There is another sense of "responsibility" that should be mentioned in passing—the one in which we tend to call responsible only those acts we judge to be good, or at least good in intent. We shall not be concerned with that sense in this book. In the sense we shall be discussing, we are responsible for acts that are disapproved or punished as well as for those that are approved or rewarded. A crime, then, would be a responsible act, although in the sense of "responsible" we are not concerned with, a crime might be called irresponsible.

2. Iris Murdoch, *The Sovereignty of Good over Other Concepts* (Cambridge: At the University Press, 1967). For a related piece, published later but based on a paper delivered in 1966, see her "On 'God' and 'Good,' " in *The Anatomy of Knowledge*, ed. M. Grene (London: Routledge & Kegan Paul; Amherst: University of Massachusetts Press, 1969).

3. The OED gives "transeunt" as a variant spelling of "transient" when it is intended in the sense we are concerned with, "passing out or operating beyond itself" (OED's sense 2). The earliest occurrence in English is 1613. An early OED example that gives the contrast immanent-transeunt is 1625, Gill, *Sacr. Philos.* I, 98: "You may observe a difference of actions, of which some are immanent, or indwelling in the 'doer . . . : some againe are transeunt, or passing from the doer upon that which is done." The source of all this is a medieval distinction of which St. Thomas's contrast of *actio manens* with *actio transiens*, or of *operatio manens* with *operatio transiens*, is typical. A passage in which Thomas makes the contrast and goes on to apply it to God will serve as an example: "Est autem duplex rei operatio. . . . Una quidem, quae in ipso operante manet et est ipsius operantis perfectio, ut sentire, intelligere et velle; alia vero, quae in exteriorem rem transit, quae est perfectio facti quod per ipsam constituitur, ut calefacere, secare et aedificare. Utraque autem dictarum operationum competit Deo. Prima quidem, in eo quod intelligit, vult, gaudet et amat; alia vero, in eo quod res in esse producit et eas conservat et regit" (II *Contra Gentes*, I). From this it is clear (a) that not all immanent operations (of men at least) give rise to transeunt ones; (b) that making and (in the case of God) creating and conserving are transeunt operations; (c) that any transeunt operation is dependent upon an immanent one, being nothing more than an exercise of an immanent power beyond the agent. Thomas reinforces this last point a little later in the same passage: "prima dictarum operationum sit ratio secundae. . . ." When Spinoza uses this distinction, he must naturally maintain that God is the immanent cause of the world but not its transient (transeunt) cause, since he holds that there is nothing external to God (*Ethics*, I, prop. 18). Chisholm warns us that he is using the borrowed terms "in a way that is slightly different from that for which they were originally intended." For the sense he gives "transeunt" he uses Aristotle's example of a staff moving a stone, as distinct from the man who holds and moves the staff and thus the stone (*Physics* VII, 5, 256a, 6-8.) The difference is much more than slight, for the medieval tradition would take the *man's* moving the stone (with or without a staff) as an example of transeunt causation. I do not quarrel with Chisholm's use of Aristotle's example as a

way of distinguishing agent causation from event causation (or my originative causal power from transmitted causation), but the use of the terms "immanent" and "transeunt" to make the distinction only confuses the issue and incidentally erodes the useful distinction originally made with the aid of those terms. R. M. Chisholm, "Freedom and Action," in *Freedom and Determinism*, pp. 17–18.

4. Bertrand Russell, "On the Notion of Cause, with Applications to the Free-Will Problem," in *Our Knowledge of the External World*, 2d ed. (New York: W. W. Norton, 1929), p. 239. The chapter so titled was originally delivered as one of the Lowell Lectures in 1914, but much of the material in it first appeared in 1913. See next note.

5. Russell, "On the Notion of Cause," in *Mysticism and Logic* (London: Longmans, Green and Co., 1917), p. 180. The paper was the presidential address to the Aristotelian Society in November 1912, and was first published in their *Proceedings* for 1912–13.

6. Op. cit., n. 4, p. 242.

7. Op. cit., n. 5, pp. 207–8.

8. Op. cit., n. 4, p. 240.

9. It appears to me that Harré and Madden, who argued in the earlier part of *Causal Powers* for the reality of causal power (at least in a sense approximating the working view of c→e causality), entertain in the latter part of it the possibility that what seems to be a particular causal power is in fact a particular "region" of one great field of which time itself is one of the dimensions. R. Harré and E. H. Madden, *Causal Powers;* chap. 9, esp. pp. 175–83.

10. *Nichomachean Ethics*, II, 1.

11. R. E. Hobart (Dickenson S. Miller), "Free Will as Involving Determination and Inconceivable Without It," *Mind* 43 (1934): 1–27. Hobart on close scrutiny turns out to be no typical compatibilist, as his choice of the expression "free will" rather than "freedom" to juxtapose with "determinism" tells us. Most compatibilists seem willing enough to suppose that the term "freedom" belongs to an ordinary and unexamined mode of discourse, while the term "determinism" applies at some deeper and more "scientific" level. Compatibilists of that kind tend to accept physical determinism as a working hypothesis, and they are not disturbed by the thought that our use of such terms as "could," "power," "freedom," and "act" must then have a merely Pickwickian sense. Other compatibilists, those with a more innocent faith in ordinary language, suppose that its mere persistence in the face of the language of an encroaching physical determinism is in itself a guarantee that the two languages are indeed compatible in some more significant sense. Miller-Hobart fits readily into neither group. He speaks of an act-source and its exercise of free will with so much confidence that we should not be surprised to find him defending an indeterminism like that of his friend and mentor William James, of whom, incidentally, Miller's bluff, hearty, and vivid prose often reminds us. There are, of course, other passages in which Miller seems to be saying no more than what Hume was saying.

12. The difference between a radical, or categorical, sense in which an agent could have done otherwise and the various hypothetical senses entertained by compatibilists was explored thoroughly and agreed upon some time ago by two writers who agree about little else concerning the freedom of the agent. See C. A. Camp- ·

bell, "Is 'Freewill' a Pseudo-Problem?" *Mind* 60 (1951): 446–65, and C. D. Broad, "Determinism, Indeterminism, and Libertarianism," in *Ethics and the History of Philosophy* (London: Routledge & Kegan Paul, 1952), pp. 195–217.

13. Virginia Woolf, *Moments of Being: Unpublished Autobiographical Writings*, ed. with an intro. by Jeanne Schulkind (New York and London: Harcourt Brace Jovanovich, 1976), pp. 70–72, 81–84, 93, 114–15, 122.

14. B. F. Skinner, *About Behaviorism* (New York: Knopf, 1974), pp. 16–17, 248–49.

15. Wilson, *The Mental as Physical*, pp. 54–55.

16. Ibid., pp. 286–88, 305, 354.

17. Kenny, *Freewill and Responsibility*, pp. 3–5.

III

The Foundation Question Reopened:
The Circle of Action and Knowledge

1. Although Plato makes an important distinction between the sensible and the intelligible world, he believes that we can make a gradual progress upwards in our grasp of reality. His metaphors for this progress are chiefly those of sight: even the Form of the Good can, in principle, be "seen" by the mind's eye. See *Republic* 533A 5. The various terms for knowledge are of course applied only to the intelligible world, but it is clear that he wants to bring out the gradual disclosure of the "really real" rather than its absolute sequestration behind appearances.

2. Richard Rorty's attack on the representative theory in his *Philosophy and the Mirror of Nature* (Princeton: Princeton University Press, 1979) may come as news to those analytic philosophers who took the linguistic turn and have since wandered in the labyrinths of language without understanding how important the representative theory was in making that turn seem the right one to take. But it should be noted that there is another tradition to whose adherents this report of the malign influence of the representative theory does not come as news—a tradition more "realist" than "representative" in its views about *what* we know *when* we know. It has roots in Greek thought that Heidegger and Rorty both overlook; it persists as one strand in medieval philosophy; it manifests itself in dissenting philosophy like that of Reid; and it has been visible enough to some twentieth-century historians of philosophy who have felt no need to write as historicists. I welcome Rorty's book, but not as one from whose eyes the scales have fallen because of it: in 1963 I called for the dismissal of such metaphors for knowledge as representing, picturing, and mirroring and for the recognition that our cognitive engagement with the real is *sui generis*. The "realistic" theme in this chapter is a continuation of that earlier criticism. See *The Recognition of Reason*, pp. 55, 83, 86, 88, 110, 127, 143. Rorty's book is the more welcome because it comes from a professional analytic philosopher of considerable standing, and so will be widely read and perhaps bring about some changes in analytic orthodoxy. Later in the chapter I suggest that despite his criticism of the representative doctrine there is some evidence that he is not entirely free of that doctrine's obsessive power.

3. Rorty has, I think, conflated the two doctrines (*Philosophy and the Mirror*

of *Nature*, pp. 38–44). He seems to suppose that because Plato uses ocular images about knowledge, because mirrors are in some sense ocular, and because the mirror metaphor is sometimes used in connection with the representative theory, Plato is therefore ultimately responsible for that theory. If Plato's views on the relation between Nous and the Forms could really be expressed in terms of what Rorty calls "knowing general truths by internalizing universals" (p. 41), we might well conclude that he was in fact responsible. Plato's views on the matter are, however, quite different. Whether or not his doctrine was sound is not the issue; the issue is what the doctrine was. And it was—need one really cite chapter and verse?—in flat opposition to everything the representative doctrine says. The Forms are said to be not copies but originals and to be directly known as such; and they are not thought of as located within Nous (which in any event can scarcely be equated with consciousness or a Cartesian *res cogitans*) but as being independently real in a region distinct from the knower. Plato's use of the term *"idea"* as equivalent with *"eidos"* should not confuse us, for though ocular enough, it has in Greek none of the sense of being internal to the knower that its transliteration "idea" has for us—especially since Descartes.

As for the metaphor of the mirror as applied to the mind, it is hard to see how anyone would be tempted to blame Plato for it. In the only reference to mirrors I can recall, Plato is concerned to make a point that forbids our taking the *mind* as a mirror. The cognitive relation, as he sees it, is never one between the mind and some copy, yet in the passage in question—it is *Republic* 596D8-E3, part of the famous discussion in which what we should today call representative art is ranked much lower than knowledge because it produces mere copies of copies—he points out that a mirror is the simplest and quickest device we have for making copies of visible things, i.e., for making copies of copies: we have merely to turn a mirror this way and that to produce copies of all sorts of things. The mind, on the contrary, looks for and is capable of "seeing" entities that are wholly original; so whatever else the mind was for Plato, it could not have been a mirror.

The Platonic use of the mirror as a metaphor for representational art has of course an important role in the history of aesthetics, but that role is independent of its use as a metaphor for the mind *in the sense required by the representative theory of ideas*. In that sense, the proper description of the cognition relation is that the knower looks into his mind, or consciousness, and there finds ideas that represent the original things he wishes to know but can not know directly. (How these ideas got into the mind is another question, and the empiricist and rationalist wings of the representative tradition are divided on this matter; it need not concern us here.) It is obvious that we could hold the view that the cognitive relation was different and more "direct," and still find the mirror metaphor useful in a different sense. We might, for instance, say of some brilliant and learned person that his mind mirrored all of nature, meaning by this only that in talking with him we can learn many things about nature. We might nevertheless suppose that that person knew nature directly, not by means of representative ideas; we might suppose that we ourselves knew that person directly rather than by way of representative ideas; and none of this would be incompatible with our finding his intelligence rather like a mirror. If we are not obsessed by the representative doctrine we do not invoke it every time we use a mirror metaphor.

The history of the mirror metaphor, much of which depends ultimately upon the Platonic use of it to criticize representational art, is immensely complicated, and I have no intention of trying to tell it in a note. It is simply an exaggeration, however, to suppose that whenever the mirror metaphor turns up in the centuries before Descartes it brings with it some anticipation of his representative theory of ideas. The most that can be said is that there are some things in the history of the metaphor that contributed to making it natural to put it to the more narrow epistemological use that is not infrequent after Descartes. Three uses of the metaphor, all of which probably owe something to the Platonic tradition going back to the *Republic* passage cited above, come to mind. One was the application of the term "mirror," or "*speculum*," to a book of some kind, usually something compendious enough to purport to be a written representation of some significant portion of reality. Another was its application to nature as a whole, regarded as a representation of either some version of the Platonic "really real" or some version of a God more radically creative of nature than the *demiourgos* of the *Timaeus*. To suppose oneself to be seeing God in nature, as in a glass, darkly, is by no means to bring in the representative theory of ideas. Yet another use of the metaphor was its application to man, regarded as a microcosm in which the various perfections of the macrocosm could be found. But it was usual for man as a whole, and not just his mind, to be considered a mirror in this sense. This is true even of the rather late occurrence of the metaphor in Nicholas of Cusa, although his imaginative synthesis does indeed give the mind a special role that suggests what we later find in Leibniz. In any event, by Nicholas's time (1401–1464) other epistemological considerations are already setting the scene for the entry of the representative doctrine as we know it in Descartes. But it is interesting that even Leibniz, who often gives the mirror metaphor the sense required by the representative theory of ideas, also uses the metaphor in the more extended sense in which Nicholas uses it: each monad mirrors all other monads, but for Leibniz not all monads are conscious minds.

4. Wilfrid Sellars, *Science, Perception and Reality* (London: Routledge & Kegan Paul; New York: Humanities Press, 1963), p. 173. Sellars, it should be noted, goes out of his way to make the point that he is speaking as a philosopher.

5. This may seem an odd thing to say about a writer whose spare and elegant prose abounds with commonsense remarks and even with some explicit appeals to common sense. "Science," he says in "Two Dogmas of Empiricism" (p. 45), "is a continuation of common sense, and it continues the common-sense expedient of swelling ontology to simplify theory." But references to experience in a phenomenalist spirit also abound, for instance in "On What There Is," pp. 16–19. Commonsense physical objects are dealt with as "posits" and "myths" in "Two Dogmas" (p. 44), despite the remark quoted above from the same essay, the ultimate objective of countenancing such myths being the empiricist one of "predicting future experience in the light of past experience." Between the ontology required by the physicalist conceptual scheme gradually elaborated by science (it will require posits of a different kind) and the ontology implicit in a phenomenalist attitude towards experience, the world of common sense itself has no ontological authority. (Despite what Quine says in "On What There Is," there are other ontological commitments besides those a *theory* is committed to by what its bound variables are capable of

referring to.) For the two essays quoted—they are surely Quine's most influential ones, aside from his work in mathematical logic—see *From a Logical Point of View*, 2d ed., rev. (New York and Evanston: Harper & Row, 1961).

6. For the manifest image doctrine see chap. 5 and its notes.

7. Bertrand Russell, "The Philosophy of Logical Atomism," *The Monist* 28 and 29 (1918–1919). For another version of his views on logical atomism, see "Logical Atomism," in *Contemporary British Philosophy: Personal Statements*, 1st ser. (London: Allen & Unwin; New York: The Macmillan Co., 1924), pp. 356–83. Both versions were reprinted in *Logic and Knowledge*, ed. R. C. Marsh (London, 1956). Ludwig Wittgenstein, *Tractatus Logico-Philosophicus* (1922) trans. D. F. Pears and B. F. McGuinness (London: Routledge & Kegan Paul, 1961).

8. Ludwig Wittgenstein, *Philosophical Investigations*, trans. G. E. M. Anscombe (New York: The Macmillan Co., 1953).

9. The claim that rigorous philosophy must suspend and go beyond the natural standpoint is a continuing theme in Husserl's work from the first decade of the century. The notion of the life-world becomes prominent in the thirties. See especially *Krisis*, cited chap. 1, n. 22. For a slightly earlier lecture out of which *Krisis* was later developed, see "Philosophy and the Crisis of European Man," in Edmund Husserl, *Phenomenology and the Crisis of Philosophy*, trans. with an intro. by Quentin Lauer (New York: Harper & Row, 1965).

10. Rorty, *Philosophy and the Mirror of Nature*; see esp. pp. 131–82.

11. Pols, *The Recognition of Reason*, pp. 38–41.

12. G. E. Moore, "A Defence of Common Sense," in *Contemporary British Philosophy*, pp. 193–223 cited n. 7; reprinted in his *Philosophical Papers* (London and New York, 1959).

13. B. Russell and A. N. Whitehead, *Principia Mathematica*, 2 vols. (Cambridge: Cambridge University Press, 1910, 1912).

14. There have been many retrospective surveys of logical positivism. See especially A. J. Ayer's introduction to the collection of essays he edited, *Logical Positivism* (New York: The Free Press, 1959). The most influential, and certainly the clearest, statement in English of the movement's aims is Ayer, *Language, Truth and Logic* (1936), 2d ed. rev. (London: Gollancz, 1946).

15. For Quine, besides the material cited in n. 5, see W. V. Quine, *Word and Object* (New York and London: Technology Press of M.I.T. jointly with John Wiley & Sons, 1960); "Ontological Relativity," in *Ontological Relativity and Other Essays* (New York: Columbia University Press, 1969). For Sellars, see chap. 5 and its notes.

16. Quine, "On What There Is," in *From a Logical Point of View*, pp. 12–13.

17. Ibid., pp. 15–19. Quine's views about the relation between notation and ontology discussed in the text are illuminated by a much later remark in *Word and Object*, at the end of the section "Aims and Claims of Regimentation": "The quest of a simplest, clearest overall pattern of canonical notation is not to be distinguished from a quest of ultimate categories, a limning of the most general traits of reality. Nor let it be retorted that such constructions are conventional affairs not dictated by reality; for may not the same be said of physical theory? True, such is the nature of reality that one physical theory will get us around better than

another; but similarly for canonical notations" (p. 161). The concluding section of *Word and Object*, "Semantic Ascent," pp. 270–76, should also be consulted. There is, incidentally, no more telling example of the spirit of the consensus of linguistic enclosure than the paragraph with which Quine ends that book. Note especially how the connection between language and the sensory is characterized: outside the enclosure there is only "non-verbal stimulation," or the "surface irritation" with which ontological issues make connection through a "maze of intervening theory."

18. Wilfrid Sellars, *Science and Metaphysics: Variations on Kantian Themes* (London: Routledge & Kegan Paul, 1968), p. 150. But see also the discussion of the manifest image doctrine in chap. 5 of the present book.

19. *Tractatus Logico-Philosophicus*, 6.53, 4.12–4.1212.

20. *Philosophical Investigations*, 89, 90.

21. Ibid., 109, 119, 125. For some of the discussion of the continuity of doctrine from the *Tractatus* through the *Investigations* I have drawn upon an article I wrote in response to the reception of the *Investigations*, "To Live At Ease Ever After," *Sewanee Review* 66, no. 2 (1958): 229–51.

22. *The Recognition of Reason*; see n. 2.

23. Nelson Goodman, *Ways of Worldmaking* (Indianapolis: Hackett, 1978). The metaphor of worldmaking expresses a contemporary version of Kant's epistemology that is in some debt to Cassirer's doctrine of symbolic forms. See chap. 5, n. 9.

24. Woolf, *Moments of Being*, p. 93.

IV

The Conditions Fulfilled: A Reflexive Vindication

1. See chap. 3, n. 9.

2. See *Meditation on a Prisoner*, as indexed under "Act-temporality."

3. Ibid., as indexed under "Causality, C→E."

4. I use the abbreviation "PB" here because it is used throughout chap. 6 in a detailed discussion of the identity theory.

5. *Phaedo*, 98B–99D. The phrase that usually produces the translation "real cause" is τὸ αἴτιον τῷ ὄντι (99B); a little earlier (98E) there is the phrase τὰς ὡς ἀληθῶς αἰτίας, which is sometimes translated "real causes" and sometimes "true causes."

V

Manifest Image vs. Ontically Significant Appearance

1. Wilfrid Sellars, *Science, Perception and Reality*, chap. 1, "Philosophy and the Scientific Image of Man." Sellars gives the history of the chapter on p. vii.

2. Ibid., pp. 6, 9, 8, 19.

3. Ibid., p. 18.

4. Wilfrid Sellars, *Science and Metaphysics*, p. 1.

5. Sellars, *Science, Perception and Reality*, p. 28.

6. Ibid., p. 40.

7. Sellars, *Science and Metaphysics*, pp. 50, 143, 150.

8. Ibid., pp. ix–x.

9. Some readers may well feel that an outlook dominated by the metaphor of worldmaking is incompatible with physicalism. I think that depends on how much ontological weight one gives to scientific as against other kinds of worldmaking; and surely among several ways of worldmaking it is possible to attach more onto-logical significance to one than to another. Cassirer certainly gives science a heavy weight, so much so that (to use his own terminology rather than Goodman's) reli-gion and artistic symbolic forms seem to belong to the youth of the race. Ernst Cassirer, *Philosophy of Symbolic Forms*, trans. Ralph Mannheim, 3 vols. (New Haven: Yale University Press, 1953, 1955, 1957). For Goodman, see chap. 3, n. 23.

10. For the persistence of this claim through the radical change from the *Tractatus* to the *Philosophical Investigations*, see the article cited ch. 3, n. 21.

11. Rorty, *Philosophy and the Mirror of Nature*.

12. Kuhn, *The Structure of Scientific Revolutions*.

13. The doctrine of the *clinamen atomorum* is known chiefly from Lucretius' *De Rerum Natura*, Book 2, 216–93, although the word "*clinamen*" itself occurs only at 292. There is no discussion of the swerve in the surviving fragments of Epicurus, but there is no doubt that the doctrine goes back to him. For a clear summary of the matter see T. Lucreti Cari, *De Rerum Natura*, ed. with intro. and commentary by William Ellery Leonard and Stanley Barney Smith (Madison: Uni-versity of Wisconsin Press, 1942), pp. 332–33, n. to ll. 216–93; p. 336, n. to ll. 251–93.

14. For an English translation of the fragments of Leucippus and Democritus, based on the fifth edition of Diels, *Fragmente der Vorsokratiker*, see Kathleen Freeman, *Ancilla to the Pre-Socratic Philosophers* (Cambridge: Harvard University Press, 1957), pp. 90–120. For another translation, which also incorporates the *testimonia* of later philosophers, see Philip Wheelwright, *The Presocratics* (New York: Odyssey Press, 1966), pp. 175–99.

15. That Parmenides himself was not a materialist seems clear enough. The best English versions of his *Way of Truth*, to my mind, are Cornford's and Wheel-wright's. Francis M. Cornford, *Plato and Parmenides: Parmenides' Way of Truth and Plato's Parmenides* (London: Routledge & Kegan Paul, 1957). Wheelwright, *The Presocratics*.

16. Freeman, *Ancilla to the Pre-Socratic Philosophers*, p. 104, no. 125; Wheel-wright, *The Presocratics*, p. 183.

17. Wheelwright, *The Presocratics*, p. 190.

18. R. W. Sperry, "A Modified Concept of Consciousness," *Psychological Review* 76, no. 6 (1969): 532–36; "Changing Concepts of Consciousness and Free Will," *Perspectives in Biology and Medicine* 20, no. 1 (1976): 9–19.

19. Dean E. Wooldridge, *The Machinery of the Brain*, pp. 219–28.

20. See, for instance, the causal account of epiphenomenalism given in Jerome A. Shaffer, *Philosophy of Mind* (Englewood Cliffs, N.J.: Prentice-Hall, 1968), pp. 68–71.

21. See works cited above, n. 18.

22. Paul A. Weiss, "The Living System: Determinism Stratified," in *Beyond Reductionism: New Perspectives in the Life Sciences* ed. Arthur Koestler and J. R. Smythies (London: Hutchinson & Co., 1969), pp. 3–55.

23. Michael Polanyi, *Personal Knowledge* (Chicago: Chicago University Press, 1958). For a late and very clear statement of his version of what I have called the hierarchic view of the laws of nature see "Life Transcending Physics and Chemistry," *Chemical and Engineering News*, August 21, 1967, pp. 55–66.

24. *Meditation on a Prisoner*, pp. 39–68.

25. Edgar Wilson's view inclines to the PMI doctrine to the extent that he speaks, more often than many identity theorists do, of two aspects of the physical, one being what is usually called the physical, the other being phenomenal. His own term for the "two-aspect" feature of his doctrine is "biperspectivism." See *The Mental as Physical*, pp. 72–81, 98–101, and elsewhere. In other respects his doctrine conforms to the usual conventions of an identity theory—especially the one that assigns no explanatory value to one of the aspects.

26. Ernest Nagel, *The Structure of Science* (New York: Harcourt, Brace & World, 1961). See especially chaps. 11 and 12.

27. Hans Reichenbach, *Atom and Cosmos* (New York: Macmillan, 1933), pp. 27–29.

28. The classic case is La Mettrie's *L'Homme Machine* (Leyden, 1748). For a modern edition of the French text with an English translation, see J. O. de La Mettrie, *Man a Machine*, trans. G. C. Bussey et al. (La Salle, Ill.: Open Court, 1961).

29. Not all macroscopic things are on the same size level. It seems plausible, for instance, to regard a single cell or an organism of one cell as macroscopic in the sense that it can be seen in an ordinary (light) microscope and thus experienced as such.

VI

Rational Action and Its Physiological Basis

1. Skinner, *About Behaviorism*, pp. 16–17, 248–49.

2. *Meditation on a Prisoner*, chap. 4.

3. Most of them are at least implicit in Danto's *Analytical Philosophy of Action*.

4. The term "language" is used too loosely in contemporary philosophy. I summarize here a point made in more detail in chap. 3: where a language L_2 is embedded in another language L_1 and can only function when so embedded, and where L_1 is not so embedded in another language, L_2 is a language in a less fundamental sense than L_1. Nonetheless, such distinctions as mental language/physical language are frequent in discussions of mind-body identity. The distinction RA-language/PB-language is designed to be appropriate to contexts of that kind and does not represent my own view.

5. Contingent identity in this restricted sense is compatible with the claim that the self-identity of the single referent could not be otherwise than it in fact is—that it is, in that sense, necessary. But identity theorists often use "contingent" in a less restricted sense. See the following note.

6. For this reason, the use of the notion "rigid designator" to mount an attack on identity theory by way of an attack on the alleged contingency of identity may not be so devastating as some suppose. If, as a first step in an argument designed to show that the identity, if real, must be a necessary one, the critic claims (in the RA-PB case) that "RA" rigidly designates a referent RA, or (in Kripke's version of the M-B case) that "pain" rigidly designates pain (the phenomenon pain), the identity theorist may well concede the point. In the mind-body case, no identity theorist worth arguing with claims the total absence of subjectivity. What the theorist claims is that it is deceptive, delusive, or otherwise deficient—so much so, that it can not see that it is identical with what it supposes to be only its physical basis. If he concedes that "pain" rigidly designates the phenomenon pain, while "C-fibre stimulation" rigidly designates a physical reality, he concedes only that the first designator designates a *prima facie*, or apparent, referent rigidly, while the second designates the authentic referent rigidly. If he does this, he is not claiming that pain is merely apparent, except in the trivial sense that it is indeed a phenomenon. The subject's pain is real enough. The theorist is claiming rather that the *prima facie* referent pain has the apparent status of being authentically distinct from C-fibre stimulation. The identity theorist need not, therefore, be discomfited when told that a necessary identity should be manifest in the confrontation of the two rigid designators in the case where it is claimed that they designate only one authentic referent. It is science, he is entitled to say, and not an intuitive inspection of *prima facie* referent and authentic referent combined with a scrutiny of the logic of designators, that persuades him that there is only one authentic referent, the physical; and in that sense, the identity is contingent. What he need not, and indeed should not, concede to be contingent is the self-identity of the single referent. He should maintain that it could not be otherwise than it in fact is, although its own inner necessities only emerge in the laws of science and are only necessary in whatever sense of "necessity" we are prepared to attribute to the laws of science. Granted the presence of a referent (pain) distinct only in a *prima facie* sense from C-fibre stimulation, the identity theorist should not say that some other *prima facie* referent (say, pleasure) might have been in its place. For all these reasons, I have decided to take seriously the claim of the analogous RA-PB identity theory that the identity is contingent. My refutation, therefore, deals directly with the empirical claims thus attributed to the theory. See S. A. Kripke, "Naming and Necessity," in *Semantics of Natural Language*, 2d ed., ed. D. Davidson and G. Harman (Dordrecht, Holland and Boston: D. Reidel, 1973), pp. 253–355.

A more basic objection to inferences drawn from the notion of rigid designator is the dependence of that notion on the notion of possible worlds. In the absence of a theological framework in which the Deity contemplates a number of such worlds from which he selects one to actualize, the latter notion is of dubious worth. It is not surprising that the Deity so conceived looks somewhat like a logician writ large, for logicians do tend to confuse their system-building with a God-like world-building. We are more often told, by those who deal in the notion, what a possible world is not, rather than what it is. A close observation of how the notion is actually used in such discussions suggests that it is a logical object in somewhat the sense in which mathematicians speak of mathematical objects. It is difficult enough to say what things are possible within this actual world, let alone whether other worlds (in any plausible sense of "world" and "possible") are possible.

7. I do not mean to imply that this straw man is a legitimate version of the distinct reality of mind. It is, however, the usual version of those who hold the theory of the physicalist identity of mind and body.

8. See Eugene Wigner, "Two Kinds of Reality," in *Symmetries and Reflections* (Bloomington: Indiana University Press, 1967); and "Epistemology of Quantum Mechanics: Its Appraisal and Demands," in *The Anatomy of Knowledge*. See also Arturo Rosenblueth, *Mind and Brain: A Philosophy of Science* (Cambridge: M.I.T. Press, 1970). A more unusual case is J. C. Eccles's attempt to use similar ideas derived from Karl Popper in a defense of such notions as free will and the efficacy of consciousness. See Eccles, *The Understanding of the Brain*, 2d ed. (New York: McGraw-Hill, 1977), esp. chap. 6.

VII

Participant Powers: The Ontology of the Rational Agent

1. Aristotle, *Metaphysics*, 1042b 9–11, 1043a 19–21, 1050a 22–24; *De Anima*, 412a 12–31.

2. See especially *De Anima*, II; *Nichomachean Ethics*, II, III, 1–5.

3. The story depends upon the entanglement of the words "ousia," "hypokeimenon," and "hypostasis." As noted in the text, Aristotle is responsible for the association between "ousia" and "hypokeimenon." He uses the latter (literally, that which lies under) sometimes to refer to matter as that which persists through change, and sometimes to refer to an individual being—a man, for instance— regarded as persisting, as the same individual entity, through the change it undergoes. (The individual, in that restricted sense, can be regarded as the *matter* in which the privation of a certain qualitative *form* is succeeded by its presence.) The word "hypostasis" (literally that which stands under, or is placed under) was first used in a philosophic sense by the Stoics, who made it synonymous with "ousia." It is not surprising that they should have done so, because "hypostasis," like "hypokeimenon," has materialist overtones, and theirs was a materialist metaphysics; but when "ousia" is associated with "hypostasis," its Platonic and Aristotelian sense is blurred in much the same way as when it is associated with "hypokeimenon." Irenaeus (i, 5, 4) says that "hypostasis" was introduced into theology by the Gnostics, and there also associated with "ousia." The meaning Plotinus gives it in due course is plainly not a materialist one, but his doctrine of the three Hypostases is such an important contribution to the development of the doctrine of the Trinity, that "hypostasis" becomes a key word in the controversy about it. As late as the Nicene Creed, "hypostasis" and "ousia" are interchangeable in talk about the threefold nature of Deity, but because of the Arian dispute Athanasius in his later writings uses "ousia" for God considered as a unity, and "hypostasis" for each of his three personal manifestations. After the Council of Alexandria (362), this becomes standard. In Latin the Trinitarian formula of one Ousia in three divine Hypostases then became one Substantia in three divine Personae. This is an odd result, because in its literal meaning "substantia," though not a good translation

for "ousia," is a plausible one for "hypostasis." Our Latin-based "subject" is cognate with "hypokeimenon," and so "subject" sometimes turns up in the literature in place of "substance."

4. Despite his interest in dynamic development, Leibniz more often than not allows another view, more suited to the requirements of his subject-predicate logic, to dominate the dynamic one.

5. *Physics* I, 7.

6. *Meditation on a Prisoner*, pp. 327–35, 336, 337, 348, 349.

7. Because Hope's use of "primary being" to translate Aristotle's "ousia" influenced my choice of that expression, it may be wise to point out again that a primary being, as defined in the present book, has only a slight resemblance to Aristotle's *ousia*. See *Aristotle: Metaphysics*, trans. Richard Hope (New York: Columbia University Press, 1952).

8. See chap. 1, n. 7.

9. All this can not be dealt with adequately without a discussion of the ontological status of the laws of nature. I have considered this in some detail in *Meditation on a Prisoner*, chap. 2, "Action, Entities, and the Laws of Nature," pp. 28–68.

10. Whitehead's refusal to regard men and women as actual entities (in his special sense of the term) is very curious indeed. To show just how strange it is I must in what follows place a number of his technical terms in italics so that I may contrast the sense he gives them with their more usual sense. *Actual entities* are *organisms* that undergo *growth*; they are *subjects* and have *feelings* with more or less *subjective intensity*; they engage in a *self-creation* that is an *integration*; they make *decisions*; they have *aims*; they may or may not accept *persuasions*; they may entertain *propositions*; they form *societies*; they enjoy *satisfactions*; and some of them are even *conscious*. Any Whiteheadian can easily add to this list of anthropomorphic terms. Whitehead has deemed the features of human life upon which these italicized technical terms are based so important that much of his philosophy is designed to protect their authenticity from materialistic attacks. But at the same time he is unwilling to ascribe to the creature in which he has found these features the kind of extreme self-identity he feels any ontologically fundamental entity should have. He therefore postulates *actual entities* that have the requisite absolute self-identity, and he ascribes these features to them. The *actual entities* being what they are, however, these features undergo the sea change that italicizing them as technical terms indicates.

Going back to the "ordinary" organisms in which the original important features were found, Whiteheadians must now deal with them in a truly extraordinary way. They can no longer attribute to them these same important features, for their standard for these features is now given by those italicized technical terms. The features they were originally interested in are now only to be found in the strict technical sense in the postulated *actual entities*. Thus, if *decision* is something carried on by *actual entities*, human decision takes on a Pickwickian sense: we can at best only reconstruct human decision as a derivative of *decision*. The result is a profound confusion in our understanding of human nature. Designed to protect the reality of human subjectivity from materialistic encroachment, this philosophy now tells us that a human subject is not a *subject* but rather a *society* of *actual entities*, these latter being true *subjects*. The ordinary organism from which our root metaphor comes is not an *organism*, but once more, a *society of organisms*. A man's feelings can not be *feelings*, because *feelings* are what *organisms* (*actual entities*) have, and the person is a *society* rather than an *actual entity*; feelings do not belong to the *society* but to the *actual entities* that make it up.

I have a good deal of faith in human ingenuity. If philosophers are persuaded that they must give an account of human nature, and, ultimately, responsible human action, in terms of Whiteheadian *actual entities*, *societies*, and the like, I am sure they will produce some ingenious constructions. Given the strange restrictions under which their makers must work, the constructions already produced are marvels of ingenuity, although a creature so constituted is probably more plausible as a sensitive observer of sunsets than as the creative agent who, in a surprisingly short burst of intense activity, produced *Process and Reality*. But marvel as we may, we shall still be puzzled about why one should have to undertake such an *Aufbau* of something that was originally deemed so important that in a very real sense the postulated *actual entities* are in fact constructions out of *it*.

The present book is not in the least directed against Whitehead, to whom I owe a great deal. Its target, like his own, is a materialistic view of nature and of human nature. But I have taken a quite different course about human nature, calling the agent itself an entity, or being, and furthermore a primary one. Its actions, including those in which rational and responsible decisions are taken, are acknowledged to be ontologically fundamental, which means that they are not dealt with reductively and need not enter our philosophy by way of an *Aufbau*. This does not hinder our use of the term "action" in metaphor. Thus, if I call some microevent actlike or ascribe act-temporality to it, as I did in *Meditation on a Prisoner*, it is the natural home of the term in its human context that provides the sanction for the metaphorical extension of it to the microevent. (This note is taken, with a few changes, from my article "Human Agents as Actual Beings," in *Process Studies* 8, no. 2 [1978].)

Index

Library of Congress Cataloging in Publication Data
Pols, Edward.
The acts of our being.
Includes bibliographical references and index.
1. Agent (Philosophy)   2. Responsibility.
3. Knowledge, Theory of.   I. Title.
BD450.P577   128'.4   81-16319
ISBN 0-87023-354-8   AACR2

Arguing that we are the responsible rational agents that the law and our self-awareness tell us we are, the author explains that the *prima facie* features of action are what they purport to be and not mere appearance of some deeper reality. Thus, though science can explain important features of the infrastructure of action, rational human acts—just as we know them—are profoundly important explanatory factors.

This positive thesis of the authenticity of the rational agent is developed by way of a reflexive exercise in which rational action turns back upon itself in a series of concrete and direct acts of cognitive attention, rather than by way of conceptual analysis of theory-building. In the first stage rational action is used to develop a set of nine metaphysical conditions that must hold if agency is what it purports to be. The conditions of ontic dependence, causal power, ontic power, explanatory ultimacy, explanatory opacity, partial determinateness, positive indeterminateness, rational obligation, and ontically significant appearance define what the author calls ontic responsibility —a responsibility that includes but is not limited to moral responsibility. In this fresh setting, many of the tired and inconclusive arguments about free will and determinism can be dispensed with.

In the next stage, the *prima facie* mode of knowledge (nonscientific) we use to attend to our *prima facie* rational action is itself considered to see whether its "structure" might give it the authority to adjudicate the rival claims of science and our direct awareness of ourselves in action. This argument confronts and challenges the contemporary prejudice against such "foundational" efforts. The confrontation occasions a reexamination of the role of language in knowledge in general and in philosophy in particular. From all this emerges a "realistic" view of the mode of